Josiah Dwight Whitney

The United States

Facts and Figures Illustrating the Physical Geography of the Country, and it's

Material Resources

Josiah Dwight Whitney

The United States
Facts and Figures Illustrating the Physical Geography of the Country, and it's Material Resources

ISBN/EAN: 9783744674089

Printed in Europe, USA, Canada, Australia, Japan

Cover: Foto ©ninafisch / pixelio.de

More available books at **www.hansebooks.com**

THE

UNITED STATES:

FACTS AND FIGURES ILLUSTRATING

THE PHYSICAL GEOGRAPHY OF THE COUNTRY,

AND ITS MATERIAL RESOURCES.

Supplement I.

POPULATION: IMMIGRATION:

IRRIGATION.

By J. D. WHITNEY

PREFACE.

THIS volume is essentially a continuation of an article originally written for the Encyclopædia Britannica, and published in part in that work, and afterwards separately, with omissions supplied, and a small amount of additional matter added, in which the statistics of certain important industries were brought up to the latest date, for which information could be procured. In this republication of the article as originally written, an appendix was added in which various topics connected with the discovery and scientific development of the country were discussed more at length than would have been admissible in the text of the work. The volume as thus enlarged was published just before the census of 1890 was taken; so that the statistics of population which it contained were necessarily unsatisfactory, inasmuch as they represented a condition of things existing nearly a decade before its publication. Hence it was, from the beginning, the author's intention to prepare a supplement in which this defect should have been remedied, and this was to be done as soon as the results of the census of 1890, so far as they related to population, became available for use. It was not, however, until 1892 that the publication of the full census returns made this possible, but it has now been done, and on the plan adopted in the original work, which was to present the important facts in a very condensed form, leaving details of minor importance to be sought for in the volumes of the Census Reports.

In the matter of the statistics of immigration a course similar to that adopted in regard to population was not so important or desirable, because the official publications dealing with the former are issued so promptly that it was impossible in the original work, the date of whose publication was 1889, to present the important facts relating to immigration down to a date so late as to include the whole of 1888, and a part of 1889. In the present volume, however, the statistics of immigration include the essential facts for the year 1893, and for the first half of 1894, and some matters relating to this subject in general have been discussed more fully than they were in the original work.

The subject of the increase and distribution of the population, which includes all matters connected with immigration, is also closely allied to that of irrigation, as will become evident on examining the contents of the present volume. Hence it was natural that these three topics should here be taken up in sequence. That the irrigation question should not have been opened in the original work need not excite surprise, because almost all the definite knowledge which we have in regard to it is of very recent origin, very few United States official publications relating to irrigation bearing dates less recent than 1890. When it was decided to include this subject in the present work, the author himself was not aware how important the irrigation question is to a large part of the country, and how many interesting scientific and economical problems are involved in it. For some time, indeed, it was impossible to get hold of various documents and reports bearing on this question, some of which could only be obtained after the volume had made considerable progress. This circumstance will account for the somewhat disjointed character of that part of the present work which relates to irrigation; a further difficulty has been encountered in the fact that various official documents appear not to have been issued, or at least not made accessible to the general public, until considerably later than their time of publication, as fixed by the dates which they bear on their title-pages.

J. D. WHITNEY.

CAMBRIDGE, MASS., August, 1894.

CONTENTS.

I. POPULATION.

Population and percentage of increase, at each decennial census, from 1790 to 1890, 1, 2. Effects of the Civil War on the growth of the population, 2.

Density and distribution of the population, 3. Movement of the population, 4. Positions of the centre of population, 1790–1890, 4, 5.

Division of the population by sexes, 5. Geographical distribution of the sexes, 5, 6. Alteration in various States in the condition of the population with regard to the distribution of the sexes, 6, 7. Present distribution of the sexes in various geographical divisions, 7.

Distribution of the population with reference to color, 7, 8. Relative decrease of the colored population from 1790 to 1890, 8. Past and present geographical distribution of the colored population, 8. Number and distribution of the Chinese, 9.

Distribution of the population with reference to the topographical and climatic features of the country, 9, 10. Distribution of the population by drainage basins, and percentage of the total population in the different drainage basins, in 1880 and 1890, 10. Distribution of the population in accordance with the topographical features, from 1870–1890, 11.

Distribution of the population in cities and towns, 11–13. Number of large cities, 1790–1890, 11. Cities having a population of over 100,000, arranged in numerical order, 12. Geographical distribution of large cities, 13.

Number and percentage of persons of native and foreign birth, 1850–1890, 13.

II. IMMIGRATION.

Earliest statistics of immigration, 14, 15. Immigrants entering from Canada and Mexico, 14, 15. Number and nationalities of immigrants, 1820–1893, 16–18.

Fluctuations in the number of immigrants, and changes in regard to their nationalities, 19. Distribution of immigrants through the country, 20.

Distribution of the native and foreign-born population, 21. Percentage increase of native and foreign-born population, by geographical divisions, from 1850 to 1890, 21. Percentage of foreign-born population, and geographical distribution as compared with native, from 1870 to 1890, 21, 22.

Exclusion of the Chinese, 22. Farther legislation concerning the Chinese, 22, 23.

Exclusion of convicts, lunatics, and idiots, etc., 24. Regulation of the immigrant-carrying business by Congress, 24. Restraints on immigration, 24.

III. IRRIGATION.

Distribution of the population in accordance with the mean annual rainfall, 25. Imperfection of the statistics of rainfall, 25. Scantiness of rainfall much more important than overabundance in reference to density of population, 26. Parts of the country where the rainfall is large and the population scanty, 26.

Regions thinly inhabited on account of insufficient supply of rain, 27. Slow growth, or even decrease, of the population in parts of the arid region, between 1880 and 1890, 27, 28.

Area and population of the Cordilleran division, 1880 and 1890, 28. Effects of irrigation, 28. Introduction of irrigation, 28, 29.

Appropriations by Congress for preliminary work with reference to a scientifically planned irrigational system for the arid region, by the U. S. Geological Survey, 29. Reports of work done by the Geological Survey, as far as received up to September, 1893, 30, 31. Nothing up to this time actually done by the government toward carrying out these irrigation schemes, 31.

Great expenses and difficulties necessarily to be encountered if this were to be attempted, 32. Light on this subject from the reports of the Chief of Engineers, in regard to the reservoirs built by government at the head of the Mississippi, 32, 33. Discussion of the utility of these reservoirs, 33.

Irrigation in India, 34–36. Essential differences between the conditions in India and in the United States as regards irrigation, 34–36. Density of population of India, 35. Irregularity, not scantiness, of precipitation the difficulty in India, 35, 36. Table showing the density of the population, the number of acres cultivated, and the number irrigated, with the average rainfall of the principal districts of India, 36.

Table showing the annual precipitation and local variations at stations in the arid region, 37. Contrast between conditions in India and the arid region of the United States, 38. System of irrigation of the Doab described, 38.

Injurious effects of long-continued irrigation, or so-called "over irrigation," 39. Statements of English engineers in regard to this matter, 39–41. Long-continued irrigation in various countries other than India, 41, 42.

Physical decay of certain Eastern countries, 41. G. P. Marsh's views in regard to the causes of this condition of things, 42. Reference to the present writer's investigations of this subject, 42.

E. W. Hilgard's investigations of the "reh" or alkaline deposits in California, 43–45. Origin of the "reh," 43. Attention to this matter recommended, 45. The subject of drainage in connection with the "reh," 45. Report of the Superintendent of the Geological Survey of India on this subject, 46.

Irrigation of the arid region of the United States by means of Artesian wells, 46–48. Report of F. H. Newell on "Artesian wells for Irrigation," 47. What is an Artesian well? 47, 48. Titles of United States official publications on Artesian wells, 47.

Artesian conditions in the Paris Basin, 49, 50. The Artesian well of Grenelle, 49. Of Passy, 49, 50.

Deep and Artesian wells in London, 51, 52. Failure of deep Artesian wells, and causes of this, 51. Deep borings in the London basin, 51, 52. Deep bored wells in Central and Northern England, 52. Water supply of Manchester and Liverpool, 52, 53. The Vyrnwy dam, 53.

Irrigation by means of Artesian wells in Northern Africa, 54–56. Methods of boring, and conditions in the Sahara, 55, 56. Prospects of redeeming the Sahara, 56.

Artesian wells in the Eastern United States, 56–61. Ideas formerly generally held with regard to procuring water by means of deep bored wells, 56, 57. Attempts to procure water in this way in Boston and New York, 57. Deep wells in New York, 57.

Bored wells in Alabama, and quality and quantity of the water thus obtained, 58. A. Winchell on the Artesian wells of Alabama, 58, 59.

Water-supply of Charleston, S. C., 59–61. Artesian wells at Charleston, 59–61. Analyses of the water from these wells, 60, 61.

Deep borings in the Mississippi Valley, 61–67. Artesian well at Louisville, Ky., 61, 62. At St. Louis, Mo., 62. At Columbus and Eaton, and near Cincinnati, Ohio, 63. Natural gas and petroleum in the Trenton limestone of Ohio, 63, 64. Deep borings and shallow wells in Indiana, 64. Quality of the water obtained from deep borings in Indiana, 65. Attempts to obtain Artesian water in Illinois, 65, 67. Deep borings at Chicago, 65, 66. At other localities in Illinois, 66, 67.

Mineral springs and Artesian wells of Wisconsin, 67–73. Regions in Wisconsin designated by the Geological Survey as areas of favorable probabilities for Artesian wells, 67, 78. Classification of the Artesian wells of Wisconsin with reference to the geological position of the rocks from which the water is derived, 68. Wells in the drift of Wisconsin, and quality of the water obtained, 68, 69. Bored wells in the Niagara limestone of Wisconsin, 69, 70. Wells in the Galena and Trenton limestones in Wisconsin, 70. In the St. Peters sandstone at Sheboygan, Milwaukee, and Racine, 70, 71. Wells in the Potsdam sandstone in Wisconsin, 71. Mineral springs and wells north of the Wisconsin River, 71–73. At Sparta, 71. At La Crosse and Prairie du Chien, 72, 73.

Water-supply of Iowa, 73–78. Conditions of water-supply in Iowa, discussed in the State Geological reports, 73, 74. R. E. Call's investigations of the Iowa Artesian wells, 74–77. Wells in Iowa in the glacial drift, 74–76. Deep wells in Iowa obtaining water from the St. Peters sandstone, 76. Quality of the water furnished by the Artesian wells of Iowa, 77. "Magnetic" and medicinal waters of Iowa, 77, 78.

Water-supply of Minnesota, 78–81. Shallow wells in Minnesota, 78. Shallow flowing wells, or "fountains," in Minnesota, 78, 79. Quality of the water from the "fountains" of Minnesota, 79. Artesian wells at Red Wing, 79. Near St. Paul, 80. At Mendota and Hastings, 81.

Mineral springs and Artesian wells of Missouri, 81–83. Analysis of the water of the Belcher well, St. Louis, 82. Analyses of waters from other Artesian wells in Missouri, 82, 83.

Mineral waters and springs of Arkansas, 83. Climatic conditions of Texas, 84.

Artesian wells in the Coast region of Texas, 84–86. Artesian wells at Galveston, 85, 86. At Houston, 86. Quality of the water obtained from deep borings in the States adjacent to the Mississippi River, 87.

Water-supply and irrigation in the arid region of the United States, 87–232. Position of the isohyetal marking the boundary between the sufficiently and insufficiently watered divisions of the United States, 87. Where the irrigation question is one of great importance, 88.

Table showing the percentage of irrigated area in 1890, and the density of the population in 1880 and 1890, in various States and Territories included within the arid belt, 89. Circumstances conditioning the density of the population within the arid belt, 89. Irrigation in Washington and Oregon, 90. Complete returns lacking for California and Colorado, 90. Census statistics of Artesian wells for irrigation in the western half of the United States, 91.

Sources of information in regard to the region of the Plains, 91. Additional titles of volumes relating to the irrigation of the arid lands of the United States, issued under government authority, 92. White and Aughey's report on Artesian wells on the Great Plains, 92, 93. Enumeration of the early attempts to procure water on the Plains by boring, under government auspices, 93, 94. Unfavorable conclusions of White and Aughey as to the possibility of obtaining Artesian water on the Plains, 94.

General considerations in regard to the early occupation of the arid region of the United States by immigrants and settlers, 95–100. Irregularity of the rainfall in regions where this is small in amount, 96. The Great Plains naturally a pastoral or stock-growing region, 96. How settlers were obliged to diminish the area of their ranges, 97. Results of too hasty occupation of a region of small rainfall, as shown by the census of 1890, in the case of the Dakotas, Nebraska, and Kansas, 98, 99. Additional statements to the same effect from other sources, 99.

Review of the "Progress Report" of R. T. Hinton, Special Agent of the "Artesian Underflow and Irrigation Investigation," 100–134. Nature of the "Underflow" or "Undersheet Water," as described by him, 101. The so-called "phreatic waters," 101. Supposed theoretical proof of the existence of an available undersheet of water in the Mississippi Valley, 102–105. Fallacy of these ideas, 102–105.

What portion of the Mississippi Valley is in need of irrigation? 102–105. Incorrectness of the data used, and sources from which they were obtained, 103, 104. Early and later estimates of the amount of rainfall in the Mississippi and Missouri basins, 103, 104. Table of rainfall and of percentage of discharge of the Mississippi and its tributaries, 104. Hinton's under-estimate of the percentage of the rainfall lost by evaporation, 105. Lack of precise data for the United States in regard to percolation and evaporation, 105.

Experiments with the Dalton gauge near London, and their results, 105, 106. Similar experiments in other parts of Europe, 106.

Climate of the Great Plains very unfavorable to percolation, 106, 107. The author's experience in Colorado, 107.

Results obtained by the Artesian, Underflow, and Irrigation Investigations up to 1891, 108–110. The drainage of the Rocky Mountains declared to be a great source of supply for Artesian wells over a large part of the United States, 108, 109. Catlin's ideas in regard to the underflow as the origin of the Gulf Stream, 110.

The "Artesian Wells Investigation Report" of 1890, 110–121. Names of the engineers and geologists employed, 111. Principal results of this survey, as summed up by the Supervisory Engineer, 111, 112. Groups of Artesian wells in the region examined, geographically located by the General Field Geologist, 113. Principal facts in regard to the Artesian wells of the James River Valley, 113. Quality of the water of these wells, 114. Artesian wells in Southwestern Kansas, and near the Colorado line in the Arkansas Valley, 114. Shallow wells in the glacial drift in the Dakotas, 115. The wells of the Denver Basin, 115, 116. Water-supply of the region in Colorado lying at the eastern base of the Rocky Mountains, 116. Presumptions in regard to the similarly situated region in New Mexico, 116. Failure of the wells at Denver, 116. Wells in Southwestern Kansas obtaining water from the Tertiary grit, 116. Wells at Miles City, Montana, supplied from the Laramie group, 117.

Report of E. S. Nettleton, Chief Engineer of the Artesian, Underflow, and Irrigation Investigation, 117–121. Geographical position of lines surveyed by him across Nebraska and Kansas with reference to conditions of water-supply, 118. Condensed statement of facts contained in his tables of statistical information, 118, 119. Inferences drawn from this statement as to the reality of a general underflow system, 119. The real nature of the water-supply from the superficial detritus in the region reported on by the Chief Engineer, 120. Relations of water-supply from wells in general to the amount of precipitation, 120, 121.

Possibility that the water obtained from these wells was stored in the rocks during a former period of greater precipitation, 121, 122.

Final Report of the Artesian and Underflow Investigation, and of the Irrigation Inquiry, published in 1892, 122–231. Titles of the separate volumes of this report, and names of the authors, 122, 123. Valuable results claimed by the Special Agent in charge to have been accomplished, 123. Activity in irrigation enterprises during the year 1891, 124. Increase of population in the northern part of the arid region claimed, 124. More evidence on this will be afforded by the results of the next census, 125. Slight amount of change shown by comparison of statistics given with those of the census of 1890, 125. Statistics of irrigation and population in Arizona, 125.

Ideas of the Special Agent in regard to controlling the "continental water-supply" examined and criticised, 126–134. What is meant by "continental water-supply," 126, 127. Dimensions of area drained by streams heading in Montana, Wyoming, and Colorado, 127. Size of the basin of a river and length of its course do not determine its importance as a tributary stream, 128. How it is supposed that control of the water-supply could possibly be effected, 128–130. Reservation of the forests, 130. Necessary conditions of settlement and cultivation of a forested country, 131. Conditions in this respect of the Atlantic States, 131. The climate of New England has not been changed to any perceptible degree by the removal of a large proportion of its forests, 132. The distribution of the isohyetal lines not dependent on the presence or absence of forests, 132. What causes do really determine the amount of the rainfall of any region, 132. What effects may be produced in certain localities by protecting the forests, 133. Diminution of the amount of water standing in lakes or flowing in rivers known to have long been going on over much of the earth's surface, and to be still in progress, but this desiccation not caused by the agency of man, 134. Any change of this kind necessarily most important and soonest perceived in regions of small precipitation, 134.

Contribution to the Final Report of the Artesian and Underflow Investigation, by E. S. Nettleton, Chief Engineer, 135–145. Time for completing the irrigation investigation extended to January 1, 1892, and distribution of work in accordance with this change, 135. Re-examination of surveyed lines in the valleys of the Arkansas and Platte rivers, 135. Value of the work in the Dakota Artesian Basin, 135.

Pecos Valley subterranean waters, 136–138. Water conditions in the Pecos Valley and the adjacent region, 137. Recent change in the character of the Rio Peñasco, 137. "China holes" on the table-lands of Pecos Valley, 138.

Extent and availability of the underflow in the Valleys of the Platte and Arkansas, according to the Chief Engineer, 139–141. Location of surveyed lines, 139. Negative results along Cheyenne and Sterling lines, 139. No important additions to the results previously attained on the other surveyed lines, 140.

Movement of the underflow in the river valleys, 140–141. Experiments for determining its velocity, 140. Reasons why experiments of this kind can have but little value, 140, 141.

Deep wells of the Dakota Basin, 142, 143. Location of these wells, and statistics of their depth and flow, 142. Lack of uniformity in the position of the water-bearing strata, and in the character of the lower rocks, 142, 143.

Statements of W. W. Follett, Assistant Engineer, in regard to the Red River Valley Artesian Basin, 143, 144. Geological structure of this basin, and statistics of the wells, 144. Character of the water, 144.

Belief of the Chief Engineer, that there has been a recurrence of wet and dry periods in the region examined by him, 144. Unsatisfactory character of the evidence to this effect, 144. Real nature of the phenomena of desiccation, 144, 145.

Report of the Chief Geologist of the Irrigation Inquiry, 145–155. Titles of the special reports contained in this volume, 145. Sketch of the geology of the Plains, 145–147. The superficial formations, "plains' marl," "Tertiary grit," etc., 146, 147. Difficulty of separating the Post-Tertiary from the Tertiary in the Plains region, 147. Impropriety of the use of the term "Loess" in this region, 147. Wells in the Tertiary grit, 147–148. Importance of the water-supply from the Tertiary grit, 149. The source of this water is the rainfall, 149. Discussion of the question whether this source of supply is inexhaustible, 149, 150.

Discussion by the Chief Geologist of the meaning of the word "underflow," 151–153. Exaggerated ideas of the underflow current in the arid region, and why they cannot be accepted as correct, 151, 152. How the Chief Geologist wishes to limit the use of the word "underflow," 152. Objections to this, and the real nature of the underflow explained, 153.

Remarks of the Chief Geologist in regard to the Artesian basins of the Great Plains, 153, 154. Their number has not been increased since the publication of the preceding report, but the area of several of these basins has been enlarged, 153. The James River Basin, Dakota, and the Fort Worth-Waco Basins, Texas, 153, 154. Source of the water of the wells of Coolidge, in the Arkansas Valley, 154, 155. Gas pressure and rock pressure as causes of the rise of water to the surface, 155.

Report of the Assistant Geologist for Texas west of 97°, the Indian Territory, and Eastern New Mexico, 155–198. Occurrence and availability of underground water, 155–157. Extraordinary ideas on this subject held by many in the arid region, 155, 156. Conditions controlling the distribution of the underground waters, 156, 157. Causes of the failure of various borings for Artesian water, and how water may be procured on the most sterile plains, 157.

Detailed account of the Texas – New Mexico region, 158–198. Topography and subdivisions of this region, 158, 159. Geographical limits of the Eastern Division of Texas, 160. Position of the isohyetal lines in Texas, 160, 161. Geology of the Eastern Division, 161, 162. Soil, rocks, flora, and water-supply dependent on geological structure, 161. Distribution of the forests and prairies determined by the character of the soil, 161, 162. Reference to the present author's publications on this subject, 161. Fault lines in the Eastern Division of Texas, 162.

Artesian areas in the Eastern Division of Texas, 163–183. The Coast Prairie region, 163, 164. Artesian wells of Galveston and Houston, 163, 164. The Washington County Black Prairies, 164. The Fayette sands as a source of water-supply, 164. The East Texas timbered region, 164, 165. Geological structure and water-supply of the timber belt, 164, 165.

The Cretaceous Prairie region and the Cross Timbers, 165–168. Topographic features, soil, and vegetation of this district, 165, 166. Prosperity of the prairie region, 166. The Main Black Prairie region described, 166. Nature of the "black-waxy" soil, and the cause of its dark color, 166. Geological formations underlying the Black Prairie region, 167. The Lower Cross Timbers, 167, 168. Cause of the occurrence of this belt of timber, 167, 168. The "prairie question," 168.

The Grand Prairie, 168, 169. Its elevation and geological structure, 169. The Comanche Series, 169.

Water-supply of that part of Texas which is underlain by Cretaceous rocks, 170–183. The Grand Prairie drainage system,

170–173. Geographical position of the Edwards Plateau, 170. Its value as a great water-reservoir, 171. Springs and rivers running from the Edwards Plateau, 71. The springs of San Antonio, Del Rio, San Marcos, and Austin, 172. These are all derived from the Trinity sands, 173.

Artesian well system of the Grand and Black Prairies, 173–183. Extent of this Artesian area, 173. Wells of Fort Worth, 174. Formations furnishing the Artesian water of the Black and Grand Prairie region, 174, 175. Dallas-Pottsboro group of Artesian wells, 175. The Lower Cross Timber, or Dakota, sands furnish the water of these wells, 175. Area occupied by the Dakota sands in Texas, and rainfall on this formation, 175. Artesian and non-flowing wells in the Dakota sands, 176. Artesian wells of the Fort Worth – Waco region, 176–181. Wells in this district obtaining their water from the Paluxy sands, 176, 177. Importance of these wells, 177. Wells of Waco deriving their water from the Trinity sands, 177, 178. Volume of water delivered by the Artesian wells of Waco, 177. Depth of these wells, 178. Quality of the water of the Waco wells, 178. Deep borings at Fort Worth, 179. High expectations in regard to the future importance of the Fort Worth Artesian wells, 179, 180. Asserted purity of the water from these wells, 180. Limits of the Fort Worth – Waco system, 181.

The Black and Grand Prairie region south of the Colorado, 181, 182. The Edwards Plateau, 181, 182. Springs on the eastern edge of this plateau, 182.

Value of the Artesian waters of the Black and Grand Prairies, 182, 183. Absence of information in regard to the composition of these waters, 183.

The Red Beds region of Texas, Oklahoma, and New Mexico, 183, 184. Geographical position and geological structure of the Red Beds region, 184. Scantiness and irregularity of the precipitation in this region, 185. "Red rises," 185. Water conditions of the Red Beds region, 185. Quality of the water of this region, 185.

The Llano Estacado, 185–189. Extent of the Llano, 186. Origin and meaning of the name, 185, 186. Topographic features, scenery, and drainage of the Llano, 187. Character of its superficial covering, 187. No surface water on the Llano, and reasons for this condition of things, 188. Irregularity of the precipitation in this region, 188. Water can be had on the Llano from deep wells in the mortar beds and grits, 189. No Artesian water has as yet been obtained on the Llano, 189. Absence of information in regard to the quality of the water from the wells of the Llano, 189.

The Trans-Pecos or Basin region, 189–198. Topography of the Great Basin, 190, 192. Great Salt Lake and Humboldt Lake, 190, 191. Climatic conditions of the Great Basin, 191. The Colorado River, 191. The regions south and southwest of the Great Basin proper, 192. Changes in the orography of the Rocky Mountains in this direction, 192. Development of "mesas" and "basin plains" in New Mexico and Western Texas, 193. Lack of accurate maps of this region, 193. The Organ-Hueco basin, 193, 194. The Mesilla Basin, 194, 195. Climatic and water conditions of these and other similar basins, 194–196. Records of wells on the Lanoria Mesa, 195. Depth and character of the water from flowing wells at Pecos City, 196.

Summing up of the water conditions of the inter-mountain plains or basins, 197. Death Valley and the Jornada del Muerto, 197. Sanguine expectations of a citizen of the driest part of Nevada, 198.

Examination of the Report of L. E. Hicks on the Underflow, etc. of Nebraska, 198–210. Geological structure of the region,

199. Rainfall and water conditions of Nebraska, 199, 200. The rivers of that State were once much larger than they now are, 200, 201. Explanation of this, 202, 203. The underflow described, 203, 204. Sheet waters, 204. Geology of the region examined, 204. Water conditions of the superficial detrital material, 204, 205. The annual rise of the Loup Rivers considered with reference to the question of the velocity of the underflow, 205, 206. Real character of the phenomena, 206. Irrigational possibilities in Nebraska, 207, 208. Survey of the Loup Valley, 208–210. The Loup a typical river of the plains, 208. Description of the Loup Valley, 200–210. How its climate may be ameliorated, 210.

Examination of the Report of G. E. Culver on the Dakota Basin, 210–215. Geological condition of the Dakota Basin, 210–212. Quantity and quality of the water, 212. Geology and water conditions of the Black Hills, 213, 214. Districts in which "test wells" are considered desirable, 214. Adequacy of the supply, 214, 215.

Report of J. W. Gregory, Special Agent, on the Mid-Plains Division of the Artesian and Underflow Investigation, 215–231. Boundaries of his field of investigation, 215. Special object of this investigation, 215. Surface characteristics of the region examined, 216. Its climate, 216, 217. What is needed to make it densely populous, 217. Meaning and use of the name "Great American Desert," 217. Deserts, barrens, and tundras, 217. Statistics of the rainfall of this region, 218. Minimum amount of rainfall necessary for the success of agriculture, 219. Opinions of the Chief Signal Officer on this point, 219. Irrigation of the arid region not an absolute necessity, 219, 220. Successful experiments in timber-culture without irrigation, 220. An ideal development of the Plains region described, 220. How this might have been brought about, 220, 221. What has really happened on the Plains, 221. Sanguine expectations in regard to the future development of the Plains, 222. By what means this is to be effected, 222, 223. It is the duty of the General Government to interfere in behalf of the settlers on the Plains, 223. Artesian wells on the Plains are of little or no value, 224. The underflow, 224-231. Its mode of occurrence illustrated by diagrams, 225. Attempts to determine its rate of flow, 225, 226. Statements of citizens of the Plains in regard to the abundance of the underflow water, 226. The underflow believed to appear on the Atlantic coast and in the Gulf of Mexico, in the form of fresh water springs, 226, 227. Testimony of the Superintendent of the Coast Survey in reference to this, 226, 227. Modes of utilizing the underflow or sheet waters of the Plains, 227-231. The "fountain method," 228, 229. Examples of the application of this method, 228, 229. Conditions at Garden City, Kansas, 229. Method adopted in Persia for bringing water from a distance, 229. Objections to the fountain method refuted, 230. Immense development of the Great Plains possible by means of this method, 231.

F. H. Newell; Statistics of Irrigation contained in Extra Census Bulletin, No. 23, 231, 232. Tabular statement of areas irrigated and of percentage character of irrigated crops, 232.

Fourth Irrigation Report of the United States Geological Survey examined, 233-274. Contents of the Report, 233, 234.

F. H. Newell on Water Supply for Irrigation, 234-247. Water supply available as determined by the character of the vegetation in the region requiring irrigation, 234-237. Estimate of the areas furnishing water and of the whole amount of water available for irrigation in the arid region, 237. Fluctuations of rivers and lakes, 238, 240. Seasonal or periodic oscillations, 238. Non-periodic oscillations,

239. Extraordinary amount of precipitation in 1884, and inferences therefrom, 230. Brückner's work on climatic fluctuations, 239, 240. Fluctuations of lakes and rivers due to climatic forces world-wide in extent, 240. Subsurface waters, 240–243. Statistics of irrigation by means of Artesian wells, 241. Ordinary wells on the Great Plains, 241. Nature of the underflow, 241, 242. Are the subsurface waters stationary? 242. The fountain method not a success, 243, 244. Cost and value of water-supply, 244–246. Probable sources of error in these computations, 246. Drainage basins of the Missouri, Yellowstone, and Platte rivers, 246. Character of the discharge of the principal streams gauged, 246, 247.

Report of H. M. Wilson on American Irrigation Engineering, 247–274. Object of this report, 247. Artesian wells for irrigation, 248. Definition of the term "underflow," 248. The fountain method, 248, 249. Utilization of the great rivers for irrigation, 249. Desirability of storage reservoirs, 250. The duty of water, 250. Irrigation in India, 251–256. Contrast between the conditions affecting irrigation in India and in the arid region of the United States, 251–253. Relation of the government to irrigation in the United States, 252. The conditions from this point of view in India, 253. The question of the formation of alkaline deposits as a consequence of irrigation discussed, 254–256. Discussion of the question of the character of the water to be used for irrigation, 256, 257. History of irrigation and of legislation relating to it in the United States, 257–259. Early practice of irrigation in Arizona, 257, 258. In California and Utah, 258, 259. Present condition of irrigation in California, Colorado, and Utah, 259, 260. Legislation and administration, 260, 261. Present status of the irrigational work done under the direction of the United States Geological Survey, 261. Present condition of the laws regulating the acquirement of title to irrigable lands, 261, 262. Description of various engineering works, 262, 263. Water storage, 263-270. San Diego Flume Company, 264, 265. Merced Reservoir, 265. Long Valley Reservoir, 265, 266. Walnut Grove Reservoir, 266. Castlewood Reservoir, 266, 267. Bear Valley Reservoir, 267, 268. Rainfall in Bear Valley, 267. Sweetwater Reservoir, 268. Lake Hemet Water Company, 268. Arrowhead Reservoir Company, 269. Water-supply of Denver, 269, 270. Subsurface sources of supply, 270-272. The underflow, 270. Pumping wells, 271. Submerged dams, 271, 272. American Water Company's works, 271. Submerged dam on Pacoima Creek, 272. Relative importance of pumping wells, 272. Engineering results of the Irrigation Survey, 272-274. Methods by which the work has been conducted, 272, 273. Surveys of various drainage basins, 274.

General Remarks on Irrigation, 274-282. Discrepancies in the views of writers on the arid region, 274, 275. Gradual relinquishment of some of the earlier exaggerated ideas held by irrigational officials, 275. Inadequate natural supply of water a great disadvantage, 275. Density of population as affected by dryness of climate, 275. No nation occupying a commanding position except in a region of adequate precipitation, 275. The arid part of the United States will never be densely populated, 276. Importance of certain parts of the arid region, on account of the extent and value of their deposits of metalliferous ores, 276. Duration of these deposits, 276. The Great Plains, their present condition and future prospects, 277. Artesian wells, general remarks on, 278-280. Relative importance of Artesian wells, 278. The typical basin structure not present in the Artesian wells of the United States, 278. Conditions producing Artesian pressure where the basin structure is absent, 278-280. Rock pressure, 279. Gas pressure, 280. Water supply by means of storage reservoirs, 280–282. Difficulties and dangers of storage reservoirs, 281. Plan of having the General Government build and manage storage reservoirs, 281, 282.

Supplementary Note. Artesian wells in Eastern Virginia, Maryland, Delaware, and New Jersey, 282.

APPENDIX.

A. Latest statistics of Immigration, with additional remarks on Immigration in general, and on the present status of the Chinese in the United States, 285–289.

B. Brief Discussion of the Question whether Changes of Climate can be brought about by the Agency of Man, and on Secular Climatic Changes in general, with special reference to the Arid Region of the United States, 290–317.

C. List of United States Official Publications relating to Irrigation and Matters connected therewith, 318–324.

POPULATION, IMMIGRATION, AND IRRIGATION.

I. POPULATION.

THE first census of the United States was taken in 1790, and there has been one taken every tenth year since that time. The following table shows the absolute number of inhabitants, "excluding Indians not taxed," at each decennial period, and also the rate per cent of increase during the previous ten years: —

Year.	Population.	Percentage of Increase.
1790	3,929,214	
1800	5,308,483	35.11
1810	7,239,881	36.40
1820	9,633,822	33.06
1830	12,806,020	33.55
1840	17,069,453	32.67
1850	23,191,876	35.86
1860	31,443,321	35.58
1870	38,558,371	22.63
1880	50,155,783	30.08
1890	62,622,250	24.86

The population of the United States on June 1, 1890, as shown by the final count, exclusive of Indians and other persons in Indian territory, on Indian reservation, and in Alaska, was 62,622,250; including these persons the population was 62,979,766. In 1880 the population with the same exclusions was 50,155,783. The absolute increase of the population in the ten years intervening was 12,466,467, and the percentage of increase was 24.86. In 1870 the population was stated as 38,558,371. According to these figures the absolute increase in the decade between 1870 and 1880 was 11,597,412, and the percentage of increase was 30.08.

The effect of the Civil War on the growth of population in the United States is easily seen in the diminished ratio of increase shown by the figures for the decade 1860–70. With that exception, the rate has been extraordinarily large and uniform, but less in the decade 1870–80 than in any preceding one, and still less in the decade 1880–90.[1] That this rapid growth of the population, due in so large a part to

[1] The following statement, made in the volume devoted to Population, in the Final Census Report of 1890, gives an explanation of how, in the opinion of the Superintendent of this Census, these anomalies are to be accounted for: "Upon their face these figures show that the population increased 869,055 more between 1880 and 1890 than between 1870 and 1880, while the rate of increase has apparently diminished from 30.08 to 24.86 per cent. If these figures were derived from correct data, they would be disappointing. Such a reduction in the rate of increase, in the face of the heavy immigration during the past ten years, would argue a diminution in the fecundity of the population, or a corresponding increase in its death rate. These figures are, however, easily explained when the character of the data used is understood. It is well known, the fact having been demonstrated by extensive and thorough investigation, that the census of 1870 was grossly deficient in the Southern States, so much so as not only to give an exaggerated rate of increase of the population between 1870 and 1880 in these States, but to affect materially the rate of increase in the country at large."

immigration, will continue to be maintained is in the highest degree improbable. The fact that nearly the whole of the more valuable portion of the public lands has been already taken up can hardly fail to check immigration, although the population is at present far from dense, and far from being so large that there is not ample room for a much larger number.

The area embraced within the United States at the time of taking the first census was about eight hundred and fifty thousand square miles, a precise statement of the amount being impossible, owing to the peculiar wording of that part of the treaty in which the northern and western boundaries of the country are defined. The density of the population at that time was about 4.6 persons per square mile, this population being almost exclusively confined to the Atlantic seaboard. At that time not more than five per cent of the inhabitants of the country lived west of the Appalachian range, the settlements being very closely limited to the borders of the navigable streams. At the time of taking the census of 1850, the boundaries of the United States had become definitely established, the only addition made since that time being the territory acquired in 1853 by the Gadsden purchase (about 47,330 square miles). At that time the average density of the population of the whole country was a little less than eight persons per square mile.

The following table shows the density of the population at the epoch of each census which has been taken during the time when the area of the country remained (with the exception of the purchase of Alaska, not here included) unchanged : —

Year.	Area of U. S.	Population per sq. mile.
1860	3,025,600	10.39
1870	"	12.74
1880	"	16.57
1890	"	20.70

The movement of the population has, from the beginning, been from the east toward the west, the first settlements having been made on the Atlantic coast, and the emigration to the United States having been almost exclusively from European countries. The Pacific coast had, previously to the annexation of California, received a small number of whites coming from Mexico, and since that time there have been some accessions to the population in that region by means of emigration from China; but the number added from this direction is almost insignificant in comparison with that which has come into the country from the east. Hence the centre of population has been moving westward, and the investigations of the Coast Survey and of the Census Bureau have shown that this movement has been in an almost exactly westerly direction, and that the centre of population has always remained very near the parallel of 39°. In 1790 it was in latitude 39° 16'.5, at a point about twenty-three miles east of Baltimore; in 1880 it was eight miles west by south from Cincinnati, in latitude 39° 4'.1, having moved westward 457 miles in ninety years; in 1890 it was in latitude 39° 11' 56", and in longitude 85° 32' 53", having moved westward in the preceding ten years 53' 13", or about forty-eight miles, and northward 7' 48", or about nine miles. It rests now in Southern Indiana, at a point a little west of south of Greensburg, the county seat of Decatur County, and twenty miles east of Columbus, Indiana. The most southerly point reached was that of 1830, when the centre was in latitude 38° 57'.9; the most rapid movement was in the period 1850–60, namely, eighty-one miles, this being due to the rapid transfer of a considerable population from the Eastern to the Pacific States, consequent on the discovery of the gold of California.

The percentage division of the population by sexes, as shown by the censuses of 1850–90, was as follows: —

	1850.	1860.	1870.	1880.	1890.
Males	51.04	51.16	50.56	50.88	51.21
Females	48.96	48.84	49.44	49.12	48.79

The number of females for each 100,000 males in 1870, 1880, and 1890 was as follows: —

	1870.	1880.	1890.
Number of females to 100,000 males	97,801	96,544	95,280

As a natural result of the conditions influencing emigration from the older to the newer States, it is found that females are in excess in the Atlantic States. In 1880 in the District of Columbia, Rhode Island, and Massachusetts the excess of females over males was five per cent or more; in Connecticut, New Hampshire, North Carolina, South Carolina, New York, Virginia, and Alabama it was from two and a half to five per cent; in Maryland, Georgia, New Jersey, Louisiana, Tennessee, Pennsylvania, and Maine it was less than two and a half per cent. The States, on the other hand, in which the males were, in 1880, considerably in excess of the females, were those situated in the

Cordilleran region, where mining is the chief pursuit, and where the conditions of life are such as are more easily borne by men than by women. In Michigan, Minnesota, Kansas, and Nebraska, which are not Cordilleran States, but which are on the extreme northern, western, or southwestern borders of the Central region, the number of females was from eighty to ninety per cent of that of the males, and New Mexico was in the same category. In the Pacific Coast States in 1880 the number of females was from fifty to eighty per cent that of the males; and the same was true of Colorado and Dakota, which are situated on the eastern borders of the Rocky Mountains, and which are partly agricultural and partly mining States. In those States in which mining and stock-raising are by far the predominating interests, and which are entirely enclosed in the Cordilleras, namely, Idaho, Nevada, Wyoming, Arizona, and Montana, the inequality in the numbers of the sexes is greatest, there being in 1880 in these Territories less than half as many females as males.

Since 1880 the conditions of the population of several of the States in regard to sex have altered materially. Thoughout the country at large there has been an increase in the proportion of males, and this increase has resulted in transferring from the list of States in which in 1880 females were in excess, to those which in 1890 males were in excess, no fewer than six States — namely, Maine, Pennsylvania, Georgia, Alabama, Louisiana, and Tennessee: in general it has increased the proportion of males in the Northern and Southern Central States. The development of more settled conditions in the extreme western group of States and Territories has, on the other hand, reduced the proportion of males in that region. The whole number of States and Territories in which, in 1890, the females exceeded the males was eleven, as against seventeen in 1880. All of the States and Territories which, in 1890, showed an excess of females are found in the North Atlantic and South Atlantic divisions, as was also true of the States and Territories having, in 1880, an excess of females over males, with the exception of Alabama, Louisiana, and Tennessee in the South Central division. In 1880 there were five States and Territories in which the number of females was less than fifty per cent of that of the males — namely, Idaho, Nevada, Wyoming, Arizona, and Montana; while in 1890 there was no State or Territory in which there were not at least half as many females as males. In 1890 there were eleven States and Territories, mainly in the Cordilleran division, in which the number of females was between fifty and eighty per cent of that of the males, as against five States and Territories under like conditions in 1880.

Of the colored population the census of 1880 showed the number to be 6,580,793 to 43,402,970 whites, or 15,162 colored in every 100,000 whites. The census of 1890 showed that, out of a total population of 62,622,250, the persons of African descent numbered 7,470,040. In addition there were enumerated 107,475 Chinese, 2,039 Japanese, and 58,806 Indians competent to be enrolled among the general population, making the total colored element of the country 7,638,360, as compared with a total white population of 54,983,390.

The percentage of the white and colored population (including in the latter only those of African descent) was, from 1790 to 1890, as follows: —

	1790.	1800.	1810.	1820.	1830.	1840.	1850.	1860.	1870.	1880.	1890.
White	80.73	81.12	80.97	81.61	81.90	83.16	84.31	85.62	87.11	86.54	87.89
Colored	19.27	18.88	19.03	18.39	18.10	16.84	15.69	14.13	12.66	13.12	11.92

The uniform slowness with which the colored population has decreased from being nearly one fifth of the total to being only a little more than one tenth is indeed remarkable.

The colored population is still, in spite of some slight emigration, almost entirely confined to the former slave States, and in three of them — South Carolina, Mississippi, and Louisiana — the colored are in excess of the whites. In Alabama, Georgia, Florida, Virginia, and North Carolina the colored represented, in 1890, more than fifty per cent of the white population, and the same was true of these States in 1880. In four States — Arkansas, Tennessee, Texas, and Maryland — the colored population represented, both in 1880 and in 1890, from twenty-five to fifty per cent of the white. In the District of Columbia, in 1880, there were more than half as many colored as white, and in 1890 there were 48.85 of the former to 100 of the latter. In Kentucky and Delaware, both in 1880 and in 1890, the colored represented between ten and twenty-five per cent of the white population. Of the remaining States and Territories ten had in 1890, as against eight in 1880, a colored population representing from two to ten per cent of the white, while in twenty-four the colored element represented less than two per cent of the white, both in 1880 and in 1890.

The number of Chinese in the country increased only to a trifling extent between 1880 and 1890,—namely, from 105,465 to 107,475. As in 1880, so in 1890, by far the greater portion of them are found in the Cordilleran division, although a perceptible amount of distribution over the country in general has taken place. In 1890 the number of Chinese in the Cordilleran division was 96,844, and in 1880, 102,102. Of the total number of Chinese in the country in 1890, a little over two thirds (72,472) were in California, 9,540 in Oregon, while the remainder were scattered widely over the country.

The distribution of the population in reference to the topographical and climatic features of the country is such as naturally arises from the constant operation of two causes, both acting in the same direction. Emigration and overflow from a more thickly settled region toward one more thinly inhabited takes place, with insignificant exceptions, from the east toward the west. Immigrants arrive from Europe, are landed on the Atlantic coast — about three fourths at one point, New York — and thence in large part find their way westward in the direction of lands unoccupied or only thinly settled. To the east of the Mississippi the land is almost everywhere exceptionally fertile, and the climatic conditions are over a large area very much the same, and on the whole highly favorable. Soon after crossing the Mississippi River, however, we find that this favorable condition of things begins to change. Not only is the immigrant getting farther and farther from his home, but he is finding his environment less and less suited to the development of those conditions which favor the existence of a dense population. Never by any possibility can the region of small rainfall and in large part of rugged mountains, extending from the first belt of States beyond the Mississippi to the belt lying directly on the Pacific coast, become a densely populated portion of the country. This dryer region is throughout its entire extent also the most elevated. The results of the conditions thus indicated are sufficiently shown by the following figures.

DISTRIBUTION OF THE POPULATION OF THE UNITED STATES IN 1880 AND IN 1890, BY DRAINAGE BASINS.

Drainage Basin.	Area in sq. miles.	1880.		1890.	
		Total.	Per sq. mile.	Total.	Per sq. mile.
New England Coast	61,830	3,811,102	61.6	4,486,813	72.6
Middle Atlantic Coast	83,020	9,646,057	116.2	11,482,411	138.31
South Atlantic Coast	132,040	3,705,807	28.1	2,248,466	32.18
Great Lakes	175,340	5,377,019	30.7	7,009,839	39.98
Gulf of Mexico	1,725,980	26,167,367	15.2	32,993,234	19.12
Total Atlantic	2,178,210	48,707,352	22.4	60,220,763	27.65
Great Basin	228,150	210,998	0.9	256,130	1.12
Pacific Ocean	619,240	1,237,433	2.0	2,145,357	3.46
Total	3,025,600	50,155,783		62,622,250	

PERCENTAGE OF TOTAL POPULATION OF THE DIFFERENT DRAINAGE BASINS.

Division.	1870.	1880.	1890
Atlantic Ocean	97.79	97.11	96.16
New England Coast	8.52	7.60	7.16
Middle Atlantic Coast	20.85	19.23	18.34
South Atlantic Coast	7.26	7.39	6.78
Great Lakes	10.96	10.72	11.19
Gulf of Mexico	50.20	52.17	52.69
Great Basin	0.33	0.42	0.41
Pacific Ocean	1.88	2.47	3.43

GEOGRAPHICAL DISTRIBUTION OF THE POPULATION OF THE UNITED STATES IN ACCORDANCE WITH THE TOPOGRAPHICAL FEATURES, 1870–1890.

	Population per square mile.		
	1870.	1880.	1890.
Coast Swamps	15.3	18.7	21.5
Atlantic Plain	47.0	60.2	74.4
Piedmont Region	45.8	55.8	69.5
New England Hills	35.4	38.6	40.7
Appalachian Mountain Region	34.3	41.7	49.8
Cumberland Alleghany Plateau	40.7	49.4	59.3
Interior Timbered Region	31.3	38.8	44.3
Lake Region	12.1	17.6	25.1
Ozark Mountain Region	10.3	16.0	22.8
Alluvial Region of the Mississippi	12.2	18.2	23.6
Prairie Region	14.6	21.2	28.3
Great Plains	0.1	0.4	1.4
North Rocky Mountains	0.2	0.4	1.1
South Rocky Mountains	0.7	1.7	2.1
Plateau Region	0.2	0.5	0.7
Basin Region	0.5	0.9	1.4
Columbian Mesas	0.2	0.8	1.9
Sierra Nevada	3.8	4.6	4.9
Pacific Valley	3.5	5.2	9.1
Cascade Range	0.9	1.7	5.5
Coast Ranges	5.8	9.8	14.3

In regard to the distribution of the population of the United States in towns and cities, and the positions of those centres, the following may be stated: —

In 1790 there were in the country four cities having a population of from 8,000 to 20,000, and two above 20,000, but not one surpassing 75,000 in number. Fifty years later, there were forty-four towns and cities having a population of 8,000 and over, and one of about 500,000. In 1880 there were 286, and in 1890 there were 448 towns having over 8,000 inhabitants.

In 1870 there were fourteen cities having over 100,000; in 1880, twenty; in 1890, twenty-eight, as shown in the following table.

POPULATION OF THE CITIES.

Over 1,000,000.

Name.	Population in 1880.	1890.
New York	1,206,299	1,515,301
Chicago	503,185	1,099,850
Philadelphia	847,170	1,046,964

Over 500,000 and under 1,000,000.

Brooklyn	566,663	806,343

Over 200,000 and less than 500,000.

St. Louis	350,518	451,770
Boston	362,839	448,477
Baltimore	332,313	434,439
San Francisco	233,959	298,997
Cincinnati	255,139	296,908
Cleveland	160,146	261,353
Buffalo	155,134	255,664
New Orleans	216,090	242,039
Pittsburg	156,389	238,617
Washington	147,203	230,392
Detroit	116,340	205,876
Milwaukee	115,587	204,468

Over 100,000 and less than 200,000.

Name.	Population in 1880.	1890.
Newark	136,508	181,830
Minneapolis	46,887	164,738
Jersey City	120,722	163,003
Louisville	123,758	161,129
Omaha	30,518	140,452
Rochester	89,366	133,896
Saint Paul	41,473	133,156
Kansas City	55,785	132,716
Providence	104,857	132,146
Denver	35,629	106,713
Indianapolis	75,056	105,436
Allegheny	78,682	105,287

According to the census of 1880, there were thirteen cities having a population of more than 50,000 and less than 100,000, making a total of thirty-three cities having over 50,000 inhabitants, of which three are situated south of the parallel of 38° — namely, San Francisco (which, however, is very near that parallel), New Orleans, and Richmond. In 1890 there were twenty-nine cities having a population of more than 50,000 and less than 100,000 inhabitants, making a total of fifty-eight cities having over 50,000 inhabitants, of which eight are south of the parallel of 38° — namely, San Francisco, New Orleans, Richmond, Nashville, Atlanta, Memphis, Charleston, and Los Angeles.

The following table shows the number and percentage of persons of native and foreign birth in the United States, as given by each census since such statistics began to be collected: —

Date.	Population.		Percentage.	
	Native.	Foreign.	Native.	Foreign.
1850	20,947,274	3,244,602	90.32	9.68
1860	27,304,624	4,138,697	86.84	13.16
1870	32,991,162	5,567,229	85.56	14.44
1880	43,475,840	6,679,943	86.68	13.32
1890	53,372,703	9,249,547	85.23	14.77

II. IMMIGRATION.

The subject of immigration into the United States has recently been reported on very fully by the Bureau of Statistics,* and from that report the following con-

---

* See Quarterly Report of the Bureau of Statistics, No. 2, 1892-93, page 301 *et seq.*

densed statement of the more important facts connected with this matter has been compiled.

No official records of immigration into the United States were kept prior to 1820, but the number of arrivals from the close of the Revolutionary War up to that date has been estimated at 250,000. Previous to 1856 there had been no attempt made to distinguish immigrants, or those who came intending to remain permanently in this country, from those who came simply as visitors or as transient passengers. From 1856 to 1868 a step in advance was made by giving the total number of immigrants, separating them from transient passengers; but since 1868, not only the number, but the nationality, of the former has been carefully recorded. Of course absolute accuracy cannot be expected in statistics of this kind. Thus, for instance, some persons come to this country not intending to remain, but do become permanent residents, while the converse of this occasionally happens. Moreover, since there is no law providing for the collection of the statistics of immigration by land, arrivals from British North America and from Mexico can be only imperfectly given. Previous to 1885 the attempt was made, however, to include among the immigrants reported as arriving in the United States those who came by land; but since that time this has been given up as impracticable, owing to the difficulty of collecting information on the numerous railway trains arriving from Canada and Mexico. It is believed that the number of immigrants from Mexico, or passing through that country on their way to the United States, is very small, but the number coming by way of Canada is very considerable. The number of immigrants reported by the Canadian officials as having passed through that country on their way to the United States is given as 567,557 for the eight years ending with 1892, an average of nearly 71,000 per year, and this fact should be taken into consideration in connection with what here follows.

During the entire period from 1820 to 1892 much the greater portion of the immigration into the United States has come from Europe, the proportion of European immigrants increasing from 68.89 per cent in the decade 1821-30 to 89.99 in the decade 1881-90. In the very earliest period of this immigration movement, from 1820 to 1830, nearly all the countries of Europe were represented to some extent, but the total number during that time was comparatively small, having increased from about 8,000 in 1820 to a little over 23,000 in 1830. In the forty years from 1821 to 1860, inclusive, over one half of the immigration into this country was from England and Ireland, and the greater portion was from the last-named country. In the decades 1831-40 and 1841-50 one quarter of the entire immigration, and from 1851 to 1870 about one third, was from Germany. Between 1871 and 1892, the proportion of German immigrants has varied between a third and a fifth; in 1891 and 1892 it was 20.65 per cent, and the average of the entire period from 1821 to 1892 was 28.59 per cent of the total immigration. The United Kingdom and Germany have, therefore, together furnished the bulk of the immigration into the United States.

During the last two decades the flow of population into this country from Scandinavia, Austro-Hungary, Russia, and Italy has been pretty steadily increasing in magnitude. During the decade 1881–90, the first named of these countries furnished about the same percentage of the total immigration as did Ireland. In the years 1891 and 1892, Austro-Hungary, Italy, and Russia together contributed more than two fifths to the total immigration into the United States.

The following tables illustrate the more important points connected with this subject: —

In the first table the total immigration into the United States from 1821 to 1892, inclusive, is presented, and also the division of this total among the various countries which have been the principal contributors to it.

TOTAL IMMIGRATION INTO THE UNITED STATES FROM 1821 TO 1892 INCLUSIVE, AND ITS DISTRIBUTION AMONG THE MORE IMPORTANT NATIONALITIES.

Germany	4,748,440
Ireland	3,592,247
England	2,534,955
Norway and Sweden	1,032,188
Austro-Hungary	586,666
Italy	526,749
Russia	517,507
France	379,687
Scotland	347,900
China	296,219
Switzerland	185,488
Denmark	163,769
All other countries	2,700,295
The grand total is	16,611,060

In the following table the number of immigrants arriving in the United States is given for each decade from 1821 to 1890, with a classification in which the relative importance of the immigration from the United Kingdom in the earlier decades is conspicuously manifested, as also the remarkable increase in the years 1881 to 1890.

IMMIGRATION—NUMBER AND ORIGIN.

STATEMENT OF IMMIGRANT ARRIVALS IN THE UNITED STATES FOR THE DECADES 1821–90.

From	1821–30.	1831–40.	1841–50.	1851–60.	1861–70.	1871–80.	1881–90.
British Islands	75,803	283,191	1,047,763	1,338,093	1,106,970	989,163	1,462,839
Rest of Europe	23,013	212,497	549,739	1,114,564	1,073,429	1,357,801	3,258,743
China	2	8	35	41,397	68,059	122,436	61,711
Rest of the World	44,621	103,429	115,714	104,160	349,756	475,295	463,320
Total	143,439	599,125	1,713,251	2,598,214	2,466,752	2,944,695	5,246,613
Yearly Average	14,344	59,912	171,325	259,821	246,675	294,469	524,661

Still further light will be thrown on this subject by the following table, in which the nationality of the immigration into the United States is given in considerable detail for the years 1881 to 1887, in percentages of the total amount. From this table it will be seen that Germany furnished during those seven

PERCENTAGE TABLE SHOWING THE NATIONALITY OF IMMIGRANTS INTO THE UNITED STATES FOR THE YEARS 1881–87.

	1881.	1882.	1883.	1884.	1885.	1886.	1887.
Great Britain	13.10	12.11	12.92	13.69	15.92	18.75	20.04
Ireland	9.85	9.99	14.67	12.70	14.21	13.47	14.06
Austro-Hungary	3.92	4.10	5.30	6.81	7.31	10.22	7.56
Belgium	.27	.15	.29	.37	.39	.42	.58
Denmark	1.24	1.75	1.71	1.65	1.07	1.69	1.80
France	.78	.76	.70	.80	.90	1.04	1.08
Germany	34.66	31.80	32.33	33.72	30.72	21.96	21.53
Italy	2.79	4.03	5.18	3.14	4.42	7.78	8.99
Netherlands	1.50	1.08	.86	.81	.71	.68	1.02
Norway and Sweden	11.51	12.00	9.45	8.22	9.47	11.73	13.46
Russia	2.01	3.07	1.78	4.32	5.72	8.45	5.95
Spain and Portugal	.06	.66	.16	.11	.26	.13	.01
Switzerland	1.62	1.62	2.00	1.78	1.40	1.15	1.26
Other European countries	.06	.06	.06	.23	.19	.64	.25
China	2.87	4.87	.07	.02	.02	.00	.00
British North America	13.22	11.90	11.74	10.38	5.22	....	....
All other countries	.54	.65	.78	1.25	1.41	1.89	1.81
	100.00	100.00	100.00	100.00	100.00	100.00	100.00

years somewhat less than one third of the total immigration; Great Britain and Ireland somewhat more than a quarter; Norway and Sweden about a tenth; British North America about a tenth; Austro-Hungary a little over six per cent; Russia (including Poland) from four to five per cent; and Italy nearly the same. These nationalities together furnished during the six years 1882–87 about ninety-five per cent of the total. The immigration from Italy and Russia shows a moderately rapid, but pretty uniform, increase from year to year. From France, Spain, and Portugal the immigration has been, during the entire period, almost insignificant in amount.

This subject is still further illustrated by the following table, which gives the number of immigrants into the United States for the years 1890, 1891, and 1892, with a detailed statement of the various nationalities.[1]

Country.	Years.		
	1890.	1891.	1892.
England and Wales	57,689	54,048	50,527
Scotland	12,041	12,557	11,520
Ireland	53,024	55,706	55,467
Total United Kingdom	122,754	122,311	117,514
Denmark	9,366	10,659	10,593
France	6,585	6,770	6,521
Germany	92,427	113,554	130,758
Italy	52,003	76,055	62,137
Netherlands	4,326	5,206	7,260
Austro-Hungary	56,199	71,042	80,136
Russia	46,671	74,923	117,692
Sweden and Norway	41,002	49,448	57,709
Switzerland	6,993	6,811	7,408
All other countries	16,976	23,340	25,356
Total	455,302	560,319	623,084

[1] For later statistics of immigration see Appendix A.

The total immigration into the United States for the twelve years 1881-92 has been as follows: —

1881	669,431	1887	490,109
1882	788,992	1888	546,889
1883	603,322	1889	444,427
1884	518,592	1890	455,302
1885	395,346	1891	560,319
1886	334,203	1892	623,084

The above figures indicate a considerable fluctuation in the total immigration into this country, the reasons for which cannot easily be given. The maximum of the last twelve years was in the year 1882, 788,992 persons, and the minimum in 1886, with 334,203 persons; since the latter date there has been a pretty steady rise in the number, those for 1892 being nearly the double of those for 1886. The yearly average for the decade 1881-90 was 524,661, which is nearly the double of the average of the preceding decade.

The table on the preceding page, showing the number and the nationalities of the immigration for the three years 1890-92, exhibits, in the main, facts similar to those indicated in the percentage table of the nationality of immigrants for the years 1881-87, given on page 17. A slight decrease in the immigration from the United Kingdom from year to year is evident, the average of the three years being only a little more than a fifth of the total. The immigration from France and Denmark remained nearly stationary; that from Sweden and Norway and Germany increased rapidly and quite regularly; that from Russia very rapidly and regularly; that from Italy rapidly and irregularly. Russia furnished in 1892 as large a number of immigrants to the United States as the United Kingdom, and nine tenths as many as Germany.

The immigration into the United States is very unequally distributed over the surface of the country. An inspection of the census tables and the accompanying maps shows that immigrants in very large proportion seek Northern regions. In the Southern States, with the exception of Florida, Louisiana, and Texas, the foreign element is practically null. North Carolina, South Carolina, Alabama, Georgia, and Mississippi have less than one per cent of foreign-born population; Virginia, Tennessee, and Arkansas less than two per cent. No State south of Maryland and the Ohio River east of the Mississippi has as much as five per cent, with the exception of Florida. In the North Atlantic, Northwestern Central, and Cordilleran States and Territories, on the other hand, the foreign element is most strongly represented. Thus, in Rhode Island, Wisconsin, Minnesota, North Dakota, Montana, and Nevada the foreign-born population is over thirty per cent of the native; in Massachusetts, Connecticut, New York, Illinois, Michigan, South Dakota, Idaho, Wyoming, Colorado, Utah, Washington, Oregon, and California, over twenty but less than thirty per cent. Texas forms an exception to the other Southern States, the foreign element being of some importance — 6.84 per cent — especially in the southwestern portion of the State.

The following table shows by geographical divisions the percentage of the native and foreign-born of the total population in 1890, as well as the percentage of native white persons born of foreign parents.

Division.	Native.	Foreign.	Native white of foreign parents.
North Atlantic	77.66	22.34	25.03
South Atlantic	97.65	2.35	3.64
North Central	81.84	18.16	25.08
South Central	97.07	2.93	4.62
Cordilleran	74.54	25.46	23.45

The distribution of native white persons of foreign parentage follows very closely that of the foreign-born element, showing that those States and Territories which a generation ago attracted European immigrants still continue to attract them in practically the same degree.

The following table shows the percentage increase of native and foreign-born by geographical divisions, and for the whole country, for each census since 1850.

Division.	Percentage Increase of Native.				Percentage Increase of Foreign.			
	1850–60.	1860–70.	1870–80.	1880–90.	1850–60.	1860–70.	1870–80.	1880–90.
North Atlantic	17.38	14.09	19.58	19.57	17.68	30.51	20.46	34.10
South Atlantic	13.73	9.31	20.53	16.52	51.89	2.67	4.44	19.66
North Central	58.91	40.97	35.68	26.68	137.30	51.18	25.01	39.20
South Central	32.93	11.96	39.41	23.20	68.13	1.39	17.65	17.34
Cordilleran	189.84	53.91	87.20	78.02	562.50	75.06	59.58	54.16
United States	30.35	20.83	31.78	22.76	84.38	34.52	19.99	38.47

There were in the United States as a whole in 1890 17,330 foreign-born persons to each 100,000 native-born, as against 15,365 in 1880, and 16,875 in 1870. There has been an increase in the number of foreign-born to each 100,000 native-born for the North Atlantic division from 24,070 in 1880 to 28,773 in 1890, and in the North Central division from 20,189 to

22,184. In the Cordilleran division there has been a decrease in the number of foreign-born to each 100,000 native-born from 39,448 in 1880 to 34,161 in 1890. In the South Atlantic and South Central divisions the foreign-born element is not numerically of importance, there being only 3,021 foreign-born to each 100,000 native-born in 1890 in the South Central division, and but 2,411 in the South Atlantic division.

Early in 1882 an Act was passed by Congress suspending Chinese immigration into the United States for the term of twenty years. This was vetoed by the President, and another one was passed having nearly the same provisions as the first, but limiting the time of its operation to ten years. This Act was not vetoed: but became a law May 6, 1882. This second Act is entitled "An Act to execute certain treaty stipulations relating to Chinese." From and after ninety days after the passage of this Act the entrance of Chinese "laborers" into the United States was forbidden, and any master of a vessel bringing them here was punishable by a fine of $500 for each laborer so brought, and also by imprisonment for a term not exceeding one year. The pretext for this unprecedented act was "that the coming of Chinese laborers to this country endangers the good order of certain localities" within the territory of the United States. The term "laborers" was held to mean "both skilled and unskilled laborers, and Chinese employed in mining."

Further legislation relating to the exclusion of the Chinese from the United States was had by Congress in 1888. Two Acts were passed, the first having been approved Sept. 13, 1888, and a second, supplementary to this, October 1 of the same year. The object of these two Acts was to prevent the Chinese who were then in the United States from returning after having left this country. The first Act (approved September 13) allowed a native of China to leave the country and return, provided he had "a lawful wife, child, or parent within the United States, or property therein of the value of one thousand dollars, or debts of like amount due him and pending settlement." This privilege was entirely cancelled by the supplementary Act, approved October 1; and as the matter now stands, only "Chinese officials, teachers, students, merchants, or travellers for pleasure or curiosity are permitted to enter the United States." Futhermore, it is provided that in order to become entitled to such entrance they must "obtain the permission of the Chinese Government or other Government of which they may at the time be citizens or subjects." This permission, and the personal identity of the party having obtained it, must be authenticated by the diplomatic or consular representative of the United States at the port or place from which the party comes. It is farther provided that any master of a vessel landing, or attempting to land, any Chinese laborer, "in contravention to the provisions of this Act, shall be deemed guilty of a misdemeanor, and, on conviction thereof, shall be punished with a fine of not less than five hundred nor more than one thousand dollars, in the discretion of the Court, for every Chinese laborer or other Chinese person so brought, and may also be imprisoned for a term of not less than one year, nor more than five years, in the discretion of the Court."

Provisions have also been made by Act of Congress for the regulation of the immigrant carrying business, and rules have been prescribed as to food, water, light, space occupied, etc. A tax of fifty cents is also imposed on all immigrants landing in this country to be used "in defraying the expense of regulating immigration under this Act, and for the care of immigrants arriving in the United States, for the relief of such as are in distress, etc."[1]

By an Act of Congress approved August 3, 1882, it is provided that no convict, lunatic, idiot, or person "unable to take care of himself or herself without becoming a public charge," shall be permitted to land. Under the provisions of this Act it appears that from 1883 to Jan. 30, 1893, 11,421 immigrants had been returned from the United States to their own countries,— or an average of about 1,000 persons a year. Of those thus returned from 1883 to June 30, 1893, inclusive, there were 120 convicts, 486 lunatics, and 151 idiots. The remainder (10,664 persons) were returned as "liable to become a public charge."

A very stringent Act was passed by Congress in 1885, prohibiting the importation and immigration of foreigners and aliens "under contract or agreement to perform labor in the United States, its Territories, and the District of Columbia." Under the provisions of this Act there had been returned to their own countries, up to 1888, 7,764 persons. During the fiscal year[2] ending June 30, 1893, 464 persons were thus returned.

---

[1] Not collected from immigrants coming from Canada or Mexico.

[2] For further remarks in regard to the general subject of immigration into the United States, its distribution etc., as also in reference to the exclusion of the Chinese and other unwelcome persons, see Appendix A.

III. IRRIGATION.

The following table is given by the census of 1890, as illustrating the distribution of the population in accordance with the mean annual rainfall.

Inches of Rainfall.	Population per square mile.			Increase in Population per square mile.	
	1870.	1880.	1890.	1870-1880.	1880-1890.
Below 10	0.3	0.6	0.8	0.3	0.2
10 to 20	0.4	0.8	1.8	0.4	1.0
20 " 30	1.6	4.7	8.1	3.1	3.4
30 " 40	28.6	35.5	43.1	6.9	7.6
40 " 50	39.4	49.2	59.0	9.8	9.8
50 " 60	15.5	20.9	25.1	5.4	4.2
60 " 70	11.9	14.5	18.1	2.6	3.6
Above 70	0.8	2.1	4.1	1.3	2.0

It must be remembered, in consulting the above table, that the statistics of rainfall where this is very scanty are never satisfactory, and this is emphatically the case in the arid region of the United States, where the stations at which meteorological observations are taken are few in number, and the topographical conditions such that the rainfall is very irregularly distributed, and extremely variable in amount from year to year. Only by means of a very long series of observations at many stations, plotted on accurate topographical maps made on a large scale, could even approximately accurate hyetographic curves be drawn.

Nearly three fourths of the population of the United States inhabit a region over which the rainfall is between thirty and fifty inches in amount, and on either side of the area thus favored the number of persons to the square mile diminishes very rapidly, as shown by the figures given in the above table. But the extent of country where these conditions are more or less influential is very unequally divided between areas of abundant precipitation and of excessive dryness. Only over a very small part of the country does the rainfall exceed fifty inches, while considerably more than two fifths receives less than twenty inches. But it is by no means true that the scantiness of population over the region having more than fifty inches of rainfall is due to that excess of precipitation. There is no part of the United States where the rainfall is so large as to be the essential cause of a thinly distributed population. Many large areas of the earth's surface are densely inhabited even where the precipitation is much larger than it is in any part of the United States. The regions of very large rainfall in this country are parts of Mississippi and Louisiana adjacent to the Gulf of Mexico, and the southern portion of Florida. There is also a narrow belt similarly conditioned along the Pacific coast in Oregon and Washington. Here it is clearly the case that other causes than excessive precipitation connect themselves with and are responsible for the scantiness of the population. The coast of Oregon and Washington is bordered by high mountains, not easily cleared and cultivated, and coming close down to the sea. Most of the peninsula of Florida lies too low for easy drainage: the delta of the Mississippi and the adjoining regions have similar disadvantages. The Southwestern Central division of the United States (including Arkansas, Oklahoma, Louisiana, and Texas), much the larger portion of which receives over twenty but less than fifty inches of rainfall, has, according to the census of 1890, only 10.3 persons to the square mile, while the table given above shows that in the belt in which the precipitation ranges from fifty to sixty there were 25.1 to the square mile in 1890, and in the belt ranging between sixty and seventy 18.1 to the square mile.

Far otherwise is it in regard to the scantiness of the population over a very considerable fraction of the United States as conditioned at the present time in large part, and likely to be so in the future, by the insufficient supply of rain. This so called "Arid Region" comprises two fifths of the whole area of the country, but contains only three per cent of its population. Moreover, there was during the interval between the census of 1880 and that of 1890 but very little change in the density of the population of this region. Of the three subdivisions of the Cordilleran division of the country, the Plateau is most scantily supplied with water, and in that region (comprising the State of Nevada and the Territories of Arizona and Utah) the density of the population increased between 1880 and 1890 only 0.3 (or from 0.7 to 1.0) per square mile. In the whole Cordilleran division, comprising 39.3 per cent of the total area of the United States (exclusive of Alaska), the density of the population was raised between 1880 and 1890 from 1.5 to 2.5 per square mile. In the State of Nevada during that interval there was a considerable decrease of the population. The following table gives the essential facts regarding the area, distribution, and number of the population of the Cordilleran region, as reported by the census of 1880 and that of 1890.

AREA AND POPULATION OF THE CORDILLERAN DIVISION OF THE UNITED STATES IN 1880 AND 1890.

Subdivision.	Area.		Population.			
	Square miles.	Per cent of total.	Per cent of total.		Per sq. mile.	
			1880.	1890.	1880.	1890.
Rocky Mountain. .	555,275	18.4	0.8	1.3	0.7	1.8
Plateau	308,690	10.2	0.5	0.5	0.7	1.0
Pacific Coast . . .	323,570	10.7	2.2	2.9	3.4	5.7
Total	1,187,535	39.3	3.5	4.7	1.5	2.5

Irrigation has done something to mitigate the unfavorable condition of the arid belt, but no artificial assistance can do more than palliate to a limited degree, and that only within certain favorably situated areas of small extent, the discomforts and disadvantages of those who live in and attempt to cultivate a region where the rainfall is insufficient.

Irrigation was employed in California almost from the beginning of the placer-mining excitement; but at first, of course, only on a very small scale. The canals (usually called "ditches") which were originally built solely for the purpose of bringing water for use in gold washing, soon began to be used in part for irrigation, and chiefly for raising fruit and vegetables. As the mines became exhausted the water was more and more used for agricultural purposes. Later on, the construction of canals or ditches for irrigation solely, and on a more extensive scale, was successfully attempted, especially along the base of the foot-hills in the southern part of the Sierra. The same thing was done in the more southern part of the State, in the western and southwestern border region or foot-hills of the Coast Ranges. As the towns grew larger, dams began to be built to hold back water for their supply. At the eastern base of the Rocky Mountains, in Colorado, the natural advantages for irrigation are great, and this business has there become of considerable importance. This had all been done under authority of the various States, but after a time the general government took the matter into consideration, and Congress decided to do at least a certain amount of preliminary work, with the idea of laying the foundation of a more comprehensive and scientifically planned system of irrigation for the whole arid region of the country.

With this end in view, an appropriation was made in 1888 of $100,000, and one of $250,000 in the next year, and others in succeeding years,[1] the expenditure of which was placed in the hands of the Director of the United States Geological Survey. The objects to be attained by the work thus authorized, as stated in the Joint Resolution of Congress approved March 20, 1888, and in various Acts of that body, are: " to investigate the practicability of constructing reservoirs for the storage of water in the arid regions of the United States; also to classify the public lands, and furnish a map or maps showing the various divisions of the public domain suitable for agricultural, mineral, and other purposes; and particularly to segregate the lands susceptible of irrigation, where irrigation is required, from other lands, and designating places for reservoirs, canals, and other hydraulic works."

[1] For the fiscal year ending June 30, 1891, $41,500.89.

Up to the present time (September, 1893) three reports of the irrigation survey work thus authorized and set in operation have been published or are available for reference.[1] From these the following data have been compiled.

During the first season of this survey the necessary preliminary topographic and hydrographic work was begun: in Montana, at the head-waters of the Columbia and Missouri Rivers; in Nevada, near the head-waters of the Truckee, Carson, and Walker; in Colorado, on the South Platte and the Upper Arkansas; in New Mexico, in the drainage basin of the Rio Grande.

In the second year of this work, engineering surveys were carried on in Montana, principally along the Sun River; in Colorado, on the head-waters of the Arkansas, and in Kansas farther down that river; on the Rio Grande, principally in the vicinity of El Paso; in California, around Clear Lake and in the Sierra Nevada; in Nevada, on the Truckee and Carson Rivers; in Utah, around Utah Lake; and in Idaho, on the lava plains adjoining Snake River. In Montana, ten reservoir sites were surveyed, and on the head-waters of the Arkansas, eight. Work of a similar kind was done in the other localities mentioned above, especially near El Paso, where the position of a proposed large dam was fixed, at the outlet of Donner Lake in California

---

[1] Report I., in the Tenth Annual Report of the U. S. Geol. Survey. Part II. Irrigation. 1890.

Report II., in the Eleventh Annual Report of same. Part II. Irrigation. 1891.

Report III., in Report of the Secretary of the Interior (52 Cong. 1st Sess., Ex. Doc. 1, Part 5), containing Twelfth Annual Report of the U. S. Geol. Survey. Part II. Irrigation. 1892.

and of other lakes in the same vicinity. Furthermore, in the Snake River division surveys were made "demonstrating the practicability of diverting the waters of that river upon the lava plains upon both sides of the stream," etc., etc.

In the Third Report of the Irrigation Survey, the results of the previous years' work are summed up in the statement that 147 reservoir sites were surveyed and reported for segregation, of which 33 are in California, 46 in Colorado, 27 in Montana, 39 in New Mexico, and 2 in Nevada. The total area segregated for these reservoirs was 165,932 acres. The aggregate contents of all these reservoirs are given as being 2,847,815 acre-feet, supposed or assumed to be sufficient to irrigate 1,898,544 acres. Of these reservoir sites, diagrams are given in the report, which was prepared by A. H. Thompson, who was in charge of this department of the work. In addition there is a special report "On the Hydrography of the Arid Region" by F. H. Newell, and one by H. M. Wilson on "Irrigation in India," occupying nearly 200 royal octavo pages.

Nothing has yet been done toward the accomplishment of any of these gigantic schemes, involving an immense expenditure, if they were actually to be carried out. With any such attempted carrying out, the practical difficulties which would arise, aside from the question of cost, would be great and manifold. The engineering difficulties of large dams, not only those of construction, but those of preservation after building, have been sufficiently shown in the numerous catastrophes which have occurred in this country during the past few years, resulting from the giving way of these structures, and by which thousands of lives have been lost. The legal difficulties involved in the distribution of the water and the right to purchase the land about to be benefited by the irrigation works of any particular district, as well as the question of conflict between United States and State or Territorial authorities, would not be the least of the obstacles which would have to be met and overcome, if the United States should really embark in any such irrigation enterprise as seems to have been contemplated by Congress at the time of the inception of this irrigation scheme.

The question of the probable cost of dams and storage basins in the arid region receives some light from the examination of what has been expended by the United States government in building reservoirs at the head-waters of the Mississippi River. The object of these reservoirs is defined by the Chief of Engineers to be "to collect surplus water, principally from the precipitation of winter, spring, and early summer, to be systematically released so as to benefit navigation upon the Mississippi River below the dams." [1]

This reservoir project was the outcome of surveys and examinations made in 1869, 1874, 1878, and 1879. Up to the close of the fiscal year ending June 30, 1891, the sum of $619,850.20 had been expended on this work, and a further sum of $1,034,683.50 was estimated as required for the completion of the project. Up to the year 1886 four of the proposed reservoirs had been completed, and during the months of May and June, 1891, men and materials had been assembled for

[1] Annual Report of the Chief of Engineers, U. S. Army, 1892, Part I. p. 257.

the erection of a fifth at Sandy Lake. The completed reservoirs are said to have been operated from 1885 to 1891, during seasons of low water, "to the benefit of navigation on more than 165 miles of the Mississippi River." The "true effectiveness" of the system does not seem yet to have been ascertained, since the officer in charge of the work recommends that appropriations be continued "for the operation and maintenance of the five reservoirs, and for hydrological and meteorological observations, to determine the effect of the reservoir water." The latter purpose is said to be "specially worthy of consideration, for the result of the observations extending over a period of several years would determine the true effectiveness of the reservoirs."[1]

[1] There is an elaborate discussion of the question of the utility of the reservoirs at the head-waters of the Mississippi in the Report of the Chief of Engineers cited above. It contains a condensed history of the reservoirs, proposed and built, at the head-waters of the Mississippi River and its tributaries, with a brief *résumé* of the results up to the close of the season in 1887, with additional matter by the engineer in charge of the work, bringing the whole subject down to the end of the fiscal year ending June 30, 1892. The question whether the benefits realized are sufficient to justify the enormous expenditures incurred in this work does not seem to have been satisfactorily answered. It is claimed that by the release of the stored-up water of the four completed reservoirs (at Lake Winibigoshish, Leech Lake, Pokegama Falls, and Pine River, this last completed in 1886) there was an increase in the channel depth at St. Paul of one foot during the low water season of 1888; but "the effect of the reservoirs on the navigable depths of the water in the channel of the Mississippi River above the Falls of St. Anthony is not as clearly shown as it could be." Practically the navigation of the Mississippi ends at St. Paul, above which point there are numerous falls and rapids. The upper part of the river appears to be chiefly used for rafting logs during the season of high water, and it seems that the system of dam construction for the purpose of increasing the depth in the channel during low water season is opposed by the lumbermen as being decidedly in conflict with their interests. Should this prove to be the case, it is to be feared that

Frequent reference is made in the various United States and State reports on irrigation to the condition of things in India, and to the vast irrigational engineering operations which have been carried on there by the government; which, however, are to a considerable extent merely a continuation, systematization, and amplification of what the natives had been doing for centuries.

There are very great and essential differences between the condition of things in India and the United States, with reference to the governmental control of irrigation. The Indian government has the means of repaying itself, in large part at least, for its expenditures in this department of the public works. It is the land which furnishes the chief source of Indian revenue, and the collection of the land tax forms the main work of Indian administration.[1] The rate of assessment, however, varies with the quality of the land, and with the advantages, natural or artificial, which it possesses. The average rate is 9s. 6d. per acre on irrigated land, as compared with only 2s. 3d. per acre on unirrigated land.[2] Any similar method of repayment to the United States government for the expenditures incurred in engineering irrigational works would be impossible.

---

the dams, unless carefully defended from attack by the United States authorities, will be more or less completely destroyed by those who consider that their natural rights to use the river for rafting purposes have been interfered with by the general government.

[1] "That the state should appropriate to itself a share of the produce of the soil, is a maxim of finance which has been recognized throughout the East from time immemorial. . . . No other system of taxation could be theoretically more just, or in practice less obnoxious, to the people." W. W. Hunter, in "Our Indian Empire," London, 1882, page 334.

[2] W. W. Hunter, loc. cit., page 424.

But, furthermore, the conditions of the two countries, British India and the arid region of the United States, both as to climate and population, are, if not entirely different, at least so essentially unlike, that no safe conclusion can be drawn from a comparison of their irrigational possibilities.

And, first, as to population: India is a densely populated country, as compared with the United States as a whole, and much more so as contrasted with the arid region of the last named country. The census of 1891 showed a population of 287,234,849 on 1,557,484 square miles of British territory — that is, including the feudatory states. Here, as will be seen from these figures, we have almost five times the population of the United States on about half its area. But the portion of the latter country which it is proposed to irrigate has, as will be seen from the table on page 28, only from one to two persons to the square mile, while British India as a whole (excluding the native states) has a little over 233 to the square mile.

Again, India, on the whole, is a region of large precipitation, only small portions of that country having a scanty supply of rain. It is irregularity of precipitation, or exceptional seasons of drought, rather than a small average amount, for which provision has chiefly to be made. Sind, which derives its supply mainly from canals filled by the floods of the Indus, and where the percentage of irrigated as compared with non-irrigated land is largest (80 per cent), has only a little more than 2,000,000 acres under cultivation, the total of British India being nearly one hundred times greater. Sind, however, has been exceptionlly free from famine uuder British rule. Orissa, on the other hand, where the average rainfall exceeds sixty inches, was, a few years ago, the scene of one of the most severe famines of recent times.

The annexed table gives a pretty good idea of the comparative density of the population, as well as of the relative amount of irrigation and the amount and variability of the rainfall in the most important provinces of British India.[1]

Province.	Population to square mile.	Acres of area ordinarily cultivated.	Acres of area ordinarily irrigated.	Per cent of cultivated land irrigated.	Rainfall in inches.	
					Average Annual.	Local Variation.
Punjab	187.4	21,000,000	5,500,000	26.2	22	6–30
N. W. Provinces and Oudh	442.2	36,000,000	11,500,000	32.0	36	25–50
Bengal	473.5	54,500,000	1,000,000	1.8	West. 49	43–61
					Lower 66	54–112
Central Provinces	127.4	15,500,000	770,000	5.0	51	43–79
Berar	163.5	6,500,000	100,000	1.5	35	21–69
Bombay	150.4	24,500,000	450,000	1.8	..	...
Sind		2,250,000	1,800,000	80.0	..	...
Madras	248.3	32,000,000	7,300,000	23.0	..	...
Mysore	196.6	5,000,000	800,000	16.0	29	18–36

The following table shows the annual average precipitation at certain stations in the arid region, those being selected at which the observations have been continued during the greatest number of years.[2] Arizona, New Mexico, Colorado, and Utah are represented,

[1] This table is compiled chiefly from data furnished by H. F. Blanford, in "Climates and Weather of India, Ceylon, and Burmah," London, 1889, and W. W. Hunter's "Indian Empire," London, 1882.

[2] The information presented in this table has been compiled from the Report of the Chief Signal Officer on Irrigation and Water Storage in the Arid Region (1891), 51st Cong. 2d Session, Ex. Doc. No. 287.

RAINFALL OF ARID REGION. 37

no very recent available data for other Cordilleran States and Territories having been obtained. The scantiness and irregular yearly distribution of the precipitation in the region which the table covers are

ANNUAL PRECIPITATION AND LOCAL VARIATION AT CERTAIN STATIONS IN THE ARID REGION.

Station.	Average Annual Precipitation.	No. of Years observed.	Precipitation.		Local Range.
			Greatest.	Least.	
Casa Grande, Arizona	4.28	10	10.70	1.73	8.97
Maricopa, "	5.17	15	11.96	0.38	11.58
Fort McDowell, "	10.38	24	20.95	4.94	16.01
Fort Mohave, "	5.99	17	5.99	21.38	2.16
Phœnix, "	7.88	16	12.83	5.17	7.66
Tucson, "	12.11	15	18.37	5.26	13 11
Fort Verde, "	13.13	22	27.53	4.82	22.76
Whipple Barracks, "	17.06	20	26.75	10 02	16.73
Fort Craig, New Mexico	10.84	24	24.58	4.63	19.95
Santa Fé, "	14.69	39	24.80	7.75	17.05
Fort Selden, "	8 57	18	12.60	3.49	9.11
Fort Stanton, "	19.05	23	28.70	12.63	16.07
Fort Collins, Colorado	13.75	16	14.48	9.70	4.78
Colorado Springs, "	14.79	17	18.56	9.12	9.44
Denver, "	14.32	21	20.12	9.51	10.61
Pike's Peak, "	28.65	18	44 57	9.28	35.29
Fort Garland, "	12.74	12	42.34	7.44	34.90
Fort Lyon, "	11.07	11	13.47	4.54	8.93
Blue Creek, Utah	8.27	14	11.94	4.13	7.81
Corinne, "	11.58	21	18.95	5.41	13.54
Camp Douglas, "	17.41	24	28.00	6.73	21.27
Ogden, "	13.46	21	20.60	6.54	14.06
Promontory, "	7.61	21	14.67	3.30	11.37
Salt Lake City, "	16.85	29	38.20	10.94	27.26
Terrace, "	4.29	21	10.04	0.76	9.28

here most strikingly manifested. There is not a single station (with the exception of Pike's Peak, at an elevation of over 14,000 feet) where a series of observations of any considerable length has been taken, in the arid region, where the annual precipitation averages as much as twenty inches: in all but five of these stations it falls below fifteen, and in one-third of them below ten.

This scantiness of the rainfall in the arid regions of the United States is in striking contrast with the abundance of the precipitation over a large part of India where irrigation is extensively employed. Thus, in the Northwest Provinces, including Oudh, where one third of the cultivated land is irrigated, the average annual rainfall is thirty-six inches, or about the same as that of Western New York and Northern Ohio, Indiana, and Illinois.

The most gigantic of the Indian system of irrigation works is that by which the districts of the Doab, or the high ground lying between the Indus and the Ganges, are supplied with water. For this purpose nearly the whole visible stream of this river in the winter and spring, before it has been swollen by the melting of the snows of the Himalaya is taken, at the point where it leaves the mountains and enters the plains (Hurdwar), and conveyed in an artificial channel two hundred feet wide and twenty feet in depth, the water itself being ten feet deep. This canal, after passing through a region where the engineering difficulties were tremendous, finally reaches the water-shed between the Ganges and the Jumna. This and another canal, taken out of the Ganges 200 miles lower down, are capable of discharging 10,000 cubic feet per second, and this great body of water is distributed by means of a main channel more than a thousand miles long, with four thousand miles of distributing channels.

There is an important question connected with the

subject of irrigation, namely, that of the effect on the soil of a long continuance of the process, or of what has sometimes been called "over irrigation," which really means "long continued irrigation." The saline ingredients which are contained in the water used are left behind, of course, as evaporation takes place, and this residuum accumulates with greater or less rapidity according to the quantity and purity of the water supplied to the soil. The smaller the rainfall of the irrigated regions the more rapid will be the accumulation of the saline matter, other things being equal, since this deposit is liable to be dissolved and carried off by the rain-water, which is itself almost chemically pure. Hence, in regions like the larger part of India, where irrigation is practised on a large scale coincidently with a very considerable amount of precipitation, the results of a long continued artificial supply of water to the surface are manifested only to a comparatively small extent, the surface soil being cleansed, as it were, by the occasional heavy falls of rain.

But even in India this deleterious effect of extensive irrigation seems already to be manifesting itself, and, in certain districts, to an alarming degree. This fact is admitted by some of the best authorities on Indian engineering matters. In support of this statement the following quotations are given from a work the object of which is to call attention to the extravagance of the Indian government, and the injury which this enormous expenditure on public works, especially on irrigation, is doing to that country. "Secondly — and this is a still more serious set-off, affecting alike the North-West Provinces and the Punjab — there has been a great loss of land revenue owing to increased exudation of *reh* or saline efflorescence, in many of the canal-irrigated districts. This is what Mr. A. O. Hume writes: 'In Oudh, the Punjab, and the North-West Provinces the soils contain an appreciable mixture of saline particles. With the construction of high-level canals the subsoil water-level is raised, the surface flooded, the earth yields up its soluble salts to the water, which again restores them (but on the surface) as it passes in vapour. At first the result may be good, and marvellous are the crops that have been raised in the Doab on the first introduction of canal-irrigation, owing to the first slender doses of potash and chloride of sodium. But nature works on blindly and unceasingly. The water below searches out one by one each soluble particle in excess of the particular soil's capacity of retention, and, as it slowly creeps up by capillary attraction, leaves these ever behind it on the surface. Time passes on; some crops begin to be unprofitable. In the hottest time of year a glimmer as though of hoar frost overspreads the land. . . . Along the little old Western Jumna Canal thousands of fields are to be seen thus sterilized. Along the course of the mighty Ganges Canal, a work as it were but of yesterday, the dreary, wintry-looking rime is already in many places creeping over the soil. . . . The time must come when some of the richest arable tracts in Northern India will have become howling saline deserts.' And this terrible fact is admitted by the engineers themselves. Thus Sir Andrew Clarke, late Public Works Minister in India, writes of the 'vast *oosur* plains, within easy reach of the canal, lying waste and barren,' and the white patches called *reh*. 'They represent a serious loss to Government, the *reh* especially so, for it is found to spread in a most alarming way with the extension of irrigation.' . . . It is to be hoped that this canal [the Sirhind] will prove a real blessing to the Punjab, but the note of warning, struck by Lord Ripon in declaring it open,. points to serious dangers ahead. 'I am,' he said, 'a warm friend of irrigation, but I must express my belief that it is possible to have too much of a good thing. . . . It is found that, although for a few years after the opening of a new canal the increase of fertility of the irrigated country is great and striking, a time comes when the crops begin to fall off, and the land commences to show signs of decline.' . . . Anyhow, till the *reh* difficulty is satisfactorily solved, it seems absurd for the Famine Commission to propose a further extension of the Western Jumna Canal through the districts north-west of Delhi."[1]

Similar facts connected with the subject of long continued or excessive irrigation have been frequently observed in other parts of the world, and have been more or less carefully investigated. The decay, loss of fertility, and consequent partial or entire abandonment of extensive areas of the earth's surface, once densely populated, is a matter which has excited much comment. Various districts not very far removed from the Mediterranean, and farther east, in Syria, Armenia, and Mesopotamia, are the localities where these changes of physical conditions within the historical period have been most clearly perceived and most generally ad-

[1] A. K. Connell. The Economic Revolution of India, and the Public Works Policy. London, 1883, pp. 121, 122, 127, 128.

mitted to have taken place. The most popular opinion in regard to the cause of these changes is, that they have been, in large part at least, the result of neglect or hostility on the part of man.[1]

The present writer is of opinion that the physical decay of the regions in question has been chiefly caused by a change in its climatic conditions, a positive diminution of the precipitation having taken place, and that this change has manifested itself over a large part of the earth's surface, having been begun long before the historic period, and being still active.[2] This desiccation, of course, connects itself intimately with the subject of irrigation, since the more widely the diminution of an already scanty rainfall has been felt, the more extensive have been the efforts to remedy this growing deficiency by artificial means.

The subject of the deterioration of the soil as a consequence of long continued irrigation has also been discussed in this country in connection with what has been observed in California, and especially in the southern part of the San Joaquin Valley, where, to use the

[1] Thus Mr. G. P. Marsh, in "The Earth Modified by Human Action," (New York, 1874,) makes the following statement: "The decay of these once flourishing countries is partly due, no doubt, to that class of geological causes whose action we can neither resist nor guide, and partly also to the direct violence of hostile human force; but it is, in a far greater proportion, either the result of man's ignorant disregard of the laws of nature, or the incidental consequence of war and of civil and ecclesiastical tyranny and misrule." The countries to which reference is here made are "Northern Africa, the greater Arabian peninsula, Syria, Mesopotamia, Armenia, and many other provinces of Asia Minor, Greece, Sicily, and parts of even Italy andSpain." *Loc. cit.*, pp. 4, 5. The same statements are repeated in the edition of 1885, pp. 3, 4.

[2] See the author's "Climatic Changes of Later Geological Times," (Cambridge, Mass., 1882,) Chapters II. and III., where this question is discussed at very considerable length.

words of the principal scientific investigator (Professor E. W. Hilgard) of this matter, " it was not until it began to be noted that in the irrigated districts of the Kern and Tulare Valley, the alkali was continually extending its area, and seriously damaging the wheat crop where before there had been no signs of it, that public interest was aroused." [1]

The phenomena exhibited in the San Joaquin Valley are thus described by Professor Hilgard : [2] "The rainfall in this region is usually so small (from five to six inches) as to suffice only for the moistening of the soil to the depth of a few feet; and during the time required for the evaporation of this natural moisture the short-lived vegetation of the region rapidly passes through its development. That vegetation consists of a comparatively small number of species of bright spring flowers, which in their season cover the entire country with a dense beautiful carpet, one and the same flower occupying the ground almost exclusively at times for many square miles by virtue of the law of the 'survival of the fittest.' Were there any crop of a habit similar to these flowers that could be profitably grown on these plains, irrigation could obviously be dispensed with. The settlers of the region have tried what seems to be the next best thing, viz.: to grow grain crops of a short period of growth, and therefore needing irrigation only during a small portion of the dry season. In so

---

[1] See "Alkali Lands, Irrigation, and Drainage in their Mutual Relations," by E. W. Hilgard, Professor of Agriculture and Director of Experiment Station. Sacramento, 1892. This is a pamphlet published by the College of Agriculture, University of California. It is a second edition of an Appendix to the Report for the year 1890.

[2] *Loc. cit.*, p. 15.

doing, they have moistened the soil to a considerably greater depth than was reached by the rain-water before, and as a consequence the annual evaporation has greatly increased. The irrigation water, moreover, has brought with it from these depths all the supply of alkali salts that before had gradually been washed beyond the reach of the ordinary rainfall by an occasional wet season. Each succeeding irrigation, followed by evaporation, tends to accumulate the salts nearer the surface, so that finally the root-crowns of the grain crops are 'burnt up' before even beginning to head. The evil will, of course, be greatly aggravated if the water used for irrigation originally contains any considerable amount of alkaline salts, which are superadded to those already in the soil strata."

The subject of the origin of the "reh" or alkali on irrigated lands is discussed at some length in Professor Hilgard's report, and the following quotation from that document will give, in a few words, his most essential conclusions, so far as they relate to the question of the difficulties of the irrigation problem: "From the facts above given regarding the alkali soils and irrigation waters of California, the importance of investigating thoroughly not only the quantity but also the quality of the water available for irrigation in the arid regions, is sufficiently obvious. The facts as nature has made them should be elicited and plainly set before the people, so that money may not be invested in useless undertakings, or damage done which it may be difficult to undo thereafter. There are probably but few rivers in the world of such composition or natural purity that continued irrigation without correlative under drainage can be practised without in the end causing an injurious accumulation of soluble salts in the soil. In India, according to the testimony of official reports, quoted herein, the evil effects of such practice have become painfully apparent, and to such an extent that after the expenditure of enormous sums for bringing the water upon the fields, the Government now finds itself face to face with the costly problem of its economical removal, by drainage, so as to relieve the soil of the accumulated 'alkali,' which has rendered it unfit for cultivation. An early attention to this matter, with such foresight as will prevent the occurrence of similar difficulties, cannot be too earnestly recommended to all interested in lands needing irrigation, from the Pacific coast to Colorado and Kansas." [1]

The desirability of drainage as a prevention of the accumulation of alkali on and near the surface depends on the fact that this seems to be brought about, to a considerable extent at least, not so much by the actual evaporation on the surface of the irrigation water as by the bringing up from below by capillary attraction and evaporation of the subsoil water holding saline matter in solution. The effect of irrigation is to raise the water level, thus bringing fresh alkaline particles to the surface, from which, in a hot and dry climate, evaporation is exceedingly rapid, and the deposit of saline mater proportionally large. The remedy for this, in the opinion of the Indian officials, is deep drainage, the object of this being, as expressed by the most concise and comprehensive term, the *remedying* of *defective water circulation*. The great difficulty and ex-

[1] *Loc. cit.*, page 56.

pense of any system of deep drainage in India has been repeatedly admitted by various officials. That there is still considerable uncertainty in regard to the causes of the development of alkali or "reh" on irrigated surfaces seems pretty evident, and in proof of this statement the following quotation is offered. It is an extract from a report of the "Reh Committee" for the Aligarh District, by the Superintendent of the Geological Survey of India, Mr. H. B. Medlicott.

"Observation and experiment cannot be profitably made by men, however otherwise intelligent, without any scientific knowledge of the matter under investigation. The almost total absence hitherto of this element in *reh* investigations, is the most instructive point in its history; and I would express a hope that the Aligarh Committee may mark a turning point in this report. . . . The resulting information will depend chiefly upon the amount of informed intelligence applied from the beginning. Unless the proposed experiments are conducted by some competent head, the question will drift helplessly, as it has up to this day. I would therefore advise that a well qualified agricultural chemist be engaged for five years under the Department of Agriculture, to devote himself to this special investigation."

The question of the possibility of irrigation in the arid region by means of Artesian wells is one of great scientific interest, and of some practical importance. This matter has received considerable attention in the course of the various State Geological Surveys, as also on the part of the United States Geological Survey, and the Department of Agriculture. Census Bulletin No.

193 (Census of 1890), by Mr. F. H. Newell, is devoted to the subject of "Artesian Wells for Irrigation."[1]

An Artesian well is properly a boring of considerable depth, from which water rises to the surface and overflows, without the necessity of pumping. Deep wells from which the water does not rise to the surface, but has to be raised by means of a steam-engine or some other mechanical contrivance, were formerly called "deep wells," or "bored wells"; but at the present time, especially in the United States, any bored well, even if not very deep, is frequently designated as an "Artesian well."[2]

The presence of water-bearing strata at some depth beneath the surface is a fact of quite common occurrence in various parts of the world; but the conditions favoring a rise to the surface or an overflow of this water, when such a stratum has been reached by a bore-hole, are much less frequently met with. To cause water to rise to the surface and overflow it, the water-

[1] This paper bears the date of June 11, 1892. Besides this, there may be mentioned, as having been published by the Department of Agriculture, a report on "Artesian Wells upon the Great Plains," drawn up by a Commission appointed "to examine a portion of the Great Plains east of the Rocky Mountains, and report upon the localities deemed most favorable for making experimental borings." This report, signed by Messrs. C. A. White and Samuel Aughey, Commissioners, was published in 1882. A paper "On the Requisite and Qualifying Conditions of Artesian Wells," by Thomas C. Chamberlin, is contained in the Fifth Annual Report of the U. S. Geological Survey, published in 1885. The reports of Richard J. Hinton, "Special Agent [of the Department of Agriculture for] Artesian, Underflow, and Irrigation Investigation" (1887–91), deal largely with the question of irrigation by means of Artesian wells in various sections of the Arid Region, as also on the Great Plains.

[2] "The term Artesian was originally only applied to wells which overflowed, but nearly all deep wells are now so called, without reference to their water-level, if they have bore-holes." Ernest Spon, in "The Present Practice of Sinking and Boring Wells," 2d Edition, p. 2. London, 1885.

bearing bed must be both covered and underlain by impermeable strata, and there must be hydrostatic pressure due to the fact that the outcrop of the bed so situated is at a higher level than the orifice of the bore-hole through which water is to rise. The extent of the uncovered surface of the permeable stratum, and the average quantity of rain which falls upon it, are the essential factors determining the amount of water which can be obtained by an Artesian boring penetrating that stratum, and on the elevation of the source of supply or outcrop of permeable rock depends the solution of the question whether the water will rise to the surface, and, if so, with what amount of pressure; that is, to what height it will rise if confined within a tube and not allowed to flow away at the orifice of the bore-hole.

What is commonly designated by geologists as a "basin structure" is, therefore, an essential feature of a region in which a flow of what may properly be called "Artesian water" can be obtained. Such a structure is typically well developed in the Paris basin, where the Lower Greensand — an assemblage of permeable strata — is covered by a thick mass of chalk, between which and the underlying water-bearing beds there is a series of impermeable strata, representing the Gault of the English geologists, of no very great thickness, but sufficiently argillaceous to prevent the escape of water from the underlying greensand.[1]

[1] For some remarks in regard to possible modifications of the typical conditions under which Artesian water is obtained, see further on, in connection with the descriptions of various wells in the Mississippi Valley, Wisconsin, Minnesota, and California.

The well of Grenelle, at Paris, begun in 1833 and completed in 1841, draws its supply from the Lower Greensand, at a depth of about 1,800 feet beneath the surface, above which it rises to the height of 120 feet, having a temperature of 82°. This is the most famous of all Artesian wells, because it was the first to furnish water from so great a depth. Before this well was bored a considerable amount of water had been obtained from the Tertiary strata in the vicinity of Paris, as well as in various other localities in the North of France. Some of these borings yielded a large supply of water, but in no case as much as that furnished by the Grenelle well, nor did it in any instance rise to a considerable height above the surface, the geological conditions for obtaining an Artesian flow of water from the Tertiary not being as favorable as those governing the supply from beneath the chalk.

The outcrop of the Lower Greensand, from which formation the well of Grenelle is fed with water, is in a zone lying about a hundred miles east of Paris, and at an average elevation of about 300 feet above the orifice of the bore-hole. The average rainfall of the region is probably about twenty-two inches, and the area over which the water-bearing stratum is exposed is not far from one hundred square miles.[1]

The success of the Grenelle well led to various efforts on a much larger scale to obtain Artesian water from the strata beneath the chalk of the Paris basin. The well of Passy is the most famous of these, chiefly on account of the great diameter of the bore-hole, which

[1] See "A Geological Inquiry respecting the Water-bearing Strata around London," by Joseph Prestwich, Jr., London, 1857, p. 304.

is about three and a quarter feet, while that of the Grenelle well was only eight inches. The Passy well was begun in 1856, and completed, after surmounting many difficulties caused by the caving in of the upper strata, in 1861, when, from a depth of 1,914 feet, water rose to the amount, at first, of about three and a third million gallons a day. This afterwards increased, for a time, to five and a half million, and afterwards declined to about four million, at which figure it continued for some time. Owing to the defective character of the tubing of the Passy well its yield has fallen off greatly, and at latest accounts was not so much as half a million of gallons a day. Had the tubing been made of iron, and sufficiently strong to stand the pressure of the water, the original yield of four or five million gallons would have been continued, in all probability, until the present time.[1]

Water supply from deep bored wells which are not properly Artesian, but from which water is raised to the surface by pumping, are very common in different parts of the world, and especially in England. In London many wells bored in the beds of the Lower Tertiary, lying under the London clay, at a depth of from a hundred to two hundred feet below the level of the Thames, were originally Artesian, — that is, their water rose above the surface. After some years, this source of supply having been drawn upon too heavily, the water level sank to from sixty to seventy feet below high-water mark.

London, from a geological point of view, is not as favorably situated as Paris for procuring Artesian

[1] See Spon, *loc. cit.*, pp. 224-232.

water. There is a notch in the lip of the London basin made by the passage of the Thames out of it, and this is at a level of about a hundred feet below the rest of the rim. This, of course, diminishes the capacity of the basin as a reservoir. Again, various deep borings made in and near London, which have passed entirely through the chalk, have in most cases failed to reveal the presence of the Lower Greensand, which is the chief water-bearing formation in the Paris basin. In all the London deep borings the Upper Greensand and the Gault succeeded each other in due order, but beneath the latter a great variety of beds has been found. Of thirteen deep borings of which the records are given in the publications of the English Geological Survey,[1] only one (that at the brewery of the Messrs. Meux) seems positively to have passed through any appreciable thickness of the Lower Greensand, which there had a thickness of somewhat over sixty feet, but which was lithologically very different from that formation at its outcrop, being composed of a limestone of oölitic structure. In most of the other localities where deep borings have been made in the London basin, much older rocks have been reached by the drill after passing through the Gault. These rocks have been shown by examination of the cores obtained with the diamond drill to be of various ages: in one case, Lower Carboniferous; in two, Devonian; in one, Upper Silurian; and in two others, probably Triassic or Devonian. In short, there is

[1] See W. Whittaker's "Guide to the Geology of London and its Neighborhood," (a publication of the Geological Survey of England and Wales,) Third Edition, London, 1880, p. 19.

abundant evidence that there is a range of old rocks under London which has unfavorably affected the development of the formation which has been so prolific of water in the Paris basin.

There are, however, numerous deep bored wells in London and its vicinity, which draw their supply from the chalk: these, however, all have to be pumped. But a small part of the water supply of this great city is obtained from this source, most of it being taken from the Thames and the Lea.

In former years many large towns in Central and Northern England were supplied in large part with water from deep bored wells in the New Red Sandstone, — a formation underlying a large area in that region. Birmingham and Liverpool were among the cities which depended on this source of supply. The water furnished by these wells was never very satisfactory as to quality or quantity, and they have been gradually abandoned, as far as it was possible for this to be done, in favor of water obtained by means of storage reservoirs, in which the water is collected from some suitably situated drainage area.

The water supply of Manchester for a long time came from deep wells in the New Red Sandstone; but this having been found to be an entirely unsatisfactory method, a tract of high land lying between that city and Sheffield, and drained by the river Etherow and its tributaries, was selected as a gathering ground, and seven reservoirs formed there, having a collective capacity of about 4,590 million gallons, and capable of supplying eighteen million gallons a day. Even this quantity proved insufficient, so that, as long ago as 1879, it was decided to seek an additional supply, and Lake Thirlmere was finally fixed upon as the locality from which it was to be obtained. From this lake, the level of which was raised by a dam, water is conducted by tunnels or a covered conduit for a distance of a hundred miles to the vicinity of Manchester, which city will thus be supplied, when the works have been entirely completed, with fifty million gallons a day. Liverpool, which also had long been furnished with water from deep wells in the New Red Sandstone, finally, after much investigation, selected the valley of the Vyrnwy River, a tributary of the Severn, as a site for a large storage reservoir. Here a dam has been built capable of holding back a body of water having an area of 1,121 acres and a maximum depth of eighty-four feet. This work, begun in 1880, was completed in 1889, and is calculated to furnish forty million gallons per day.[1]

The Artesian and deep wells of which a brief notice has thus been given are intended for the water supply of large cities, and not at all for irrigation. Indeed,

[1] As this work is one of great importance, and excelled by few, if any, of a similar kind in the world, the following particulars may be appended in regard to it. This dam, of solid masonry throughout, is about 140 feet high and 1,172 long across the top. The foundation extends, in the middle of the valley, 60 feet beneath the surface to solid rock, where the bottom of the dam is 132 feet below the level of the lake; its height from the lowest part of the foundation to the parapet of the roadway along its edge is 161 feet. The lake thus artificially formed is $4\frac{3}{4}$ miles long, and from $\frac{1}{4}$ to $\frac{3}{8}$ of a mile wide. The main portion of the aqueduct which conveys the water of the lake to the service reservoirs will consist of three lines of cast-iron pipes, one of which, $42\frac{1}{2}$ inches in diameter, has already been laid. The distance between the lake and the service reservoirs, near Liverpool, is over sixty-eight miles. The lake, at its lowest available level, is 496 feet higher than the top level of the service reservoir at Prescot.

it is not known to the present writer that this use of water obtained from great depths is anywhere practised on a scale of any magnitude, either in Europe or Asia. There are, however, Artesian wells in Northern Africa, the water of which is used for irrigational purposes, and which are quite celebrated on account of the peculiarities of their geographical position and mode of use. The wells in question are by no means novelties, for it is known that the Romans, and, before their time, the Egyptians, obtained by various methods water which they used for cultivation, and in other ways, on the northern and eastern borders of the Sahara. Rivers were dammed, and reservoirs constructed, from which the water was taken in canals, in a manner quite similar to that practised in modern times. It is believed that various districts which now are entirely dry and deserted, but which once were celebrated for the beauty of their vegetation and somewhat densely populated, were formerly supplied in this way, and possibly with Artesian water obtained from deep wells.

When the French took possession of Algiers, they found that the natives in certain localities on the borders of the Sahara had long been in possession of the art of digging wells, some of which were more than 200 feet deep. The region where the water thus obtained had been, and was still, of some importance, lies to the southeast of the city of Algiers, distant some two hundred miles, between Biskra and Tuggurt, in the valley known as the Wadi Rihr. Here various wells have been sunk, the well-digger usually coming, at the bottom of his excavation, on a bed or kind of crust of hard gypsum, on breaking through which the water issued with great force, and in considerable volume. This operation was attended with considerable danger. Moreover, the wells thus sunk usually began within a few years after their completion to become choked with sand brought up from below or washed in from above. To remove this was a very difficult matter, as the work had to be done by divers, who were able to remain under water for as much as five or six minutes while clearing away the obstruction to the flow of the water.[1] In spite of the efforts of the divers to keep the wells open, many of them have become useless, and several once flourishing oases had been more or less completely abandoned at the time the French took possession of the country. Engineers acquainted with the modern methods of well-boring were, therefore, brought from Europe, and they were successful in procuring, without difficulty, and in various localities, a considerable supply of Artesian water, thus restoring prosperity to the region of the Wadi Rihr to such an extent that its population doubled in number between the years 1856 and 1890. The water thus obtained is chiefly used for the cultivation of the date palm, which requires a large supply of moisture, and does not suffer even when the water is strongly impregnated with saline matter, as is the case with all that obtained in this region from deep wells.

The satisfactory results of the borings in the Wadi Rihr have led to operations of a similar kind in various other districts of the Sahara, some of which have

---

[1] See, for a description of this process, E. Desor, in "La Forêt Vierge et le Sahara," Paris, 1879, pp. 108-115, quoted from "Les Puits Artésiens des Oasis Méridionales de l'Algérie," Alger, 1862.

proved successful.[1] There are indeed enthusiastic individuals who believe that by means of Artesian water the desert may be rescued from sterility, or even covered with forests and fertile meadows. Thus far, however, the progress in this direction has been extremely small.[2] The region where the most has been accomplished toward redeeming the Sahara is still very thinly populated, and the oases have but a comparatively small area and are far apart.[3]

Artesian wells, or those called Artesian, are numerous in the Atlantic States, the Mississippi Valley, and the Cordilleran region, and in certain localities they are of some importance, although, in general, their use in connection with irrigation is limited to the extreme western part of the country. A brief notice of the more important attempts made in the Eastern States to procure Artesian water may here be introduced.

Many years ago the idea was generally current throughout this country that water of good quality and abundant in quantity could be had almost any-

---

[1] See Comptes Rendus des Séances de la Société de Géographie, Paris, 1892, containing (on page 179) an account, by Mr. Georges Rolland, of borings for Artesian water at El Goléa, in the extreme southern part of the Algerian Sahara, where a military post has been established. In the volume for 1893 of the same journal (page 108), this engineer discusses the chances of success in boring at Hassi Inifel, a place situated on the travelled route from El Goléa to Ain Salah, and in the line of communication between Algiers and Timbuctoo. From information furnished by various authorities it appears that Wadi Rihr, Wargla, and El Goléa are the three localities in Algiers where Artesian borings have been most successful. El Goléa is about 250 miles southwest of Tuggurt, and Ain Salah about the same distance farther on in the direction of Timbuctoo.

[2] See, in reference to this point, H. Schirmer, in "Le Sahara," Paris, 1893, pp. 427, 428, where a quotation from Largeau's "Le Sahara Algérien" is given, with a commentary by Mr. Schirmer himself.

[3] The number of inhabitants in the Wadi Rihr was 6,700 in 1856, and 13,300 in 1890.

where by boring to a sufficient depth. In endeavoring to prove the truth of this theory, much money has been expended, and many bore-holes carried to a very considerable depth at a great number of localities. Some of these enterprises have been successful to a limited extent; but in general they have been failures, because the water obtained was either insufficient in quantity or unsatisfactory in quality. The object to be gained by these borings has been almost always a supply of water for cities, for important public institutions, or for some kind of manufactory. Nowhere east of the Mississippi, so far as known, has the water thus obtained been used for irrigational purposes or has any such use been contemplated.

Before water had been introduced into the large cities of the Atlantic Coast, by bringing it from a distance in conduits, it was very natural that it should have been sought for by means of deep borings. Various attempts of this kind were made in Boston and New York. In the former city, these efforts have been renewed within the past five years without any successful result. In New York, it is said that there are as many as forty deep wells; some of these, however, are not now in use, and nearly half of them are owned by breweries. Their depth ranges from a few feet to 2,000, and the diameter of the bore-hole from two and a half to ten inches; their capacity varies from 2,000 to 126,000 gallons per day. Details in regard to the quality of the water from these wells, and the height above the surface to which it rises, are not available.[1]

[1] See W. W. Mather, in "Geology of New York," Albany, 1843, pp. 146, 147, where it is stated that "borings have often been made for

The first deep wells of importance in the United States seem to have been bored in Alabama, where there were, as early as 1848, "in the single county of Greene upwards of forty 'bored wells,' varying between 170 and 600 feet in depth, all constructed by private individuals for their own use."[1] Of the quality and quantity of the water obtained from these wells the accounts vary considerably. Professor Tuomey, State Geologist of Alabama, says, in speaking of two wells at Finch's Ferry, "The water is the strongest that I have examined." He adds, apparently with reference to the wells of this region in general, "There can be no doubt that if these wells were not so numerous, they would become places of resort as mineral springs."[2]

Professor A. Winchell also describes[3] the Artesian wells of Alabama, and states that the water-bearing strata are alternating beds of sand and shale which underlie the well-known "rotten limestone" of the Cretaceous series of that region. A table of seventy-four wells is given, which vary in depths from 90 to 728 feet, the quantity of water which they deliver ranging from 3 to 1,200 gallons per minute. The well reported as yielding the last-named quantity is the so-called "Great Well," at Cahaba, and this is said to be 728 feet deep. Professor Winchell remarks in regard

Artesian wells in situations where the geological structure was such that they could not be expected to be successful. New York island is a good example."

[1] See M. Tuomey, in "Report on the Geology of South Carolina," Columbia, S. C., 1848, p. 247. Also, by the same author, "First Biennial Report on the Geology of Alabama," Tuskaloosa, 1850, pp. 138–140.

[2] *Loc. cit.*, p. 139.

[3] In "Proceedings of the American Association for the Advancement of Science," Vol. X., Albany Meeting, 1856, Part II., pp. 94–103.

to it: "This is truly an astonishing well, but I am sceptical in regard to the alleged quantity of water discharged." The water of this well, at the date of the article quoted, rose twelve inches above the mouth of the pipe. Some of the Alabama wells are said to be "highly saline"; others to be "strongly charged with sulphuretted hydrogen." Although no general statement to this effect is made, it is inferred that the water of all the wells described by Professor Winchell contains a large amount of saline matter, and that, at all events, it could not be used for irrigation, for which purpose it would not seem to be needed, since the region is one of large rainfall.

The subject of water-supply is one which has long occupied the attention of the citizens of Charleston, S. C. The rainfall at this place being quite large, the shallow wells in the sand, which is there about twenty feet thick and rests on a bed of impermeable clay, for a time furnished a tolerably satisfactory supply of water; but this has been steadily deteriorating in quality, so that the necessity of procuring something better has long been felt. For a time recourse was had to wells sunk to a depth of about sixty feet through the clay and into a bed of water-bearing sand which lies between that and the marl beneath. Several "sixty-foot wells," as they were called, were bored from 1820 on, and some of these are still in use.

Information in regard to the deep wells of London having reached Charleston, it was determined that an effort should be made to obtain Artesian water in that city. Acting under the advice of the State Geologist, Professor Tuomey, and encouraged by the success of similar undertakings in Alabama, a boring was begun by the City Council in 1845. Previous to this, however, the United States authorities had made an attempt to procure Artesian water at Fort Sumter. Both these undertakings failed of success on account of want of skill in the management of the work, the greatest depth reached having been 347 feet. In 1847 the city authorities renewed their efforts, however, and a depth of 1,260 feet was reached, at which water was obtained, but in small quantity, the diameter of the bore-hole being only three inches. Another well was then begun of larger bore, but was stopped, first temporarily by an accident, and later by the Civil War.

Again, in 1876, the attempt to procure Artesian water was renewed, and this time with success. The bore-hole was located on Calhoun Street, where, at a depth of a little over 1,900 feet, a group of beds of water-bearing sand was struck, and water to the amount of 360,000 gallons per day obtained. Another well was begun in George Street immediately after, and others have since been bored at various points in the city and in its vicinity. The quantity of water which these wells afford is, however, by no means sufficient for a city having already over 50,000 inhabitants; nor is the quality satisfactory, as will be seen from the following table, which shows the number of grains of solid matter to the gallon contained in the water of various Artesian wells in and near Charleston[1] : —

[1] See Artesian wells — Report of Special Committee, in "City of Charleston Year Book — 1881," pp. 257-315; also the same publication for the year 1884, pp. 147-156, where will be found a report setting forth the inadequacy of the water-supply of the city.

Locality of Well.	Grains in one gallon of water.
"Old Artesian well" corner of Meeting and Wentworth Streets	135.366
Citadel Green	65.053
Commercial Cotton Press	264.481
Chisholm Mill	214.937
Ashepoo Phosphate Company [1]	167.022
Edisto Phosphate Company [1]	149.06
Stono Phosphate Company [1]	128.941

A great number of deep borings have been made during the past thirty or forty years in the Mississippi Valley, with the expectation of procuring water suitable for the supply of some city or public institution. Since the excitement in regard to the occurrence of petroleum and natural gas, the number of these borings has increased indefinitely, and but little attention has been paid to their yield of water. In general, however, it can be said that, so far as water-supply is concerned, they have all or nearly all proved failures, often because the flow from the bore-hole was insufficient, and still more frequently because, in addition to the scantiness of the supply, the quality of the water obtained was not such as to make it suitable for any use other than medicinal. In many cases, however, these borings have been of value as throwing light on the geological structure of the region where they were made. Some of the most important of these undertakings may here be briefly noticed.

At Louisville, Kentucky, a boring was begun in 1857, and carried to a depth of 2,086 feet, with a diameter of three inches. The water obtained rose, when tubed, to

[1] These wells are all within three or four miles from the City Hall.

a height of 170 feet above the surface, and the flow amounted to 330,000 gallons per day. This water is, however, not fit for ordinary use, since it contains 915 grains of solid matter to the gallon, consisting mostly of common salt and sulphate of soda, with considerable sulphate of magnesia and sulphate of lime. The water is said to have valuable medicinal qualities, and to resemble that of the celebrated springs of Kissingen.[1]

At St. Louis, Missouri, a boring was carried to the depth of 3,843.5 feet, on the grounds of the County Insane Asylum. This well furnished water more or less saline all the way down. Below 3,545 feet it contained from seven to eight per cent of salt. This boring passed entirely through all the sedimentary formations, terminating in the granite. The supply of water which it furnishes appears to be but small, and no use has been made of it. Another boring was made at Belcher's sugar refinery, and carried to a depth of 2,176 feet. At 1,231 feet the water contained three per cent of salt. There are no details available as to its quantity furnished, or whether it rose to the surface. No practical use has been made of this water.[2]

[1] See J. Lawrence Smith, in the American Journal of Science, (2), Vol. XXVII. pp. 174–178, where it is stated that "the top of the well is now [1859] closed, and the water conducted about thirty feet to a basin with a large *jet d'eau* on the centre, from which there is a central jet of water forty feet in height, with a large water-pipe, from which the water passes in the form of a sheaf. When the whole force of the water is allowed to expend itself on the central jet, it is projected to a height of from ninety to a hundred feet, settling down to a steady flow of a stream sixty feet high." The bore-hole is five inches in diameter as far down as seventy-six feet, from that point to the bottom of the well three inches.

[2] See G. C. Swallow, in "First and Second Annual Reports of the Geological Survey of Missouri" (1855), p. 131. Also, G. C. Broadhead, in "Report of the Geological Survey of Missouri, including the Field work of 1873–1874," pp. 32–34.

At Columbus, Ohio, in the grounds of the State House, a well was bored between 1857 and 1860, to the depth of 2,775 feet. The water continued saline all the way down, and no use appears to have been made of it, nor are there any statements in the reports of the State Geological Survey as to its quantity. This boring passed through the whole thickness of the Devonian and Upper Silurian, and terminated in the Calciferous Sandrock underlying the Trenton limestone.[1] A deep well was bored in Eaton, Preble County, Ohio, some years ago, and was carried to a depth of 1,370 feet. Others have been bored in the Ohio Valley, near Cincinnati, and carried down to a depth sufficient to reach the bottom of the Trenton limestone; these wells were sunk in search of petroleum, but without success, nor is there any record of water having been obtained from them.

The fact that the Trenton limestone in the northern part of Ohio contained a large amount of both petroleum and natural gas, was not revealed until after the borings mentioned above had been executed. The occurrence of natural gas at and near Findlay, Hancock County, has been known since that region was first settled (about 1836); but its presence in large quantity was first made known in November, 1884, and immediately after that petroleum was discovered in the same formation (the Trenton limestone), since which time this region has become of great economical importance.[2]

[1] See Edward Orton, in "Report of the Geological Survey of Ohio," Vol. VI., Economic Geology (1888), pp. 106-108.

[2] All through this part of Ohio there has been, since these discoveries at Findlay were made, immense activity displayed in drilling wells for oil and gas. The following quotation from the above-cited volume of the

In Indiana there have been numerous borings made for water, some of which are in the drift, while others are much deeper; but they are all designated in the Reports of the State Geological Survey as "Artesian." As examples of the comparatively shallow wells may be mentioned numerous wells in Rush County, most of them not much exceeding fifty feet, and the deepest being 106 feet. Of the quality and quantity of the water supplied by these wells nothing definite can be stated, except that in one locality — at the west end of Rushville — the average depth being from twenty to twenty-three feet, the water is designated as being "Artesian chalybeate."[1] These are evidently simple shallow wells. The City of Marion, Grant County, is supplied with water from a boring sixty-eight feet deep. This well may properly be called Artesian, since the water overflows at the top of the bore-hole. The yield is not definitely stated, but the well is said to furnish "an abundance of good pure water."[2] The analysis of this water showed that it contained twenty-eight grains of solid matter to the gallon, mostly carbonate of lime.

Geological Reports may be appended as an illustration of the truth of this statement: "The discovery of gas and oil at Findlay has made a great impression on the western half of Ohio not only, but on all adjacent States as well. In fact, no geological discovery ever made in this country, unless the original discovery of petroleum in western Pennsylvania shall be excepted, has exerted so widespread and powerful an influence on half of the United States, or at least on the northern Mississippi Valley, as the discovery of Findlay gas. Every county in the western half of Ohio, without exception, has already drilled one or more wells to the Trenton limestone, or at least made a determined effort to reach the new source of light and heat." *Loc. cit.*, p. 117.

[1] See J. Collett, in "Thirteenth Annual Report of the Department of Geology and Natural History," Indianapolis, 1884, pp. 100–103.

[2] *Loc. cit.*, p. 140.

All the deeper wells of Indiana appear to furnish a strongly saline water; for instance, an Artesian well at Reelsville, 1,240 feet deep, "from which there resulted a strong flow of white sulphur water, highly charged with sulphuretted hydrogen gas. . . . It was considered a specific in diseases of the liver and kidneys."[1] A well bored at Corydon, in 1871, at a depth of 1,200 feet yielded brine strong enough to make one and a quarter pounds of salt per gallon. The yield of this well seems to have been very small.[2] Another well, half a mile east of Corydon, designated as the "White Sulphur Well," of which the depth is not given, yielded a water containing 450.88 grains of solid matter to the gallon. This well is, or has been, used as a mineral spring, and "cures almost magical in their results are vouched for." At Lodi, Fountain County, a boring 1,155 feet deep yielded a copious supply of water "discharged with great force," and containing 673.937 grains of solid matter to the gallon. This water is said to be nearly identical with that of the White Sulphur Springs of Virginia.[3]

In Illinois the results of deep boring for Artesian water do not seem to have been favorable, unless it be in the city of Chicago. Here there are wells which appear to furnish some water, although no definite information has been obtained with regard to their yield;

[1] Department of Statistics and Geology, Second Annual Report, Indianapolis, 1880, p. 405.

[2] E. T. Cox, in "Eighth, Ninth, and Tenth Annual Reports of the Geological Survey of Indiana," Indianapolis, 1879, p. 353.

[3] See J. Collett, in "Eleventh Annual Report of the Department of Geology and Natural History," Indianapolis, 1881, p. 114. The flow of this well at a depth of 1,051 feet is said to have been 1,500 barrels per day; the solid matter is stated to be about five sevenths common salt.

neither can anything positive be stated about the quality of the water. The borings at Chicago are said by the State Geologist to range from 700 to 1,100 feet in depth, and "to furnish an abundant supply of water for the local needs which caused them to be bored."[1] The most important of these wells are said to be at the Union Stock Yards, where the strata are described as being most probably horizontal, or nearly so.[2]

The following items in regard to deep borings in Illinois are extracted from the latest published volume of the State Geological Survey.[3] At Riverton, seven miles east of Springfield, a boring was carried to the depth of 655 feet. At Olney, in the south part of the State, a boring for Artesian water was carried to the depth of 2,000 feet without success. At Canton, in Fulton County, a boring was begun above the horizon of Coal No. 5, and extended into the Silurian to a depth of 358 feet. At Streator, in La Salle County, an Artesian boring was carried to a depth of 2,496 feet, the last 1,358 feet being in the Potsdam sandstone. Both the St. Peters

[1] See "Geological Survey of Illinois," Vol. III. (1868), pp. 244 and 256. There are but few particulars given in the State Geological reports in regard to either the quantity or the quality of the water obtained in any of the Artesian borings in Illinois.

[2] A pamphlet entitled "History of the Great Chicago Artesian Well, a Demonstration of the Truth of the Spiritual Philosophy, with an Essay on the Origin and Uses of Petroleum," by George A. Shufeldt, Jr., has been published at that place, and has gone through several editions (1865, 1867). The statements here made are astounding. The water is said to flow at the rate of about 600,000 gallons per day from a depth of 711 feet, and to be "as clear as crystal and as pure as the diamond, . . . and better adapted for drinking purposes than any other water known." So many of the statements made in this pamphlet can easily be proved to have no basis of truth, that it is not possible to accept any part of it as authority in regard to the Artesian water of Chicago.

[3] See "Geological Survey of Illinois," Vol. VII. (May, 1883), pp. 5, 7, 49, 50.

sandstone and the white sandstone of the Calciferous group were found to be water-bearing in this well, the water from the St. Peters coming to within forty feet of the surface, and that from the Calciferous to within about thirty-four feet: this latter water was reported as being sweet, and apparently free from deleterious mineral substances, while that from the Potsdam was brackish and unfit for common use, but it rose in a tube to the height of forty-five feet above the surface. At Marseilles, a depth of 2,189 feet was attained, but the flow of water, which rose to the surface, was only one and a half barrels per hour. The quality of the water is not stated.

The mineral springs and Artesian wells of Wisconsin are of much more importance than those of the adjacent more Southern States, which have been briefly noticed on the preceding pages, and they received considerable attention during the progress of the survey carried on under the direction of Professor Chamberlin during the years 1873 to 1879.[1] Some of the more important conclusions reached by this Survey may here be briefly stated.

The "areas of favorable probabilities" for Artesian wells in Wisconsin are designated as follows: I. A belt extending along the entire border of Lake Michigan, at an elevation not much above that of the lake.

[1] See Volume I. (1883) of the reports of that Survey, pp. 689-701, in which the subject of Artesian wells in general is discussed; Volume II. (1877), pp. 141-170, containing remarks on water supply, an enumeration of the various geological horizons in which springs occur and Artesian wells either have been or may be successfully bored, with chemical analyses of the water of several noteworthy springs and Artesian wells; Volume IV. (1882), pp. 57-63, containing descriptions, with analyses of the water, of various Artesian wells in the Mississippi Valley.

II. In the Green Bay Valley, from Fond du Lac northward. III. In the valley of Rock River. IV. Along the Mississippi River. V. Along the shore of Lake Superior.

Farther on in the series of volumes of the Geological Survey reports,[1] the numerous Artesian wells of Wisconsin are classified with reference to the formations from which they derive their flow, as follows : I. Those that flow entirely from the drift, clay layers forming the upper and lower confining strata, and sand or gravel the water-bearing seam. II. Those that derive their flow from the junction of the drift with the indurated rocks below. III. Those that originate in the Niagara limestone. IV. Those that arise from the Galena and Trenton limestones. V. Those coming from the St. Peters sandstone. VI. Those originating in the older crystalline rocks.

In the first group, or those coming from the drift, the following wells are among those more particularly noticed : — Those of Taycheedah, from sixty to seventy feet deep, and not reaching the bed-rock ; the water of some of these is said to be strongly impregnated with sulphuretted hydrogen. At Calumet, on the shore of Lake Winnebago, two fine wells are mentioned, about ninety feet deep, "giving a copious flow of clear, cold, sparkling water, impregnated with considerable iron, and some sulphuretted hydrogen." At Whitewater, various "flowing wells," owing their origin to the fact that a bed of lacustrine clay rests upon the flank of drift hills to the southeast, admirably adapted to serve as collecting areas. One of these wells, fifty-two feet

[1] Volume II. pp. 150, 151.

deep, in a stiff blue clay, is described as having a copious flow, "the water being charged with iron and sulphuretted hydrogen." At Oshkosh there is a considerable number of shallow wells, varying from fifty to 150 feet in depth, some of which derive their flow from within the drift, while others come from the junction of the detrital formation with the rock in place beneath. Some of the flowing wells at Fond du Lac also have an origin similar to that of the shallow wells at Oshkosh. There are also numerous wells at Rushford, Aurora, Poysippi, and vicinity, included in what is designated as the "Poygan Lake system," which all belong to a common depression filled by a continuous lacustrine deposit, and are essentially alike in nature and origin. They all originate in the drift, and owe their existence to the alternate porous and impervious character of the red clay and associated beach deposits. Their flow is said to be in some cases very copious, and the water excellent, rather soft, but occasionally impregnated with sulphuretted hydrogen. It is evident that no very sharp line of distinction can be drawn between the wells the water of which is derived from the drift itself, and those drawing their supply from the junction of the detrital formation with the bed-rock. The water of the various Fond du Lac, Oshkosh, and Oakfield wells comes from both these horizons.

Of wells bored in the Niagara limestone and obtaining their yield of water from that formation, those of Manitowoc are cited. The drift here appears to be about sixty feet deep, and the borings at several of the wells penetrated the rock to the depth of ninety feet.

An analysis of the water of one of the wells in this geological position shows it to contain a large amount of saline matter (192.7 grains to the gallon), the sulphates of lime, soda, and magnesia predominating.

Some of the wells at Oshkosh and Fond du Lac, and most of those at Watertown, derive their water from the fourth horizon mentioned above — the Galena and Trenton limestones; but in general this source of supply seems to be of comparatively little importance, by far the larger part of the deep-seated wells — of Eastern Wisconsin, at least — receiving their water from the St. Peters sandstone. This rock is porous, and also much fissured in various directions, so that water easily penetrates it, while the overlying Trenton limestone forms an effective impermeable cover. From this source comes the water of the deeper wells at Watertown, some of those at Fond du Lac, the Sheboygan well, and others at Milwaukee, Racine, and Western Union Junction. The well at Sheboygan is 1,475 feet deep; the discharge is 225 gallons per minute; the water contains 589.25 grains of solid matter to the gallon, consisting chiefly of common salt and sulphate of lime. The pressure at the surface is sufficient to raise the water 104 feet. The Milwaukee well is 1,048 feet deep; the pressure is sufficient to fill a four-inch pipe at sixty feet above the surface. Nothing is stated in regard to the quality of the water of this well. Another well, in the suburbs of Milwaukee, is 1,200 feet deep, and delivers 300 gallons of water per minute; its flow may be carried to a height of more than fifty feet above the surface. The water of this well contains 42.34 grains of solid matter to the gallon, consisting mostly of the sulphates of lime and soda, and the bicarbonate of magnesia. The Racine well is 1,240 feet deep; at 888 feet in depth the St. Peters sandstone was struck, which is there forty-eight feet thick. Beneath this is 100 feet of the Lower Magnesian Limestone, underlain by a considerable thickness of the Potsdam sandstone. When the St. Peters sandstone was reached a flow of water was secured, which was increased in volume on penetrating — to the depth of 204 feet — the Potsdam group. The water rose in a tube sixty-five feet above the surface: regarding its quality nothing is stated. The well at the Western Union Junction was also continued down into the Potsdam sandstone for a distance of 157 feet, the total depth reached being 1,263 feet. There are no details given in regard to the volume or quality of the water obtained.

In that part of the Wisconsin Survey reports which is devoted to the "Geology of the Mississippi Region North of the Wisconsin River,"[1] a brief notice is given of the mineral springs and wells existing at various points within the district described. At Sparta there are said to be twelve Artesian wells within a distance of two miles from the central part of the city. Their depth is uniformly about 300 feet, and the water rises from six to ten feet above the surface. "It is claimed that these mineral waters will cure a large and varied list of diseases; but of this we have no personal knowledge."[2] The source of the water of these wells is be-

[1] See "Geology of Wisconsin, Survey of 1873-1879," Volume IV. (1882), pp. 57-62.

[2] *Loc. cit.*, p. 57. An analysis of the water from one of these wells shows that more than one half of the solid matter which it contains is carbonate of iron. Too much confidence should not be placed in the cor-

lieved to be from near the junction of the Potsdam and Archæan (Azoic). The Artesian well of La Crosse is said to be 573 feet deep, but no details of its yield are given. The well of Prairie du Chien is 959 feet deep, and its water rises in the tubing to the height of sixty feet above the surface: its discharge is 869,916 gallons per day. The water is said to be clear and sparkling, but "a little brackish to the taste." The La Crosse deep well obtains its water from the granite, which, however, it penetrates to the depth of thirty-six feet only; that of the Prairie du Chien well seems to come chiefly from various strata in the lower part of the Potsdam sandstone.

The results of the chemical analyses of the Wisconsin Artesian waters show that these are, almost without exception, hard. Few of these waters, however, seem to have been carefully and accurately analyzed. Besides the analyses mentioned in the preceding pages, the following are cited in a tabular statement of analyses of the waters of Wisconsin, reprinted in 1877 from the Annual Report for 1873:[1] Artesian well, Madison, 21.12 grains of solid matter to the gallon; Wild's Artesian well, Fond du Lac, 20.84 grains; Artesian well, Court House Square, Sparta, 9.05 grains. This last is the only water cited in the table of analyses of twenty-three specimens from the springs, wells, rivers, and lakes of Wisconsin, which shows less than twenty grains of solid matter to the gallon, with the exception of that from Milwaukee River (17.02 grains) and that

rectness of this piece of chemical work, the results of which are carried to the fifth place of decimals.

[1] See "Geology of Wisconsin, Survey of 1873–1877," Vol. III. pp. 31, 32.

from Lake Michigan (8.46 grains). It seems not to be possible to make any positive general statement connecting the quality of the waters of Wisconsin with the geological horizon from which they are obtained; the evidence appears, however, to favor the idea that, on the whole, the best water comes from the shallower wells: that of some of the very deep ones is certainly entirely unsatisfactory.

The conditions of water-supply in Iowa are briefly discussed in the State Geological Report.[1] The drainage system of this State is such that the streams are numerous and pretty uniformly distributed, while springs are frequent in the valleys. Water is almost always obtained from the drift which covers so large a part of Iowa by sinking not more than a few feet, so that deep wells do not seem to be much needed. All the water of this State is, however, hard, so that rain-water collected in cisterns is commonly used for household purposes. The rainfall in this region is amply sufficient to make it possible to secure water enough for ordinary domestic use, away from the large cities, by using sufficient care in the construction of proper cisterns.[2] The scarcity of water at certain seasons of the year, and the occasional recurrence of especially severe periods of drought, however, have led to numerous attempts to secure a supply more satisfactory in quality or quantity by means of Artesian wells. Up

---

[1] See C. A. White, in "Report of the Geological Survey of the State of Iowa," Vol. II. (1870), Des Moines, pp. 331-334 and 354-357.

[2] The annual rainfall of the State of Iowa, as determined by the various series of observations collected by the Iowa State Weather and Crop Service, is about thirty-five inches. Monthly Review of the Iowa Weather and Crop Service, Vol. III. No. 3 (1892).

to the time of the publication of Professor White's report, few of these undertakings seem to have been even moderately successful. Such deep borings as were begun primarily with the expectation of discovering petroleum were entirely unsuccessful, while those made especially for water were in most cases failures, because that which was obtained was too impure to be used in any way, unless possibly for medicinal purposes.

In later years, in spite of these difficulties, increased attention has been paid to Artesian wells in this State, as is shown by the appearance in various scientific periodicals of articles devoted to this subject.[1] Professor Call has recently published a tabular statement giving certain facts in regard to eighty-six Artesian wells in Iowa.[2] Of these wells about forty are described as ending in the "glacial drift," eight in the Carboniferous, four or five in the St. Peters sandstone, and two in the "Silurian"; in regard to all the others no satisfactory information is given as to the source from which the water is derived. In fourteen cases it is said to be "soft"; in forty-five to be "hard"; further than this there is nothing said as to the character of the water. The wells ending in the St. Peters sandstone are from

---

[1] See R. Ellsworth Call, in "Proceedings of the Iowa Academy of Sciences for 1890, 1891," Vol. I. Part 2, pp. 57–63; also, by the same author, various articles in the "Monthly Review of the Iowa Weather and Crop Service," Vol. III. Nos. for February and March, 1892. The main grounds on which Artesian waters are sought in Iowa are stated by Professor Call to be, "first, the convenience of such flows for farm and urban use, and, second, the supposed purity of such waters."

[2] The details of this statement are vague and unsatisfactory. No analyses of the water are furnished, and no clue to its character is afforded other than that indicated above. Only in regard to about half the wells noticed is any information given as to the amount of flow.

676 to 1,400 feet deep; the two in the "Silurian,"[1] 1,640 and 2,000 feet. Throughout the region where large "glacial wells" occur, water is usually found at depths varying from twenty-five to 170 or 180 feet. The southwestern part of Hancock County, along the smaller tributaries of Boone River, is mentioned as being an "Artesian hydrographic basin." Another area of glacial wells is that lying within the drainage of Raccoon River, the Des Moines River dividing this from the Boone River area, the latter being described as furnishing by far the greater number of wells, as also the stronger and more permanent flows of water. The greatest reported flow of any well in the Boone River area is said to be 3,000 gallons per hour; a few hundred gallons per hour is the maximum in the Raccoon Valley. These areas of glacial wells are said to lie within the terminal moraine, while that of Belle Plain is beyond it, some seventy-five miles to the southeast. Within this area, in Benton, Tama, Poweshiek, and Iowa counties, there are said to be sixty-three flowing wells, and others in which the water does not rise to the surface. The depth of the detrital material in this basin is indeed most remarkable. A well, named "Jumbo," was bored here, and water struck at the depth of 193 feet, the lower 172 feet being "blue clay, with layers or pockets of sand or gravel." The condition of this well at the present time is not stated; but it is said of it that, during its period of greatest flow, "8,267,040 gallons in twenty-four hours came from this

---

[1] By "Silurian" appears here to be meant some formation older than the St. Peters sandstone: in one instance "Magnesian limestone of Silurian age" is specified; in the other, simply "Silurian rock."

monster well." The entire thickness of the interstratified clay and sand at this point is not known; water was found in a stratum of gravel and sand at a depth of 209 feet, and this was bored into for a distance of twenty-five feet, without passing through it. The water gave on analysis 133.68 grains of solid matter per gallon, about three fifths of this being sulphate of lime and one fifth chloride of magnesium. The great depth to which the so called "glacial deposits" in the vicinity of Belle Plain extend is thought to indicate the existence of an "extensive subterranean hydrographic basin, or the presence of an immense ancient river valley, now entirely filled and obliterated." Of the "glacial wells" in general, it is said that "they are all relatively shallow, the catchment basin which feeds them relatively small, and their 'life,' which is at best precarious, sustains a definite relationship to the mean annual precipitation of the region."

Besides the shallow or glacial Artesian wells of Iowa, of which the above brief notice has been given, there are numerous deep ones. Those which lie along the Mississippi River all, or nearly all, end in the St. Peters sandstone; and this formation is said to be the source of the water of most of the deep wells of the State. This rock underlies, at depths varying from 1,000 to 1,200 feet, that part of Iowa which is north and east of a line drawn from Keokuk to Sioux City. The conditions in the northwestern and southwestern portions of the State seem to be unfavorable for procuring Artesian water.

So far as can be determined from the small number

of analyses of Iowa Artesian water available, the earlier statements of Professor White in regard to its very unsatisfactory character seems to be upheld. Professor Call remarks that "with one or two exceptions, and it is quite doubtful if these are correctly reported, the water of all glacial wells belongs to the class called hard water; the water of all the wells that end in the Carboniferous rocks or in the St. Peters sandstone is soft." The analyses furnished do not, however, substantiate the correctness of this statement. Thus the water of an Artesian well in the city of McGregor, descending to the St. Peters sandstone, contained 136.8 grains of solid matter to the gallon, mostly common salt with sulphate of soda, and some sulphate and carbonate of magnesia; that of the well at the Asylum near Council Bluffs, 1,100 feet deep, was shown by analyses to contain 89.433 grains of solid matter to the gallon; that of an Artesian well at Des Moines, penetrating the Carboniferous strata to the depth of 380 feet, 181.37 grains of solid matter to the gallon; that of the well at Boone, the boring of which ends at 3,011 feet in a white sandstone, 86.48 grains to the gallon; that of the water of an Artesian well at West Liberty, 1,968 feet deep, ending in the sandstone, 64.8 grains to the gallon; that of a well at Fort Madison, 763 feet deep, and probably ending in the St. Peters sandstone, 115.13 grains to the gallon. In short, it does not appear from published documents that any water has been obtained in Iowa by Artesian borings suitable for use either for household purposes, or in the boilers of steam-engines. The waters of some wells in this State are said to be "strongly magnetic," and have been extensively advertised as possessing high medicinal value. The same statement has been made in regard to many other wells, springs, and Artesian waters of the Mississippi Valley, and of the region of the Great Lakes.

As in the adjacent States in the Mississippi Valley, so in Minnesota, attempts have been made to procure water by means of Artesian wells. It would appear from the various reports published by the Minnesota Geological Survey that water can be obtained with ease over a large part of this State by means of shallow wells in the drift. In some of the counties, however, the superficial detrital material contains a considerable proportion of calcareous matter, so that the water from these wells is hard. Some deep wells have been bored in the hope of procuring a better supply, but these attempts appear to have been only partially successful. Thus a deep well at Mankato, Blue Earth County, sunk to the depth of 2,204 feet, "furnished no Artesian flow of water, and is not used."[1] Many shallow wells in the same county, sunk to but slight depths in the drift, furnish Artesian water in considerable quantity, these flowing wells being locally denominated "fountains." More than a hundred of these fountains have been obtained in Blue Earth County upon the area drained by the head streams of Maple River, from Sterling Centre fifteen miles southeastward, including Sterling and Mapleton townships, and reaching into Faribault County. At Wells, in this last-named county, occur the most remarkable of this class of wells which have been discov-

---

[1] "Geological and Natural History Survey of Minnesota. Final Report," Vol. I. (1884), pp. 422, 452.

ered in Minnesota. These wells are sunk in the drift to the depth of from 110 to 120 feet, the water rising in them to the height of fifteen or twenty feet above its surface. About twenty of these wells have been sunk within a radius of one mile, the bore-holes being in most cases two inches in diameter, but reduced to half an inch or less at the top. The water thus obtained is said to be of excellent quality, but somewhat chalybeate. Other Artesian wells, or fountains, are said to have been sunk in Faribault County, the water coming from beds of gravel and sand at depths of from thirty or forty to nearly a hundred feet. Of these fountains it is stated that "All these Artesian wells, as also the common wells of the county, . . . invariably have good water and nearly always in ample amount within twenty-five or fifty feet from the surface. It is, however, hard water, holding the carbonates of lime and magnesia in solution, and requires cleansing with ashes or otherwise before it can satisfactorily be used for washing with soap."[1]

At Red Wing, Goodhue County, two Artesian wells have been drilled, one at the station of the Chicago, Milwaukee, and St. Paul Railway, the other about eighty rods from this. This latter well is 260 feet deep, the first 160 feet of which is in the drift, and the remainder in the sandstone.[2] The yield of this well is 300 barrels per day, the water rising thirty feet

---

[1] *Loc. cit.*, Vol. II. p. 471.

[2] This sandstone belongs to what is called by the Minnesota Geological Survey the "St. Croix sandstone," — one of the many names applied to the formation originally named "Potsdam sandstone" by the geologists of the New York Survey, and from which it differs in no important respect, either lithologically or palæontologically.

above the surface. The well at the railway station is 450 feet deep, discharging 800 gallons per minute, the water rising when tubed seventy-five feet above the surface. Nothing is said of the quality of the water of this well, except that it deposits "a considerable irony sediment," while that furnished by the other well, near the station, is described as being "soft and pure." A similar statement is made in regard to the water of another Artesian well, a few miles farther west, which is 355 feet deep and also terminates in the sandstone. An Artesian well at the hospital in Saint Peter, Nicollet County, on the Minnesota River, is 200 feet deep, the water rising seven feet above the surface: nothing is said as to its quality or quantity.

The Artesian wells near St. Paul appear to be the most successful and important in the State. There are several at West St. Paul, varying in depth from 200 to 275 feet, the water in which rises from twenty to thirty feet above the surface, and is said to be "very soft, pure, and wholesome": it comes from the Potsdam sandstone. There are also deep wells at St. Paul, one at "Elevator 13," 850 feet deep, and one at the "St. Paul Harvester Works," 671 feet deep; in neither of these does the water rise to the surface. It is suggested by the Geological Survey that Artesian water, which is already used for fire protection on the west side of the river, could be had at St. Paul in sufficient quantity for the supply of the entire city "by sinking several large wells to this sandrock [the St. Croix] and by the construction of pumping-stations and reservoirs."[1]

[1] *Loc. cit.*, Vol. II. p. 364.

At Mendota, also on the Mississippi River, a few miles southwest of St. Paul, there is a well 857 feet deep, the water of which, coming from the Potsdam sandstone, rises a few feet above the surface, and flows at the rate of 300 gallons per minute. Still farther down the Mississippi, at Hastings, Dakota County, there is an Artesian well, 1,160 feet deep, in the Potsdam sandstone, the water from which will rise when tubed fourteen feet above the surface, flowing at the rate of about a hundred gallons per minute.

Recent publications of two of the Geological Surveys of the Mississippi Valley States, Missouri and Arkansas, furnish considerable information in regard to the mineral waters obtained from springs and bored wells in those States.[1] The mineral springs of Missouri are very numerous, and many of them are believed to possess "undoubted medicinal value." They are classed by Professor Schweitzer as furnishing muriatic, alkaline, sulphatic, chalybeate, and sulphur waters. Under the heading, "List of Mineral Waters of the State, examined, sampled, and analyzed by the Geological Survey during the Years 1890 to 1892," thirty-five counties are cited as possessing mineral springs, eighty-three distinct springs, wells, or Artesian wells being specified, and the results of the analyses of their waters given. Of the wells designated as "Artesian," which are six in number, the following details are

[1] See "Geological Survey of Missouri, A. Winslow, State Geologist, Vol. III. (December, 1892), containing a Report on the Mineral Waters of Missouri by Paul Schweitzer and A. E. Woodward," and "Annual Report of the Geological Survey of Arkansas for 1891, Vol. I., The Mineral Waters of Arkansas, by John C. Branner, State Geologist," Little Rock, 1892.

given: the "Clinton," in Henry County, is 800 feet deep, the flow 400 gallons per minute, and the water contains 106.24 grains of solid matter (mostly common salt) to the gallon; the "Louisiana" (at the town of that name in Pike County, on the Mississippi, eighty miles from St. Louis) is 1,275 feet deep, the flow of water "abundant," and its contents of solid matter 545.71 grains per gallon, nearly four fifths of which is common salt; the "Clinton Artesian Well, No. 3," also in Henry County, 913 feet deep, flowing at the rate of 2,500 to 3,000 gallons per minute, the water being classed as "alkaline," and containing 94.54 grains of solid matter to the gallon, about half of which is common salt, and the rest chiefly the carbonates of lime and magnesia with a very little (2.08 grains to the gallon) chloride of potassium; the "Jordan," also in Henry County and near Clinton, depth not given, water said to be a weak chalybeate, and the well now abandoned; the "Belcher," St. Louis County, already noticed on a preceding page;[1] the "Nevada," near the town of that name in Vernon County, 800 feet deep, flowing at the rate of 10,000

---

[1] See p. 62. The report of Professor Schweitzer having been received since that notice of the Belcher well was written, the following additional information concerning this noted well may here be added. The water contains 550.25 grains of solid matter to the gallon, of which 401.57 are common salt, 50.18 sulphate of lime, 47.49 chloride of calcium, 46.08 chloride of magnesium, 3.06 bromide of magnesium, 0.87 chloride of potassium, the remainder silica and oxide of iron. "A large amount of this water is used for home consumption [apparently for medicinal puposes] as well as for shipping, its use being free to any one who may wish to take it." The water flows from a 1¼-inch pipe at the rate of about fifty gallons per hour; it is clear and sparkling, with a perceptible odor of sulphuretted hydrogen gas, which gives rise to a white precipitate of sulphur on the stones over which it flows.

gallons per hour, the water (classed as alkaline) containing 76.01 grains of solid matter to the gallon, nearly half of which is common salt, and the remainder chiefly carbonates of lime and magnesia, together with 2.40 grains of carbonate of soda.

The distinction between Artesian wells and springs is not very closely maintained in Professor Schweitzer's report: thus, of one of the "Randolph Springs," in the county of that name, the "Sulphur Spring" is said to be "a free flowing four-inch well, 969 feet deep, bored originally . . . for the purpose of obtaining petroleum. . . . The flow is at the rate of about 120 gallons per hour. Very few of the wells or springs mentioned in this report could be employed for any other than a medicinal purpose. A few of them have, however, been used in former years for making salt, especially the so-called "Great Salt Springs" of Saline County.

In the "Annual Report of the Geological Survey of Arkansas for 1891," a volume is devoted to the mineral waters of that State.[1] In this volume a considerable number of analyses of the water of various springs and rivers, as well as of such springs as are more properly designated as "mineral," are given. Arkansas is a well-watered State, the rainfall over most of its surface being rather in excess of its needs. Irrigation is, therefore, not a question of practical importance.[2]

[1] This volume, by John C. Branner, State Geologist, bears the date of 1892.
[2] Arkansas is famous for its springs. In the language of the above cited report, "hundreds of beautiful, free-flowing springs gush from hillsides and valleys in all parts of the State. . . . Some of these springs are so big that they are utilized for driving mills and cotton gins and other

Texas is a State having an area so extensive that the climate and topographic conditions are strikingly different over various portions of its surface.[1] Along its eastern edge, in the region adjacent to Louisiana, the rainfall is copious, and not much less on the borders of the Gulf of Mexico, while the whole of the western and northwestern part of the State lies beyond the line separating the well-watered area from that scantily supplied with moisture. It was on the Llano Estacado, a vast plain lying between the Pecos River and the Gulf water-shed, that the first attempts by the government to procure Artesian water in the arid region of the United States were made, and without success.

In the coast region of this State numerous borings have been made to procure water, and, according to the investigations of the Geological Survey, the result has proved that "flowing wells can be had throughout the coast prairie region, from the Guadalupe River to the Sabine, at depths varying from sixty-four feet in

machinery, and as their discharges are subject to little or no fluctuations throughout the year, they are free from the dangers of freshets and the risks of drouths. . . . At Mammoth Spring, in Fulton County, one of the finest water powers in the country is furnished by an enormous clear water spring." The so-called "mineral springs" are, in some cases at least, remarkable for their purity. Thus the waters of the various Eureka Springs, in Carroll County, around which a town of several thousand inhabitants has grown up, and which are visited by people from all parts of the United States, contain only from five to seven grains of mineral water to the gallon, and the same is true of the almost equally famous Elixir Spring, at Elixir Spring, in Boone County. These, as well as many others in Arkansas, belong to the class of "indifferent springs," or those in which the medicinal value cannot be accounted for by the composition of the water.

[1] Texas has an area of 262,290 square miles. It is five and a half times as large as the State of New York.

De Witt County to 1,100 feet at Velasco, in Brazoria County, and that the water as a rule is of excellent quality in all wells distant from ten to fifteen miles or more from the coast."[1] It is, furthermore, stated by the Survey, that, outside of the coast prairie region and west of the Guadalupe River, the Artesian water conditions vary so greatly and continually, through the thinning out of the water-bearing sands or their entire absence in many localities, that no large area within the boundaries of the State can, at present, be designated as an Artesian water-bearing district.

The present water-supply for the city of Galveston is derived from thirteen Artesian wells, ranging in depth from 810 to 1,346 feet.[2] The water, however, contains so large an amount of impurities, chiefly common salt, "that it is unsuitable for either domestic or manufacturing purposes, although used to some extent for the latter."[3] To determine the question whether better water could be obtained at Galveston, the city authorities caused a well to be bored to the depth of 3,070 feet, of which it is said that "the water is brackish, but apparently less so than that from any other well on the island."[4]

[1] See "Geological Survey of Texas. Preliminary Reports on the Gulf Coastal Slope. By J. A. Singley." Austin, June, 1893.

[2] The flow from all these wells is collected in a reservoir and pumped into a standpipe, whence it is distributed to all parts of the city for use in case of fire. The total flow of these wells is about 2,300,000 gallons per day. "The water is used to a limited extent for domestic purposes when a drouth begets a scarcity of cistern water." It is used also in smaller manufacturing establishments, most of the larger having wells of their own.

[3] *Loc. cit.*, p. 1. (From Fourth Annual Report, 1892.)

[4] At this depth "the City Council concluded that the experiment had been carried far enough, and discontinued the work."

Various wells sunk by private parties on the island of Galveston furnish water containing from two to three hundred grains of solid matter to the gallon, most of which is common salt. In spite of this high percentage of foreign matter, the water of some of these wells seems to be used under boilers. The Artesian wells on the mainland near Galveston seem to furnish a decidedly better quality of water than those on the island.

A large number of Artesian wells have been bored in the coast region of Texas, some of which furnish water much superior in quality to that of the Galveston wells. Thus the city of Houston has nearly a hundred wells within its corporate limits, the water being derived from about six different water-bearing sands, while the depth of the wells varies from 115 to 564 feet. The "city's supply" (probably that distributed in the mains) is said to be over 4,000,000 gallons per day. A single analysis of the Houston Artesian water gives the total solid matter as being twenty-one grains per gallon, carbonate of lime being the predominating ingredient. The water from some of the other wells in the coast region is much inferior to that obtained at Houston; but in some cases these Artesian waters appear to have been used to a limited extent for irrigation. In various localities — as at Corpus Christi, where a well was sunk to the depth of 1,765 feet without finding water that could be utilized by the city — Artesian borings seem to have been entirely unsuccessful, either no water at all having been obtained, or else only that which was not fit for any use whatever.

What has been said in the preceding pages will be sufficient evidence that for the States lying adjacent to the Mississippi River on both sides irrigation by means of Artesian wells is a matter in which success is, on the whole, rarely to be expected. The quality of the water obtained from deep borings is almost everywhere such as to make it entirely unavailable for irrigational purposes, as also, indeed, for any purpose other than medicinal. While, as already remarked, water in abundance and of good quality would be extremely desirable, especially if decidedly softer than that furnished by ordinary wells or from the rivers of a region so extensively underlain by calcareous rocks, it is much less important that such a supply should be obtained for irrigational purposes in the States adjacent to the Mississippi than in those lying still farther west, where the rainfall is insufficient for successful cultivation.

The isohyetal line of twenty-six inches may be taken as approximately marking the boundary between the sufficiently and insufficiently watered portions of the Western region. This leaves to the east, or in the moister area, a large part of Minnesota, the eastern edge of Nebraska, rather less than half of Kansas, most of the Indian Territory, and about half of Texas. Through all the region to the west of this isohyetal the rainfall may with propriety be considered insufficient, although there is a belt of considerable width lying between the isohyetals of twenty-six and twenty inches in which the conditions with respect to moisture are intermediate between those of fairly sufficient and decidedly insufficient supply. In the region enclosed between the isohyetals of twenty-six and twenty inches, and still more in that beyond the latter, almost as far as the Pacific Ocean, the irrigation question is an important one, and, as shown in the preceding pages, one which has received a considerable amount of attention from the general government, as well as from some of the individual States and Territories.

The work of the Irrigation Department of the United States Geological Survey, as far as its results are accessible up to the present time, has received a brief notice in the preceding pages.[1] It now remains to give some further details with regard to what has been actually accomplished in the way of irrigation in the Western or arid region of the country. In doing this the chief guide will necessarily be the publications of the Census of 1890, together with various official documents issued by authority of the Department of Agriculture and by the Signal Service.[2]

All that has been done up to the present time toward mitigating the effects of a naturally arid climate in the more arid portion of the Cordilleran region is comparatively insignificant, as is shown both by the figures showing the density of the population of that region, and by the actual census returns of the percentage of the area of the different States and Territories actually under irrigation at the time the statistics were collected for the census of 1890. The annexed table exhibits these results, the density of the population in the States and Territories included in the list being given for the year 1880, as well as for 1890.[3]

---

[1] See *ante*, pp. 29–31.

[2] Reference has already been made to some of the more important of these documents on pages 36, 46, and 47.

[3] See also the table on page 28, in which a general statement is given

State or Territory.	Percentage of Area irrigated.	Population per Sq. Mile, 1880.	Population per Sq. Mile, 1890.
Idaho	0.4	0.39	1.00
Montana	0.4	0.27	0.91
Wyoming	0.4	0.21	0.62
Utah	0.5	1.75	2.53
Nevada	0.3	0.57	0.42
New Mexico	0.1	0.98	1.25
Arizona	0.1	0.36	0.53

The above enumerated States and Territories are all included within the arid belt of the country, and form its larger portion. The exceeding smallness of their total area under irrigation at the latest date for which statistics are available cannot fail to be noticed, as also the scantiness of the population of this region, and the slight change in this respect which took place during the period elapsing between the time of taking the census of 1880 and that of 1890. The density of the population of this region is conditioned chiefly by the development of its mining resources, what small increase there is being almost entirely dependent on this branch of industry, as has been shown by the decline of the population of the State of Nevada which has taken place since some of the more important mining districts have ceased to be worked with profit, and as is likely to be the case in other parts of the region in question, where experience has shown that the mines, as a rule, are not of a kind likely to hold in depth, a large portion of the occurrences of ore having more the nature of contact deposits than of true veins.

In two other States, and in two only, has the census

---

with regard to the area and population of the Cordilleran division and its subdivisions in the years 1880 and 1890.

of 1890 given the statistics of irrigation in such a form that the actual importance of this branch of agriculture can be distinctly stated. These two States are Washington and Oregon: in the former the percentage of irrigated area is 0.11, in the latter 0.3. Both these States, however, lie in considerable part within the best-watered portion of the country, the rainfall on all the area west of the Cascade Range being more than ample, and it is here that almost the whole increase of population in the period between 1880 and 1890 took place. This increase was large, especially in the case of Washington, the density of whose population rose in that interval from 1.12 to 5.22, while that of Oregon increased from 1.85 to 3.32 per square mile. This increase was almost entirely confined to the area west of the Cascade Range, that to the east of it belonging to the arid belt, and having for the most part a decidedly unfertile soil.[1] Irrigation in Oregon is almost exclusively confined to the counties east of the Cascade Range. In two counties to the west of that range, however, a little has been done in this direction.

Two other States are lacking in any complete statistical returns of irrigation, namely, California and Colorado, in both of which much has been done toward the improvement of the water supply with reference to mining as well as to agriculture. Furthermore, nothing is said of Dakota, Nebraska, Kansas, and

[1] This lofty and precipitous range of mountains effects a marked change of the climate of the two States, cutting off almost entirely the precipitation, which north from the northern border of California is extremely copious on the western, and almost null on the eastern side of the range.

Texas, parts of each of which States lie within the region insufficiently supplied with moisture, and where irrigation is desirable. This incompleteness of the irrigational statistics is in part remedied by another Census Bulletin,[1] devoted to the subject of "Artesian Wells for Irrigation," in which some details are given with reference to all the States and Territories lying along the eastern base of the Rocky Mountains, in the Great Basin, and on the Pacific coast.

According to this document, there were, in June, 1890, in the States and Territories forming the western half of the United States, 8,097 Artesian wells, the average depth of which is 210.41 feet, and the average discharge 54.43 gallons per minute, while the average area irrigated by each well is 13.21 acres, and the average cost of water per acre irrigated, $18.55. These wells are very unequally distributed within the area included in the investigation, for over one third of them are in California, and nearly one third in Utah. The remainder (a little less than one third) are about equally divided between Colorado, North Dakota, South Dakota, and Texas, while in the other States and Territories the number of Artesian wells is quite insignificant.

The lack of information in the general irrigation reports in regard to the belt of States lying at the eastern base of the Rocky Mountains, and which are partly within the arid region, namely, the Dakotas, Nebraska, Kansas, and Texas, is in part supplied by the reports of Mr. Hinton, of which an enumeration has already been made.[2] Besides these reports, made

[1] Bulletin No. 193, issued June 11, 1892.   [2] See *ante*, p. 47.

under the authority of the Agricultural Department of the United States, voluminous documents have been issued within the past three years by Congress, under the title of "Report of the Special Committee of the United States Senate on the Irrigation and Reclamation of Arid Lands." The first of these special reports bears the date of 1890, and is entitled "Report of Committee and Views of the Minority."[1] The second report of this committee, also issued with the date of 1890, is entitled "The Northwest."[2] The third is devoted to the "Great Basin Region of California,"[3] and the fourth to the "Rocky Mountain Region and Great Plains."[4] The fifth contains various miscellaneous papers on irrigation."[5] The sixth is essentially a reprint of Mr. Hinton's first report on "Irrigation in the United States."[6]

The report of Messrs. White and Aughey,[7] devoted to Artesian wells upon the Great Plains, and made under the auspices of the Department of Agriculture, begins by giving a general idea of the topography and surface features of that part of the United States

---

[1] Senate Document, 51st Congress, 1st Session, Report 928, Part 1. Washington, 1890.

[2] This is Part 2, Volume I., of the above cited Report.

[3] This is Part 3 of the same Report, and is called Volume II.; it contains 573 pages.

[4] Part 4, and Volume III. of the same, with 608 pages.

[5] This part, which is numbered Volume IV. of the series, contains "Statements of the Director of the United States Geological Survey, Reports of United States Consuls in Countries using Irrigation, and Miscellaneous Papers on the Subject of Reclamation," in all 384 pages.

[6] It is called, on the title-page, "A Second Edition of Miscellaneous Document No. 15, 49th Congress." All these documents, forming together "Report 928, 51st Congress, 1st Session," in six parts, bear the date of 1890.

[7] Published in 1887. See *ante*, p. 47.

which lies between the 102d meridian and the eastern base of the Rocky Mountains, this being the region assigned to the commissioners for examination, but it is more especially devoted to that part of this area which lies within the boundaries of Colorado, want of time having made an examination of the whole district impracticable. Thirteen inches is assumed to be the the mean rainfall over this region, and a meridian 100 miles east of the 102d is said to be generally regarded as, at least approximately, representing the western boundary of the great agricultural region lying directly eastward of the district explored, beyond which to the westward the successful growth of farm crops is not practicable without irrigation. From this meridian the aridity increases until the 102d meridian is crossed, from which line westward the maximum for that latitude is encountered.

Within the arid belt as thus limited the commissioners remark that several attempts have been made to secure supplies of water by means of Artesian borings, all except one of these attempts having been the work of private parties. One boring, at Fort Lyon, was done under the auspices of the Agricultural Department. This boring was made by the Commissioners the subject of a special report, which was published in connection with the general report issued a year later.[1] The boring at Fort Lyon, which was carried to the depth of 719 feet, was not a success, the flow of water being too small to be of any practical importance. All the borings made by private parties

---

[1] This special report, addressed to the Commissioner of Agriculture, bears the date of October 20, 1881.

seem also to have been failures.[1] The conclusion of the Commissioners seems to have been decidedly unfavorable to the project of obtaining water in this region by means of Artesian borings. Their statement to this effect is given in the following words: "After a careful examination of all the facts that we have been able to gather, it is our opinion that the prospects of obtaining a satisfactory supply of water by means of Artesian borings in our district are not very encouraging; but there are portions of it, which we shall designate, within which we think that success may be more reasonably hoped for than in others."

Farther on in this report the Commissioners state that "the characters of the superficial and tertiary deposits are such as to offer very little encouragement for making Artesian borings in them; and therefore borings of slight depth are not, in our opinion, likely to be successful anywhere within the proper limits of this district." It is, however, suggested that the Dakota and Triassic sandstones may prove to be water-bearing; but to reach the former a depth of from 1,200 to 2,000 feet must be attained, while to reach the deeper possibly water-bearing formations will probably require a boring 600 to 800 feet deeper.

---

[1] In the Appendix to the Report of Messrs. White and Aughey an additional statement is given by Mr. Horace Beach, who was added to the Commission "for the purpose of collecting statistics in relation to the practical work of boring Artesian wells in the region under investigation." Mr. Beach gives details in regard to borings made at or near South Pueblo, Denver, Coal Creek, Greeley, and Kit Carson, Colorado; Servilleta, New Mexico; and Cheyenne, Wyoming. These all appear to have been failures, with the exception of a second boring at Pueblo, of which it is said that at a depth of 1,200 feet "we have a flowing well of warm water, nearly pure."

With regard to the irrigational condition of the region reported on by Messrs. White and Aughey, and the so-called "Great Plains" in general, the following remarks will here be in place, in preparing which all the available sources of information have been consulted, supplemented by numerous visits to the region in question.

After the wave of population — both that arising from the natural increase and that furnished by the extraordinary immigration into the United States — had spread itself over the well-watered portion of the country, and taken possession of the most easily accessible and agriculturally the most valuable tracts offered for sale by the Government, later comers were obliged to go farther west in order to acquire cheap homesteads, and they then found themselves obliged to take up with land less favorably situated, both with regard to climate and distance from Eastern and European markets, than their predecessors had been able to secure.[1] This condition of things came about gradually. Immigrants unacquainted with the climate, and yielding in part to the pressure of necessity, or perhaps influenced by the misrepresentations of speculators in government and railroad lands, found themselves occupying a region where the rainfall is insufficient for carrying on agricultural pursuits in the manner to which they had been previously accustomed, the consequence being that in these later years there has been a constant struggle on the part of settlers within or on the

[1] See the present writer's "United States: Facts and Figures illustrating the Physical Geography of the Country, and its Material Resources" (1889), pp. 256–258.

borders of the arid region in some way or other to get over these difficulties.

Experience has shown that in the belt of land intermediate between the distinctly well watered and the decidedly insufficiently watered areas the conditions of successive seasons are variable. The rainfall for a few years may be fairly sufficient for the maturing of the crops, but this cycle of favorable years is in turn succeeded by another of less favorable character. This irregularity of the rainfall is not a peculiar feature of the region in question: the same thing happens everywhere in districts where the average precipitation is barely sufficient for successful culture. No regular periodicity has thus far been discovered in this recurrence of cycles of rainier and drier seasons in any country, nor have the causes of such irregularities been satisfactorily made out. These fluctuations in the annual rainfall are by no means limited to regions of small rainfall, but their disastrous effects are naturally much more strongly felt where the average precipitation is only just enough for the maturing of the crops.

The consequences of this condition of things in the arid and semi-arid parts of the United States have been manifold. In the first place, it was early recognized that the decidedly insufficiently watered area extending east of the eastern base of the Rocky Mountains — the Great Plains — was naturally a pastoral region, better suited to raising cattle than for any other purpose.[1] In the earlier stages of the cattle-

---

[1] This is the case all over the world. Regions of small rainfall, if not too cold, are pastoral regions, inhabited by more or less nomadic tribes. Such are the Steppes of Asia, and the Pampas of South America. The

raising business the methods of those thus engaged were simple. A locality where sufficient water for stock could be had — usually at the base of some mountain range — was taken possession of, and purchased if necessary. From this as a base of operations a "cattle-range" was established on that purchase, and by having possession of the only available water a very large district might be made available for stock-raising without the necessity of purchasing more than a small portion of it. But, as more settlers made their appearance, claiming land occupied by others who had acquired no legal rights to it, conflicts began to arise, and sometimes became quite serious. It is true, also, that the various attempts which have been made to supplement the natural supply of water by means of ditches and Artesian wells have in certain localities been sufficiently successful to lead the settlers to realize the fact that comparatively small areas well cultivated were decidedly more profitable than tracts too large to be properly developed.

The statistics of the census of 1890 show as plainly as possible the results of the over-hasty occupation of land too dry to be successfully cultivated except during the cycles of more than average rainfall. The following extract from the census documents well illustrates

---

arid part of the United States is, however, to a considerable extent, a rich mineral region, which fact modifies greatly the conditions of settlement and distribution of the population. Moreover, the mining districts within the arid region are essentially different in their topographical character from the non-metalliferous region of the Plains. The only point of agreement between the Plains and the Great Basin is lack of moisture; in all other respects the differences between the two areas are fundamental.

this condition of things, as revealed by comparison of various State censuses taken in 1885 with the results of the United States census of 1890: "During the past ten years the population of Dakota, considering the two States of North Dakota and South Dakota together, has increased from 135,177 to 511,527, or 278 per cent; Nebraska from 452,402 to 1,058,910, or 134 per cent; and Kansas from 996,096 to 1,427,096, or 43 per cent. This increase has not, however, continued uniformly throughout the decade. In 1885 Dakota contained 415,610 inhabitants, or more than four fifths of its present population. Nebraska contained 740,645 inhabitants in the same year, thus dividing the numerical increase equally between the two halves of the decade, but leaving the greater percentage of increase in the first half. In the same year Kansas by its State census had 1,268,530 inhabitants, showing that nearly two thirds of the numerical gain was acquired during the first half of the decade. The industries of these States are almost purely agricultural, and are dependent on the supply of moisture, either in the form of rain or by irrigation. Through these States passes what is known as the sub-humid belt, a strip of country several degrees in width, in which during rainy years there is an abundance of moisture for the needs of crops, while in the years when the rainfall is below the average the supply is deficient. In this region little provision has been made for artificial irrigation, the settlers having thus far been content to depend upon rainfall. Into this region the settlers flocked in large numbers in the early years of the decade, drawn thither by the fertility of the land, and by the fact that for a few years the rainfall had been sufficient for the needs of agriculture. During the past two or three years, however, the conditions of rainfall have materially changed. It has fallen decidedly below the normal, and the settlers have thereby been forced to emigrate. Thousands of families have abandoned this region and gone to Oklahoma and the Rocky Mountain region. This migration is well shown in the progress of Kansas, as indicated by its annual censuses. These censuses show a rapid increase in population from 1880 up to 1887; 1888 shows but a slight increase over 1887, while 1889 shows a reduction in the population, leading up to the further reduction shown by the federal census in 1890."[1]

Statements to the same effect have been repeatedly made in other official documents of recent date, of which the following may be offered as an example: "In the first part of the present decade population poured in upon the Great Plains region. The earlier years of sufficient rainfall were followed by years of drought, in which a large percentage of the success previously achieved was destroyed. Reaction set in, and for a time it appeared as if the entire Plains region would have to be given over to cattlemen; but slowly, however, the cattle-range business is changing as the pressure of population continues with more or less vigor, and ranchmen are becoming unable, east of the basins of the Rocky Mountains at least, to command large areas of natural grass land."[2]

The fact seems to be, however, that this large migration of the population from the arid region of the

---

[1] See "Census Bulletin No. 16," issued Dec. 12, 1890, pp. 7, 8.
[2] Hinton's Progress Report for 1890, p. 15.

Plains was due — in part, at least — to a realization of the unfavorable conditions normally prevalent there, rather than to any actual temporary decrease of the precipitation during the latter part of the decade 1880–89, since the statistics of rainfall collected by the Signal Service during that period over the region in question do not indicate that there was any perceptible change in this respect, or any noticeable difference in the amount of precipitation, during the first and second halves of this decade.[1]

The unfavorable report of Messrs. White and Aughey on the possibility of procuring Artesian water in sufficient quantity and of suitable quality for irrigation on the Great Plains did not, however, lead to any diminution of the efforts of the settlers in that region to have still further expenditures made by the Government for the purpose of elucidating this question. The documents to which reference has already been made[2] are the outcome of this additional work, so far as the results are at present available, and some critical remarks may here be introduced with reference to their contents.

We find in Mr. Hinton's "Progress Report in Irrigation in the United States, Part I., prepared under the Direction of the Secretary of Agriculture," that this work is now designated as the "Artesian, Underflow,

---

[1] For a further discussion of the question whether there is any statistical proof of a change or periodical fluctuation in the amount of precipitation in later years in the arid region of the United States, and for remarks on changes in climate in general, as having been caused by the agency of man, see Appendix B.

[2] See *ante*, p. 92. See also Appendix C, in which will be found as full a list as can be made, up to the time of the publication of the present volume, of official documents relating to the subject of irrigation.

and Irrigation Investigation," of which Mr. Hinton is the "Special Agent."[1] We find, also, that a large corps of assistants (eighteen in all) were, or had been, employed in this work at the time this report was made. The term "underflow," here introduced, demands a special definition. This word seems to be used by Mr. Hinton as synonymous with "undersheet," a term also frequently employed by him in the report in question. The word "phreatic," which also often appears in this document, needs some explanation, since it is not to be found in English dictionaries.

The underflow or undersheet water, from the utilization of which so much seems to be expected, is nowhere definitely defined in Mr. Hinton's reports; but, as nearly as can be made out from various statements made by him, it would appear that, in his opinion, a very much larger volume of rain falls on the basin or catchment area of the Missouri-Mississippi than is delivered at its mouth, and that much the larger portion of this precipitation finds its way to the Gulf of Mexico under ground, as "seepage and percolation" of this river. There is, therefore, a subterranean mass of water — an "underflow" or "undersheet " — which, if penetrated by deep borings, or even by ordinary wells, is capable of furnishing a sufficient amount of moisture to allow of successful cultivation over a vast area in which the natural supply is quite insufficient for that purpose. This source of supply is designated by Mr. Hinton as "phreatic water," or water which can be utilized by means of wells.[2] The

---

[1] This report bears the date of 1891.

[2] "Phreatic" is derived from the Greek φρέαρ, which meant originally a well, and later a water-tank, cistern, or reservoir.

truth of this theory is considered as having been demonstrated both by general physical and meteorological observation, and by actual experimental methods in the arid region.

The theoretical proof of the existence of an available undersheet of water is sought for in the fact that the discharge of the Mississippi into the Gulf of Mexico is only equal to 107 cubic miles of water, while the total rainfall in the basin of that river equals 620 cubic miles, leaving 573 cubic miles to be accounted for. This amount, with some deduction for evaporation, must — as is assumed — flow in a subterranean current; and, as Mr. Hinton remarks, "if we allow one half of this huge volume to the western portion of the drainage basin we shall open a wide field for speculation."[1]

There are several reasons why these statements with regard to the supposed underflow of the Mississippi and its practical importance with regard to irrigation in the drier region of the country cannot be accepted as having any real value, or as being at all applicable to the matter under discussion. In the first place, it is by no means the whole basin of the Missouri-Mississippi which it is desirable to have irrigated, but only a minor portion of it. The basin of the Mississippi proper, both before and after the junction of that river with the Missouri, is almost entirely a well-watered region. The only part of the country which belongs to the arid region, and which is drained by any other branch of the Mississippi than the Missouri, is the head of the Arkansas. A very small area in Southwestern

[1] See Hinton's Progress Report, Part I., p. 37.

Kansas, Southeastern Colorado, and Northeastern New Mexico belongs to the Arkansas basin. Practically, the dry portion of the United States east of the Rocky Mountains is the basin of the Upper Missouri and its tributaries. The area of the drainage basin of the Missouri is a little more than two fifths of that of the Missouri-Mississippi, and about two thirds of this may be considered as being included within the arid or semi-arid region. Thus we find that a little more than one quarter of the basin of the whole Mississippi system is all with which we have to do in reference to the irrigation question, and that statistics based on the physical and meteorological conditions of the whole basin have no application here.

Again, the statistics used by Mr. Hinton are far from being correct, whether intended to be used with reference to the rainfall and drainage of the entire Mississippi basin or of any part of it. They are given on the authority of Mr. M. F. Maury, whose work was published more than thirty years ago, and who based his estimate of the average annual fall of rain in the Mississippi Valley on data published by Mr. L. Blodget in 1855, by whom it was fixed at forty inches.[1] A few years later, namely, in 1861, Messrs. Humphreys and Abbot, in their elaborate work on the Physics and Hydraulics of the Mississippi River,[2] availing themselves of much additional information furnished by Mr. Blodget and others, and coming down to as late as 1860, fixed the average annual rainfall in the Mississippi basin at

---

[1] See M. F. Maury, "The Physical Geography of the Sea," Eighth Edition, New York, 1861, p. 102.

[2] A publication of the Bureau of Topographical Engineers, U. S. War Department.

30.4 inches, which is about ten inches less than the number adopted by Mr. Maury and utilized by Mr. Hinton. The average annual rainfall in the basin of the Missouri was taken at 20.9 inches. The total area of the Mississippi basin was assumed by Mr. Maury to be 982,000 square miles: the figures adopted by Messrs. Humphreys and Abbot are 1,244,000 square miles, or 262,000 square miles more than Mr. Maury's estimate.[1] The object of this last-named author in discussing the rainfall and area of this basin was to use the facts for the purpose of showing the vast amount of water taken up in this region by evaporation. He assumed that all the rainfall which was not poured into the ocean by the Mississippi was disposed of in that way, entirely

---

[1] The latest official determination of the area of the Mississippi basin — that of Mr. Gannett, published in the Census Reports of 1880 — gives 1,240,039 square miles, a result differing very little from that adopted by Messrs. Humphreys and Abbot. The discharge of the Mississippi, or of any one of its branches, depends on various conditions, considerably complicated in their combined action. The amount of the rainfall, the character of the climate, and the nature of the soil, are the essential factors in bringing about the final result. The following table, exhibiting the amount of annual rainfall in each basin, including that of the main river as well as of its various tributaries, and the percentage of that rainfall discharged, as determined by Messrs. Humphreys and Abbot, will show that the amount discharged by any one of these streams is — to a considerable extent, at least — determined by the amount of rainfall in the basin which it drains.

Name of River.	Inches of Rainfall.	Percentage of Discharge.
Yazoo	46.3	90
St. Francis	41.1	90
Ohio	41.5	24
Red	39.0	20
Upper Mississippi	35.2	24
Arkansas	29.3	15
Missouri	20.9	15
Missouri-Mississippi	30.4	25

ignoring the fact that a portion of it must percolate the ground and be held there permanently.[1]

Mr. Hinton, on the other hand, almost entirely overlooks, or greatly underrates, the amount of the rainfall which is lost by evaporation. In commenting on Mr. Maury's figures he assumes that this loss amounts to only 170 cubic miles, or about twenty-seven per cent of the annual precipitation in the Mississippi basin. Of the correctness of this estimate no proof is offered: it seems to be merely a guess, and one which is very wide of the mark, as will here be explained.

There are no precise data by which to fix the amount of evaporation from the surface of the soil, or of percolation through it, anywhere in the United States. There is abundant reason, however, for believing the latter to be very small in amount in every portion of either the arid or the semi-arid part of the country. The most reliable and continued observations on percolation and evaporation have been made in England, and especially in the neighborhood of London, by means of the Dalton gauge.

Experiments conducted by Mr. Charles Greaves on the river Lea, at the intake of the East London waterworks, showed that as the average of twenty-two years' observation the annual rainfall was 25.837, the percolation 6.866, and the evaporation from the ground 18.970 inches. At King's Langley the Dalton gauge, observed for eight years, indicated that, the average

---

[1] Having shown, as he thinks, that the rainfall in the Mississippi basin amounts to an average of 620 cubic miles annually, and that the discharge of that river is 107 cubic miles, he adds: "This would leave 513 cubic miles of water to be evaporated from this river basin annually." *Loc. cit.*, p. 102.

annual rainfall being 26.61 inches, 42.4 per cent percolated, through the gravelly loam forming the surface at the locality, to the depth of three feet; between October and March, 10.39 inches percolated the soil out of a rainfall of 13.95; while between April and September, the average rainfall being 21.67 inches, only 0.90 inch percolated, or 7.1 per cent. The experiments of Dr. Dalton himself, at Manchester, showed that, as a mean of three years' observations, the percolation was twenty-five per cent of the rainfall: those of M. Gaspain, in the South of France, proved that the average rainfall was twenty-eight inches, of which twenty per cent percolated.

Similarly numerous long-continued observations in Europe have shown that at the time of the year when the precipitation is only moderate, with frequent intervals of dry weather, the percolation is almost null, while during the winter or rainy season, when the ground remains saturated with moisture for a considerable length of time, a large percentage of the rainfall percolates. In general, in England and Western Europe, the average annual percolation does not much exceed one fifth of the total precipitation.

The climate of the Great Plains is, however, much less favorable to percolation than that of any part of Great Britain. In the region east of the base of the Rocky Mountains the precipitation is almost exclusively limited to the spring and summer months, that in winter being almost null, as may be learned by examining the various publications of the Signal Service.[1]

[1] See, especially, "Climate of Nebraska," Senate Executive Document No. 115, 57th Congress, 1st Session, Washington, 1890; and "Irrigation

Thus, the average monthly precipitation at North Platte, Nebraska, for the five months from November to March, is only 0.50 inch, while that from April to October is 2.52 inches, or five times as much.

The condition of things in regard to evaporation in the arid region may be illustrated by the writer's experience during a summer of exploration in Colorado along the base of the Front Range, and in the region of the Parks. During the months of July and August rain fell copiously almost every afternoon, so that it only happened twice during that time that there were as much as three consecutive days without it, and the showers were frequently copious, continuing for several hours. Strange, however, as it may appear to one unacquainted with the peculiarities of the climate of this region, the ground was never wet to the depth of more than a few inches. Not one particle of water penetrated so deep as to be permanently retained. The character of the vegetation in the valley of the Upper Arkansas, where these observations were made, was such as to indicate clearly that the climate was exceedingly dry, "sage-brush" and piñon pine abounding, and an examination of the soil showed that nearly every drop of the rain which reached the earth was returned to the atmosphere within a few hours after it had fallen. The small amount of moisture which does percolate the soil in this region must come from the winter rains, or from the melting of the snow at the close of winter. Since over most of the Great Plains the precipitation in the form of snow is exceedingly small, unless in exceptional

and Water Storage in the Arid Regions," House Executive Document No. 287, 57th Congress, 2d Session, Washington, 1891.

seasons, and since most of the rainfall comes at a time when the conditions are best suited for producing a very rapid evaporation, it is clear that the total percolation in that region, under the climatic conditions now prevailing, must be very trifling in amount.

The facts here stated would seem to throw great doubt on the validity of Mr. Hinton's arguments in favor of a large supply of "phreatic water" in the arid regions. It remains now to examine into the facts brought forward by him in regard to the actual boring of numerous "Artesian wells," as he calls them, in the district investigated by him, or under his direction.

The results obtained in the course of the "Artesian, Underflow, and Irrigation Investigations," up to the time of the publication of the "Progress Report" in 1891, are thus stated by Mr. Hinton:[1] "It will be seen by an examination of the maps prepared for and published by the Artesian wells investigation report that from north to south a basin or basins of Artesian water of great power and volume have been struck and are now operating, through 1,400 wells or more, on an area not to exceed 100 miles in width. There are wells on the plains and in the foot-hills east and west of the belt defined, but they have distinct hydrographic and topographic features of their own. Within the developed Artesian regions it will be found that the deepest and most permanent wells have, taking topographical 'dip' and 'trend' into consideration, an almost uniform depth from north to south, a considerable sameness of temperature, volume, pressure, chemical character, and

[1] See "Progress Report," Part I. p. 35.

flow. This argues that they come mainly from one general source, and have about the same degree of hydrostatic pressure. If the investigation of the past year had accomplished nothing more than to bring this encouraging series of facts to the attention of the struggling settlers, and of all those interested in their maintenance and success, that would alone have been worth all it has cost. But this is by no means more than the beginning of a remarkable addition to our knowledge of physical features and facts relating to our semi-arid and arid domain. The investigation has opened up a great vista of economic possibilities and engineering development. The engineer and the geologist engaged in the work are confident that the source of supply for the Artesian wells now flowing will mainly be found in the drainage of our continental range — the Rocky Mountains. The same observation which governed their opinion of the Northwest holds equally good for similar conclusions as to the centre and the Southwest, as far at least as concerns that portion north of the Rio Grande boundary."

Again, Mr. Hinton remarks as follows:[1] "In North Dakota interest is now centered upon the prospect of obtaining more deep wells, and of storing water from the wells sunk in the glacial drift of the Red River Basin. Several hundred of these wells, all of a secondary character, are found in that section. Very little artificial application of water is necessary for the security of crops, but that little is needed very badly, and during most years. Water has been found all along the line of the Great Northern Railroad, and at very

[1] *Loc. cit.*, p. 36.

moderate depths in the Milk River Valley. There is very little doubt that Artesian water to a considerable extent, though at somewhat great depths, may be obtained from that vast reservoir, the Dakota sandstone, filled as it has been for unknown cycles from the vast precipitation falling on the Rocky Mountains and draining through the upturned edges of the stratum into the water-conserving rock below."

The idea of an "underflow" from the Rocky Mountains toward the east and south is by no means original with Mr. Hinton. George Catlin, in his remarkable work, "The Lifted and Subsided Rocks of America," long ago advocated something similar, although his ideas were different from those of Mr. Hinton with reference to the practical use of these "submontagne rivers," as he called them. Mr. Catlin believed that they were the source and cause of the Gulf Stream — a theory which up to this time has not been received with much favor by geologists or physical geographers.[1]

The "Artesian Wells Investigation Report," to which reference is made in the above quotation from Mr. Hin-

---

[1] "The vast inclines extending off and into the plains from the bases of the [Rocky] mountains, both to the east and the west, and at their axes several thousand feet above the level of the ocean, and from which (or through which) the mountain ridges rise, I shall here assume are the gradual elevations of the sedimentary system (as before suggested), caused by the successive upheavals passing through them, lifting them, and propping them at the fractured edges, and forming vast cellars or cisterns beneath them, through which, and above the granite surface, the sunken waters flow. . . . I have said that the Gulf Stream was caused by submontagne rivers from under the Rocky Mountains and the Andes, converging in the latitude of the Caribbean Sea, and discharging their combined waters into that estuary; and pouring through the Gulf of Mexico, taking with them the waters of the Rio del Norte and Mississippi, they debouch with them into the ocean at the Cape of Florida, and there become the Gulf Stream." *Loc. cit.*, p. 26.

ton's progress report, was published in 1890, and is called by the Secretary of Agriculture " a preliminary investigation made to determine the proper location for Artesian wells within the area west of the ninety-seventh meridian, and east of the foot-hills of the Rocky Mountains." [1] It is prefaced by a report of the Special Agent in Charge, Mr. Hinton, in which the possibilities of Artesian wells in the arid region of the United States are set forth in glowing terms, and descriptions are given of various regions in Europe, Asia, and Africa, where irrigation by means of water thus obtained is extensively carried on. Mr. Hinton's report is followed by a large number of special reports, especially those of Mr. E. S. Nettleton, " Supervisory Engineer of the Irrigation Survey," and of Professor Robert Hay, General Field Geologist, and of Messrs. Culver, Bailey, Hicks, and Van Diest, as well as other reports made to the special agent in charge by the division field agents, Messrs. Underhill, Updyke, Coffin, Gregory, Carpenter, and Roesler.

The principal results of this survey, up to the time of the publication of this report, are thus summed up by the Supervisory Engineer : " (1) The existence of a large Artesian basin in the Dakotas, which is indicated by the number of flowing wells scattered over an area of about 12,000 square miles. (2) The presence of an abundant supply of water in a loose sand stratum of great thickness and subjected to great pressure, which is fully maintained after being pierced by numerous wells flowing their full capacity for years. (3) The probability of an extension of this basin to westward or a con-

[1] This is Executive Document No. 222, 51st Congress, 1st Session.

siderable distance from the James River Valley developments, and having similar characteristics. (4) The probable existence of an Artesian basin in Texas similar to that in the Dakotas, and of unknown area, but lying at a greater depth from the surface. (5) The existence of several other Artesian basins in other parts of the country examined, which have similar flows, from which water is obtained in sufficient quantity for domestic use, and, in some instances, for the irrigation of small areas. (6) The existence of two Artesian basins lying in the drift where flowing water for domestic use and for irrigation is obtained at a very low cost. (7) The necessity of irrigation to prevent total loss of crops, at times, and for their full development nearly every year. (8) The existence of large supplies of subterranean waters underlying quite generally the whole territory examined. (9) The lack of knowledge of the majority of the people of the methods for utilizing the Artesian well and underground waters for irrigation purposes. (10) The need of a closer and more extended geological examination to designate, as near as possible, where it is probable that water may or may not be obtained. (11) The necessity of verifying by test experimental work some of the conclusions of the geologists. (12) The necessity of investigating the subject of utilizing the subterranean waters and the extent of country which can be reclaimed by them and to report on methods for bringing such waters to the surface and the cost therefor."

The groups of Artesian wells in the region examined, "whose waters are largely available for irrigation, being, to some extent, now so used and capable of considerable development in that direction," are geographically located as follows by Mr. Hay, the General Field Geologist.

(1) The wells of the Red River Valley in Northeastern North Dakota. (2) The wells of the James River Valley in the two Dakotas (North and South). (3) The wells of the Yellowstone Valley at Miles City, Montana. (4) The shallow wells in the drift formation on the eastern side of the two Dakotas. (5) The wells of Northern Nebraska. (6) Four groups of wells in Southwestern Kansas. (7) The wells of the La Poudre, Denver, and Pueblo basins in Colorado. (8) The Fort Worth and Waco groups in Texas. (9) The wells of New Mexico. (10) The wells of Wyoming. Some of the details in regard to these Artesian well districts, furnished by Mr. Hay, may be here appended.

The most important of the groups above enumerated is that of the James River Valley, which covers an area of 20,000 square miles, with about 150 wells. These are said to flow with considerable pressure (60 to 153 pounds to the square inch), and with considerable volume of water, some furnishing over 1,000 and one nearly 3,000 gallons per minute. The water which these wells furnish is believed to come from the sandstones of the Dakota group, belonging to the Lower Cretaceous. The outcrop of this group on the sides of the western mountains is said to be "several thousand feet higher than in Middle Dakota," and as this sandstone is followed toward the east it is covered by a thickness of from 1,000 to 2,000 feet of shales, which are more or less impervious, and thus seal in the waters at the low eastern edge of the Artesian trough, and prevent their escape. The reason why this sandstone has furnished no Artesian water farther west than the James River Valley is thought to be, that this rock is covered by too great a thickness of later deposits, making it too costly a matter to reach the underlying water-bearing rock. The existing wells of this group are said to have their waters "highly mineralized," but no analyses are given. It is thought, however, that none " so far are mineralized to the extent that they would injure vegetation." On the western side of the Black Hills, in Wyoming, the Dakota sandstone yields flowing wells of salt water, with a considerable amount of oil, natural gas being also present.

In Southwestern Kansas, and just over the line in Colorado, in the Arkansas Valley, there is a group of Artesian wells, the water of which is furnished by the Dakota sandstone, at a depth of less than 300 feet. There are, however, reasons for believing that these wells do not get their supply of water from the exposure of this rock in the foot-hills of the Rocky Mountains. One reason given for this is, that the Dakota sandstone, in that part of the foot-hills corresponding in latitude with Southern Nebraska and part of Kansas, are more or less metamorphosed into quartzite, thus losing their permeable quality to a considerable extent. The source of the water of these wells is, therefore, supposed to be "local breaks in the superincumbent strata not far to the west, or even in outcrops which occur some miles to the south." The wells in Kansas to which reference is here made, which are near Coolidge, do not have sufficient pressure to lift the water more than twenty or thirty feet, the neighboring high ground being 200 feet above them; and at Syracuse, sixteen miles south of Coolidge, the water did not rise to the surface. The facts seem to indicate, in the opinion of the field geologists, that Northern Nebraska may have an extension of Artesian conditions from Southern Dakota, and be a part of the James River district, the source of the water being the southeast flank of the Black Hills, where there has been no metamorphism of the sandstone. For the rest of Nebraska, as also Western Kansas, and part of Colorado, the Dakota sandstone is not expected to furnish Artesian water, except in limited areas where the local conditions may chance to be favorable, as near Coolidge.

The shallow wells in the eastern part of the two Dakotas get their water from the so-called "glacial drift," a sheet of which, varying in thickness from fifteen to two hundred feet, is spread over a wide extent of country east of the Missouri, extending even into Iowa.[1] Where the gravelly beds of this formation are sufficiently thick and intercalated with strata of clay, Artesian conditions are likely to be present; the flow of water being, however, not very abundant, but in quality much superior to that obtained from the deep wells.

The wells of the Denver basin, in most cases, are supplied with water from rocks of Tertiary age: a few only penetrate the Laramie or higher Cretaceous beds. The conditions here are favorable for an Artesian flow, since the edges of the upturned formations at the base of the Rocky Mountains are near at hand. The wells in and around the city of Denver are said to

[1] See *ante*, pp. 73-76.

be 300 or more in number, and the head of water to have become so reduced that few of them are now flowing; "but the pumps which have succeeded the natural flow have given no indication of reduction in the quantity of the water." The regions along the eastern base of the Rocky Mountains, in which the Platte, Fountain, and Arkansas debouch upon the Plains, is chiefly watered by irrigation canals from those rivers, Artesian water being there of only secondary importance. Conditions similar to those in Colorado as respects the procuring of Artesian water are presumed to exist farther south, in New Mexico, since the geological conditions continue essentially the same all along the base of the range, and the rainfall is not less there than it is in the same longitude farther north. At the time the report which is here under discussion was prepared, little seems to have been known with regard to Artesian water in New Mexico.[1] There is a group of wells at Fort Worth, in Texas, where the same thing has occurred as at Denver. Out of 240 wells which have been bored, only three or four are now flowing.

The wells of Southwestern Kansas, northeast of Meade Centre, are said to be about eighty in number, their flow varying from two or three gallons per minute to between sixty and seventy. The origin of the water in these wells is the Tertiary grit, and their number is said to have increased during the year which elapsed after the preparation of this report, while the flow of water had not diminished.

[1] In the Census Bulletin, No. 193, "Artesian Wells for Irrigation," dated June 11, 1892, no facts are given indicating the existence of Artesian water of any importance in this geological position.

The group of wells in the Yellowstone Valley, at Miles City, Montana, is briefly described by Professor Hay. They are from twenty to thirty in number, their flow being from one to twenty gallons per minute, and they are utilized for the irrigation of gardens and for domestic purposes. These wells obtain their water from the Laramie group, and it is thought that over the extensive area where this formation is developed to a very considerable thickness, and uplifted against the mountains, it may become an important source of water-supply.[1]

Accompanying Mr. Hinton's Report for 1890, and forming the second part of the Progress Report of the Artesian and Underflow Investigation, there is a special report by Mr. Nettleton, the Chief Engineer of the work, covering a large section of the central division of the Great Plains, embracing considerable portions of Kansas, Nebraska, and Colorado. This report is accompanied by maps and profiles, and a considerable amount of statistical information, in tabular form, with regard to wells examined in detail along certain surveyed lines. It is from these statistics, apparently, that Mr. Hinton feels himself justified in drawing the conclusion that "there is a large region south from the Niobrara to the Republican Fork in Northern Kansas wherein the phreatic waters are known to be abundant and their plane quite near the surface. A regular fall to the eastward will enable the distribution of water to be made with comparative ease in that direction. No great

---

[1] Later information in regard to the wells at Miles City is given in Mr. Hinton's Progress Report for 1890, Part I. (1891), p. 152. They are said to be from 450 to 500 feet deep, the water rising from twelve to eighteen feet above the level of the valley.

amount of mechanical power will be required to lift such phreatic waters to points where they may be more readily distributed. A very remarkable development is sure to be seen within the next year or two in the basin formed by the Republican, the Frenchman, and the tributaries of the North and South Platte." [1]

The geographical position of the lines surveyed by Mr. Nettleton, as stated above, may be learned from the following statement: (1) Across the South Platte, at Big Spring, Nebraska, to a point near the head of Frenchman River, forty-eight miles. (2) Across the Platte, Nebraska, from the South Loup River to Medicine Creek, fifty-five miles. (3) Across the South Platte, at Lexington, Nebraska, from the South Loup River to the Republican River, seventy miles. (4) Across the Platte River, at Grand Island, Nebraska, from the South Loup River to the Republican River, seventy-seven miles. (5) Across the Arkansas River, at Great Bend, Kansas, from Smoky Hill River to a point near Iuka, Kansas, seventy-five miles. (6) Across the Arkansas River, at Dodge City, from Pawnee Fork to Crooked Creek, seventy-five miles. (7) Across the Arkansas River, at Garden City, Kansas, from Ladder Creek to Loco, Kansas, eighty-five miles. (8) On the hundredth meridian, from Norton, Kansas, one hundred and thirty miles.

An examination of the tables of statistical information which accompany the sections made along the lines thus located reveals the following facts: (1) The depth of the wells varies from 12 to 1,145 feet. (2) In

---

[1] Hinton's Progress Report for 1890, Part I. p. 18.

102 cases (out of 188) the water did not rise at all in the bore-hole; very rarely did it rise more than a few feet, and in only one well to the surface. (3) From most of these wells the water is raised by means of a windmill, but sometimes by a hand-pump, and in two or three cases by steam. (4) In by far the larger number of these wells the water is used for stock or for household purposes; in one case only for irrigation, and in two for locomotives.[1] (5) The supply of water varies from less than a hundred to several thousand gallons per day, but in much the larger number of cases the quantity pumped is between one and three thousand gallons. (6) In regard to almost all these wells the geological information given is very meagre: by far the larger number are said to have been sunk in "sand" or "sandy clay"; in some cases the well ends in gravel, in other cases the absence of gravel is specially noted; in the few instances in which rock is said to have been passed through in the boring no clue is given as to its geological age.

The facts stated above seem clearly to indicate that the water from these wells belongs to no general "underflow" system: it comes from the superficial detrital material of Tertiary or Post-Tertiary age, this material being of very considerable, but also very irregular, thickness, while to draw the line which divides the two systems from each other is a matter of great difficulty, and probably in most cases an entire impossibility. An ideal section given by Mr. Nettleton in illustration of the geological conditions prevailing in

[1] These wells are of large bore. They are on the line of a railroad, and in the immediate vicinity of a river.

the region in question seems to be a fair representation of the general character of the formations intersected by these wells. It represents a thick body of clay traversed by beds of sand, very irregular in their development and position with reference to a horizontal plane, and occasionally inosculating with each other. In the masses of sand having a considerable thickness and lying obliquely in the clay, we have the necessary conditions for a supply of water, which may rise to some little height above the bottom of the bore-hole, but which cannot (unless exceptionally) be really Artesian. In a region of large rainfall such a source of supply would be highly satisfactory for ordinary domestic purposes, and such is really the character of the water-supply over a large part of the United States — as, for instance, in New England — away from the large cities, which have peculiar needs, resulting from the concentration of a large population within a comparatively small area.

The fact that the wells have to be sunk to a considerable depth in the region here under discussion depends on the smallness of the rainfall. Where the precipitation is overabundant the line of saturation lies near the surface, sinking a little during the drier part of the year, but in a region covered by thick deposits of permeable material never reaching any great depth. Over areas similarly conditioned, but less generously supplied with rain, the water-level stands lower and must be reached by deeper wells, which it may be necessary to sink into the solid rock, in which case, if the rock be permeable, a permanent supply of water may be secured which can be extensively drawn upon.[1] In regions where the precipitation is very small, and the evaporation proportionally large, as is the case in Western Nebraska and the arid or semi-arid region in general, the superficial detritus will be water-bearing only under exceptionally favorable conditions, as, for instance, in the immediate vicinity of permanent streams. The plane of saturation will be at a very considerable depth, and the supply of water limited in quantity.

The facts revealed in the sections and the accompanying tabular statements, of which a synopsis has been given above, are such as would be expected to result from the climatic and geological conditions existing in this region. Water is obtained in various localities in moderate quantity, but usually only at a very considerable depth, and that this supply would hold out if drawn upon to a considerable extent is extremely doubtful. Indeed, it seems most probable that in this region of present small rainfall the inhabitants are utilizing the water stored beneath the ground at a former period, when the precipitation was larger than it now is. There is abundant evidence to substantiate the statement that within a comparatively recent period — from the geological point of view, very recent — the climate of this part of the country has become decidedly drier than it formerly was.[2] At all

---

[1] Of this character was, until within a few years, the water-supply of a large part of the most densely populated region of England, the source of the water being the sandstones of the Permian and Triassic groups, which formations cover so large an area in that country. See *ante*, pp. 50-52.

[2] This change in the climate of the region in question is by no means a condition of things peculiar to this part of the country. There is abundant evidence that a change of this kind has taken place all over

events, it can be truthfully stated that any such "underflow" as that supposed by Mr. Hinton and his assistants to have been shown to exist over a region lying hundreds of miles to the east of the base of the Rocky Mountains is a physical impossibility. The idea has its root in the intense desire prevailing at the West to make it appear that natural defects of that part of the country are not really defects, because they can be so easily remedied by a sufficient expenditure of money on the part of the general government.[1]

In 1892 another report on irrigation was published, which, in the letter of transmittal of the Secretary of Agriculture by which it is accompanied, is called the "final report of the artesian and underflow investigation, and of the irrigation inquiry." It is in four volumes, the general scope and authorship of each of which are indicated in the note below.[2]

---

the world, the evidences of desiccation in later geological times presenting themselves in abundance in the Old World as well as in the New. In an article entitled "Whence comes the Water of the Oases of the Sahara?" by G. Rohlfs, published in the "Zeitschrift der Gesellschaft für Erdkunde" (Band XXVIII., 1893, pp. 296–305), this distinguished African explorer, after stating various rather puzzling facts in regard to the distribution of water in the Sahara, arrives at the conclusion that these can only be accounted for by admitting that the rainfall of that region is in reality much larger than has generally been supposed. The present writer has been led by long study of this subject to the conclusion that this larger rainfall is something which cannot be denied, but that it is an event which has to do with the past, and not with the present epoch. See the author's "Climatic Changes of Later Geological Times," pp. 101–154.

[1] See Appendix B, where this matter will be brought up for further discussion.

[2] This report constitutes Executive Document 41, 52d Congress, 1st Session, and bears the date of 1892. It is in four parts, numbered Part I. to Part IV., each paged separately. The first of these has, as a special title, "A Report on Irrigation and the Cultivation of the Soil thereby, with Physical Data, Conditions, and Progress, within the United

The introductory volume, by Mr. Hinton, the Special Agent in charge, is largely occupied by general considerations in regard to the subject of irrigation, not only in the United States, but all over the world. The great importance of the irrigation investigation carried on under the direction of the Department of Agriculture is insisted on, and it is claimed that highly valuable results have already been achieved. "The existence of underflow or phreatic waters of varying depths and quantities throughout the length and breadth of the great plains region has been in a large degree tentatively established by its work, and that this fact has given great encouragement to the pioneer farmers and communities in western Kansas. Encouragement has also been given, by the large work done during the past twenty-one months, to agricultural enterprise and industry in southwest Colorado, in eastern New Mexico, and throughout Texas west of the ninety-seventh meridian. The practical work of construction and cultivation which is in progress has resulted in great part from the impetus given to energy and enterprise by

States for 1891, accompanied by Maps, Illustrations, and Papers, by Richard J. Hinton, Special Agent in Charge." The second is called a "Final Report of the Chief Engineer Edwin S. Nettleton, C. E., to the Secretary of Agriculture, with accompanying Maps, Profiles, Diagrams, and Additional Papers." The third is entitled "Final Geological Reports of the Artesian and Underflow Investigation, between the Ninety-seventh Meridian of Longitude and the Foothills of the Rocky Mountains, made by Prof. Robert Hay, F. G. S. A., Chief Geologist." The fourth is the "Final Report of the Mid-Plains Division of the Artesian and Underflow Investigation between the Ninety-seventh Meridian of Longitude west of Greenwich and the Foothills of the Rocky Mountains, by Special Agent S. W. Gregory, of Garden City, Kansas, and a Special Report on certain Artesian Conditions in the State of South Dakota, by Fred. F. B. Coffin, Engineer for South Dakota."

the same influence under the small appropriation made by the Fifty-first Congress."

The year 1891 is said in this report to have been marked by great activity in the direction of irrigation enterprises on a large scale, and in the development, by means of irrigation, of numerous small localities west of the one hundredth meridian. In the region between the ninety-seventh meridian and the foothills of the Rocky Mountains, almost from north to south, there is said to have been a decided growth of settlements and a marked increase of cultivation. The increase of population through the region of Wyoming and Southern Idaho, up the valley of the Yellowstone, and over the Rocky Mountains into the Cascade Range, is said to have been "not large, but steady in character," while new and extensive areas that will soon invite occupation are to be found in Southern Idaho, Eastern Washington, and Oregon, as well as in Northern and Central Montana, both east and west of the Rocky Mountains. Over the more southern area of the arid region the movement of population is admitted to be slower.

This question of the rapidity of increase of the population in the arid region will have had more light thrown on it after the next census has been taken. The tabular statements given in the preceding pages of the present volume show clearly enough that during the interval which elapsed between the taking of the censuses of 1880 and 1890 the growth of the States and Territories in which the water-supply is scanty was extremely small, a density of population as great as two to the square mile not having been reached at the time of taking the last census either in the Plateau or the Rocky Mountain subdivision,[1] which together have 28.6 per cent of the area of the country, and in 1890 had only 1.8 per cent of its population.

The figures given in the volume under consideration, showing the number of acres irrigated and under cultivation over the whole of that part of the United States lying west of the ninety-seventh meridian, indicate only a trifling change as having taken place between 1890 and 1891: in the former year 7,577,600 acres are reported as having been irrigated and cultivated; in 1891, 8,026,526 acres.[2] If the irrigation of seven and a half millions of acres had been attended with so small an increase of population as that which had manifested itself up to the year 1890, it is not likely that a further development of the irrigated area to the amount of less than half a million of acres will have produced any considerable change in respect to the density of the population.[3]

A most extraordinary misconception of climatic and

---

[1] See *ante*, pp. 28 and 89.

[2] See farther on, for additional data, from "Extra Census Bulletin," No. 23, published September 9, 1892.

[3] The tendency to exaggeration in all these irrigation reports is well illustrated by what is said of Arizona, a Territory having, in 1890, 59,691 inhabitants (0.4 to the square mile). In regard to this Territory it is said that "the successful boring of Artesian wells in Arizona is of considerable importance, and bids fair for future development in this important direction. There is no doubt whatever that Arizona has a large supply of phreatic waters, with at least a negative Artesian character-pressure sufficient to rise in the bore if not to overflow at the surface." The statistics furnished, however, show that the increase in the area irrigated and under cultivation from 1890 to 1891 was only 4,900 acres: in the former year, according to the Census Reports, on one tenth of one per cent of the whole area of this Territory only were crops raised by irrigation.

topographical conditions is exhibited in Mr. Hinton's remarks in the volume under consideration having reference to the "controlling of the continental water-supply" by means of government reservations. What is here contemplated is thus stated: "Another step in the conservation of water within this region has been the passage of the act passed by the last Congress authorizing the President to set aside by proclamation any portion of the public domains as forest reservations as may be desired. It is to be hoped that this measure will be so administered as to include the sources of all interstate waters. The need of such reservation will become at once apparent to any one who will examine a proper map with critical eyes. It will be seen that the controlling power over a continental water supply is held both geographically and hydrographically by the minority in physical area, civic organization, and population. Three States, embraced within the area of the Rocky Mountains, holds the sources of at least 60 per cent of the western waters of the Mississippi system, and at least 90 per cent of all the flowing streams west of the one hundredth meridian. It is a subject of profound interest, and one that must command the attention of legislators, state and national."[1]

It is hardly possible to conceive that any statement connected with questions of geography or climatology could be made having a less substantial basis of truth than the above. The three States "embraced within the area of the Rocky Mountains" must necessarily be Montana, Wyoming, and Colorado, through which

[1] *Loc. cit.*, p. 17.

passes the "Continental Divide," or the watershed which separates the sources of the streams flowing into the Gulf of Mexico from those reaching the Pacific Ocean. There can be no other "continental water-supply" intended here than that which heads in the streams which run from this watershed east and west within the limits of these three States. Of this area east of the divide almost the whole is occupied by the basin of the Missouri and its tributaries; that to the west belongs to the Columbia and the Colorado. Since only a very small part of the basin of the Columbia is included within the limits of British America, (this division of the continent having about the same area as that of the United States, including in the latter half a million of square miles widely separated from the rest of this country, and entirely enclosed within British territory,) and since no part of the Colorado basin has any connection with Mexico and Central America, (which together have an area equal to about one third that of the United States proper,) it is clear that by the term "Continental," as here used by Mr. Hinton, is meant that part of this continent which is drained by the Missouri, the Columbia, and the Colorado, in all a little more than 1,100,000 square miles, or about one third of the United States, and approximately one eighth of the continent of North America; that is to say, the States of Montana, Wyoming, and Colorado have within their borders the sources of streams draining approximately one eighth of this continent, and one third of the United States.

The amount or volume of the drainage of any region

is dependent not only on the area of the drainage basin, but also primarily on the amount of the rainfall, while evaporation and percolation are also important factors. Thus, the Ohio, with a drainage area of 214,000 square miles, discharges annually into the Mississippi about one fifth more water than the Missouri, which drains 518,000 square miles, while the St. Francis River, draining only 10,500 square miles, discharges into the Mississippi considerable more than both the Ohio and Missouri together.[1]

After these preliminary remarks with reference to the extent of the continental area drained by waters heading in the Rocky Mountains, the much more important question comes up for consideration as to how a "controlling power" is to be exerted by the general government over this region, and what the nature of this power or influence may be.

The first thought in regard to this question would naturally be, that the rivers which head in the region were to be "controlled" by being dammed, so that

[1] These statements in regard to the size of the drainage areas and the volumes of discharge of the streams mentioned are taken from the already cited work of Messrs. Humphreys and Abbot, where it is said, in reference to a table of annual downfall drainage: "This table, taken in connection with a map of the region, shows that neither the size of its basin nor the length of its course is any criterion of the hydrographic importance of a tributary stream." There is no other source of information than this volume with regard to the discharge of the Mississippi and its various affluents, and these figures are, of course, only approximate, since only observations continued for a long series of years could furnish entirely satisfactory results in such a complicated investigation. The areas of the different basins might now be more accurately compiled than they could be at the time this work was published; but such later results would not differ materially from those furnished by Messrs. Humphreys and Abbot, and such differences as might be found would not be large enough to be of any practical importance in reference to the question here under discussion.

their waters could be accumulated in reservoirs, and thus made available for use in irrigation, or in such other way as might be desirable. Of plans and preparations for this kind of work, and of the enormous expense by which it would be attended, as well as of the other difficulties which would be encountered in the attempt to carry out such a project, notice has already been taken.[1] This, however, cannot be the kind of "influence" intended by Mr. Hinton, for any such enterprises, even if successfully carried out, would only "control the water-supply," and that to a limited extent, within the immediate vicinity of the locality where the work was done. This could by no means be designated as "controlling the *Continental* water-supply."

There remains, then, only the conjecture that it was assumed to be in the power of the government to influence the climate in some way, and that any such influence exerted at the heads of the streams of any country would have some special value which it would not have lower down in their courses. This is not a new idea, and it seems reasonable to suppose that this is what was intended by Mr. Hinton, since it has already been repeatedly suggested in other parts of the country, and even acted on, although

---

[1] See *ante*, pp. 29–33. Since those pages were written some of these difficulties have been practically illustrated by the giving way of one of the dams constructed in Idaho for irrigational purposes, in consequence of the sudden melting of snow in the mountains coupled with heavy rains. The same thing has happened more than once before in the arid region, as well as in the Eastern States, and even in England, sometimes as the result of a "cloud-burst," or of a long-continued heavy fall of rain, but more often in consequence of ignorance or carelessness in building or watching these dangerous structures.

only to a very limited extent. Thus it has been frequently suggested that the sources of the Hudson River should be "protected," and something has already been done in New York with this end in view by a State reservation of certain forested tracts in the Adirondack Mountains. If, therefore, "protection" or "influence" has any definite meaning in this connection, it must be putting a stop to the destruction of the existing forests, or increasing their extent or density.

In a mountainous region — like the Appalachian, for instance — where the ranges do not rise to the snow-line, and where, as a rule, they are naturally densely covered by forests, it does do much toward retaining unimpaired the beauty of the landscape to allow the trees to remain untouched by the woodman's axe; for after hill and valley have had their natural arboreal growth removed, not only is most of the attractiveness of the scenery gone, but a positive element of ugliness is introduced in the form of blackened stumps, which only after many years have passed become partially concealed by the undergrowth. In a well-watered region a second growth of forest trees gradually takes the place of the original arboreal covering of the surface, but this, so far as the present writer's observations go — in a temperate climate, at least — is never so beautiful as the natural growth. In a region of small precipitation, the renewal of the forest goes on with a proportionally less rapidity, or, as appears to be the case in that part of this country which is least favored by rainfall, so slowly as to be quite imperceptible.

But the land cannot be settled and cultivated without cutting down the forests, neither is it safe to leave any part of the original arboreal growth standing in an inhabited region, since the trees which have grown naturally in the midst of a dense forest are taller and slenderer than those which develop themselves singly at a distance from others of the same species, and are for this reason much exposed to being blown down or struck by lightning. Hence everything must be cleared away in the vicinity of a settlement, and a cultivated second growth be introduced, so far as this is considered necessary or practicable, in order that the settler may be supplied with fire-wood, or with timber for manufacturing purposes.[1]

All New England was once densely covered with forests, and the same is true of the Appalachian region in general, and of the States lying west of New England, as far as the borders of Illinois, where the prairies begin. In New England, New York, and Ohio, and south along the Appalachian belt into Pennsylvania and Virginia, and over a considerable portion of the more southern States, most of the original forest growth has been removed, the land having gone into cultivation to a very considerable extent, while only a comparatively small part of it has been allowed to become covered with a second or still later growth of timber. In no other manner

---

[1] For information with regard to the economical importance of the forests of the United States as furnishing fuel and lumber, see the present writer's "United States: Facts and Figures illustrating the Physical Geography of the Country and its Material Resources," pp. 216, 217.

could the now comparatively dense population of the North Atlantic and Northeastern Central States have found room to develop itself.[1] There is, however, no proof that this removal of much the larger part of the timber in the now most densely settled parts of the country has had any effect on the climate of this region. Statistics do not show that the clearing of the hills and mountains of New England has diminished the rainfall, or done anything else towards making that part of the country less habitable than it formerly was. Neither is there any reason for supposing that a State like Illinois, the surface of which is, in large part, "natural prairie" — that is, naturally destitute of forest vegetation — has, to any perceptible extent, had its share of the rainfall lessened. In other words, the distribution of the isohyetal lines in the naturally forested, as well as in the naturally non-forested, regions of the country is in no way influenced by this varied character of the surface vegetation. It is the direction, frequency, and force of the prevailing winds, the character of the water-surface over which they have blown before reaching land, the topographical features of the region and its distance from the ocean, which are the factors determining the rainfall of any part of the country, as becomes evident on studying the rain-charts of the various regions of the earth, and especially of the United States.[2]

[1] The density of the population of the Northern Atlantic States was, in 1890, 102.8 to the square mile; of the Northeastern Central States, 51.9; of the Middle Atlantic States, 50.3.

[2] The conditions of rainfall throughout the world, the part which forests play in reference to the moisture of the surface, as also various

The theory, therefore, that any perceptible change can be effected in the climate of a country, or of any part of it, by the removal or renewal of its forests, seems to have absolutely no basis of fact. The surface of the ground will be moister where it is shaded by trees, and where resort is not had to artificial drainage for the purpose of getting rid of standing water, or for drying up swampy regions. There are also localities where peculiar climatic and topographical conditions make the preservation of the forests a matter of great practical importance, as, for instance, in certain parts of the Alps, where the ravages of torrents can be guarded against, to a very considerable extent, by judicious protection of the forests, aided by suitable engineering works along the banks of the streams, but this has no connection with any permanent increase of the rainfall, nor with the development of a change of climate which could by any possibility benefit a distant region. It may be asserted with truth that the government has no power, by anything it can do at the sources of the streams heading in the Rocky Mountains, to influence the climate of that part of the country, or the water-supply of any distant region, to any perceptible or in the least degree beneficial extent.

Facts collected all over the world prove that there has been a diminution in the area of lakes going on for an indefinite length of time, accompanied by a marked but much less easily detected decrease in the volume of rivers, and that this desiccation is still in

---

other matters connected with climatological inquiries of this kind, will be found discussed in the present writer's "Climatic Changes of Later Geological Times," Chapter II.

progress, having been continued in historical times. This climatic change is one of the most important events in the earth's history which is known to have taken place, so far at least as the welfare and development of the human race are concerned. But this desiccation can be proved to have been begun before man could have exerted any influence over its progress, or have been in any way connected with its initiation, since this dates back to a period of immense antiquity, long before man had made his appearance on the earth; moreover, this desiccation has been continued, up to the present time, in regions where man is doing nothing, and for ages has done nothing, which could interfere with the operations of natural causes.

As measured by our ordinary standard of the duration of time, this climatic change proceeds but slowly: it cannot be said that instrumental observations made since these began to be accurately taken prove that there has been any marked change in the amount of precipitation which has taken place in any particular region; but various natural phenomena, which are more delicate indications of changes of this kind than instrumental observations, prove that such a modification of the earth's climate must now be going on, the results of which are necessarily most easily perceived in regions where the precipitation is already so small as to make any decrease in its quantity a matter of considerable importance in reference to the well-being and development of the human race.

The second part of the "Final Report of the Artesian and Underflow Investigation," now under consideration, is that of Mr. Nettleton, the Chief Engineer.

In the introduction to this report it is stated that Congress had extended the time for completing this investigation and making the final reports from July 1, 1891, to January 1, 1892. In accordance with this change of plan, it was deemed best to distribute the work which could be done in the allotted time as uniformly as practicable over the whole section included in the terms of the act designating the areas to be ininvestigated. While the geologist, Professor Hay, decided to spend his time in Texas, Nebraska, Kansas, Colorado, and Wyoming, Mr. Nettleton took the Dakotas for his principal field of operations, since there appeared here to be a necessity for an investigation of various engineering questions requiring immediate attention. In pursuance of this plan, examinations were made of the underground water along the base of the foothills from Cheyenne to Laramie City, Wyoming. Additional surveys were made of the underflow in the valley of the South Platte, the drainage valley of the tributaries of the Republican River, and across the valley of the Loup. The profiles of the surveyed lines in the Arkansas and Platte valleys, which were given in the Progress Report and of which some notice has already been taken,[1] are again submitted, with a few additional facts: in regard to these something will be said farther on. Considerable detail is gone into in the present report with regard to the Dakota Artesian basin, and it is stated that no portion of the engineering investigation has been productive of so much immediate benefit as that carried on in this region, especially in the way of instructing the

[1] See *ante*, p. 118.

people in regard to the proper methods of utilizing the Artesian water. Some details of the work which has been done in accordance with these plans may here be given.

Under the head of "Pecos Valley Subterranean Waters," some facts are stated with reference to one of the driest parts of the country, where the annual rainfall is said to average about twelve and a half inches. Of the amount of rain falling in the Pecos basin, twenty-three per cent is estimated as being carried off by that river, two thirds of which is supposed to come from "spring underflows," and one third from water flowing from the surface. Mr. Nettleton remarks that "the percentage of run-off in the Pecos Valley is considerably less than in Massachusetts and several other places where observations have been made. It is to be inferred that the percentage not accounted for here exceeds the average. This being the case, we then must have an underground flow greater than the average to carry away a portion of the seventy-seven per cent of the quantity not accounted for." Here again we have an entire misunderstanding of the fact that the amount of the rainfall evaporated depends on the character of the climate, and that in a region like the Pecos Valley the portion which percolates the soil must be but a very insignificant fraction of that which actually reaches its surface.

Borings have been made on the Texas and Pacific Railroad at Pecos City and Toyah, "some eighty or ninety miles south." At the former place there are said to be sixteen flowing Artesian wells, the largest flow from which is sixty gallons per minute. These wells are from 150 to 250 feet deep, and are in the drift, "some of them just reaching the conglomerate." There are also two flowing wells at Toyah. The valley of the Pecos River, which itself heads in a low range of mountains near Santa Fé, is bordered on the west by a broken chain of elevations of considerable topographical importance, since their dominating peaks rise from 7,000 to 12,000 feet above the sea level. It is in these ranges that the tributaries of the Pecos head, all of them coming into the main river from the west. These streams, however, all sink soon after passing out of the foot-hills, at least during the drier part of the year.[1] The quantity of water falling on these high ranges must at certain seasons be considerable, and much above the average in the Pecos Valley itself, and as the whole country between the river and the mountains is underlain by limestone, it is natural to suppose that much of this water finds its way beneath the surface, to reappear lower down and nearer the main stream.[2] A reservoir company has

[1] "The melting snows in the mountains and sudden and heavy rainfall often sends quite a large amount of water through the whole length of the Hondo to the Pecos." *Loc. cit.*, p. 13. The whole of the Pecos Valley is, on the rain-chart of the United States published in 1868, included within the area having from twenty to twenty-four inches of precipitation, the isohyetal of twenty inches reaching up that valley nearly to Santa Fé.

[2] The Rio Peñasco, which heads in the Sacramento Mountains, a group of ranges lying between the Guadalupe and Sierra Blanca ranges, and enters the Pecos about fifty miles south of the Rio Hondo, is said to present an interesting instance of what has been done — unintentionally, in part — to prevent the water from sinking and being lost in the soil and limestone of its channel. This river formerly disappeared immediately after leaving the mountains, but now it is a running stream for its entire length, even furnishing water for irrigation. This change is believed by Mr. Nettleton to have been caused in part

been organized to build a series of storage reservoirs twelve miles above Roswell, a settlement near the mouth of the Rio Hondo, at an estimated cost of $232,630, there being, as is stated, a large body of fine land below the proposed site of the reservoir, which without water is useless, and which it is proposed to reclaim.[1]

In addition to the springs in the Pecos Valley, there are numerous interesting pools of fresh water on the table-lands, lying above any water-course or storm-water channel. These are called by the settlers of the region "China holes," from their supposed great depth. Some of them are but a few feet in diameter, while others cover an area of several acres. Two of them (about twelve miles southeast of Roswell), which had been believed to be unfathomable, were found on being sounded to have a depth no greater than sixteen and thirty-four feet. Water-holes of this kind are not uncommon in various parts of the world, where limestone and gypsiferous rocks abound, even in regions where the rainfall is very small, as in the high tablelands of South Africa.

Mr. Nettleton's report at present under consideration is next occupied with what is stated to be "an investi-

---

by a successful attempt to carry the water for a distance of ten miles or more in a new channel, and in part by the continual tramping of the bottom of the river by thousands of cattle that go daily to this stream for water.

[1] There are said to be evidences of an ancient river, with here and there irrigation works, on the west side of the ranges which have been mentioned as lying to the west of the Pecos. This lost river appears once to have "carried quite a volume of water." Its course was southerly through a valley lying between these mountains and the San Andreas range, fifty miles still farther to the west.

gation of the extent and availability of the underflow in a few localities in Nebraska, Kansas, Colorado, and Wyoming," the valleys of the Platte and Arkansas Rivers having been selected "as affording the best opportunities for studying the relations between the surface and underground waters as they exist in these valleys and the higher country on each side." Twelve of these lines were surveyed as follows: five in the valley of the Platte; three in that of the Arkansas; one across the valleys of the Loup Rivers (an extension in a northeasterly direction of the Lexington line, previously surveyed [1]); a line from Sterling east, connecting with the Big Spring line.[2] These lines are essentially the same, or in the same region, with those the surveys of which were described in Mr. Nettleton's previous report,[3] with the exception of two lines situated farther west, namely, one, called "the Cheyenne line," extending from the head-waters of Duck Creek, on the Colorado-Wyoming boundary line, to the North Platte at Laramie, a distance of 110 miles, and the other, called the Sterling line, running from Akron, Colorado, northward to Lodge Pole Creek in Nebraska, striking at about ten miles west of Sydney, a distance of seventy-five miles.

Of the above surveyed lines that called "the Cheyenne" is said, taken as a whole, to have been "negative in its results." All the wells in Cheyenne are said to be such that in summer they can be pumped dry with a hand-pump in four or five hours, but not in winter

---

[1] See *ante*, p. 118, number of the section (3).
[2] See *ante*, p. 118, number of the section (1).
[3] See *ante*, pp. 117–119.

or spring. At Fort Laramie itself water is found in the gravel in the delta of the Laramie and North Platte Rivers, and at about the level of that in the rivers themselves. The Sterling line is also said to have furnished only negative results. The facts developed on the other surveyed lines have already been given and commented on, and no farther statements need be made with regard to them.

Under the head of "Movement of Underflow in River Valleys," an account is given of some unsuccessful experiments made for the purpose of throwing light on this question. A strong solution of an aniline dye was poured into a hole, below which, in the supposed line of the underflow, trenches were dug at a distance of five feet apart; "this was done with the expectation that traces of the dye would appear in the first trench within an hour or two, but twenty-four hours failed to show any colors even in the first trench."

In this connection it is stated that "some French engineers place the rate of movement of underground water in the river valleys at one mile in a year, or a little over fourteen feet per day, or one eighth of an inch in a minute," to which statement is added the remark, "I am inclined not to doubt the statement." Calculations of this kind, however, cannot be expected to lead to any definite result, or to have any practical value. Everything, in a matter of this kind, must depend on the character of the detrital or sedimentary material through which the "flow" is expected to take place, and on the opportunity offered for it to escape at some lower point. In an impervious rock, like most of the crystalline formations, there can be no motion of any fluid, except as opportunity is offered by the existence of accidental fissures; and in clay, which is also almost entirely impervious, fissures cannot easily be formed, or, if formed, they will soon be obliterated by the movement under pressure of the plastic mass. In a very porous rock, like some kinds of sandstone, wherever water under the influence of gravitation has a chance to escape it will do so, and its place will be taken by the adjacent particles with more or less rapidity according to the texture of the rock and the hydrostatic pressure exerted by the water. This texture, however, is almost always exceedingly variable, especially in the more recent detrital formations, in which beds of clay are commonly intercalated with those of sand, interposing an impassable barrier to the passage of water, unless there is pressure enough to make it rise high enough to flow over the top of the obstacle thus interposed. In consolidated or only partly consolidated sandstone, moreover, fissures will more or less frequently be formed, and these will gradually become filled with clay, and may be of very considerable dimensions, so as completely to obstruct the passage of water for a great distance both vertically and laterally. Such being the facts, it is evident that any attempt to measure the velocity of water making its way through rocks under such changeable and indeterminable conditions will be entirely futile, even where short distances are concerned, and much more so where hundreds of miles are to be taken into account.

The next subject discussed in Mr. Nettleton's final

report is that of the deep wells of the Dakota basin, of which a tabular statement is given comprising the results obtained from the examination of ninety-three wells, which number, however, does not include all the deep bores made in that basin, some having been omitted because, on account of their isolated position, time was lacking for their examination. Seventy-five of these wells are in South Dakota, and all but five of the others in North Dakota; of these five two are in Manitoba, two in Montana, and one in Minnesota. The valley in which most of these wells are located is that of the James River, a branch of the Missouri, flowing in a nearly southerly direction, between the 98th and 99th meridians, across the whole width of South Dakota and nearly all that of North Dakota. The wells of the James River basin are all represented to be "flowing wells," but there is no uniformity in the amount of their flow: four furnish less than ten gallons per minute; twelve over 1,000 gallons; one over 3,000; and fifteen between 500 and 1,000. The elevation of the surface at these wells is, in much the larger number of cases, between 1,200 and 1,600 feet above the sea-level; the greatest elevation noticed is 1,645 feet. The depth of these wells is exceedingly variable: the deepest is 1,901 feet; the shallowest, 229. Farther on, in discussing the report of the geologist of the Survey, Professor Hay, additional remarks will be made with reference to the source from which the water of the James River Artesian basin is derived.[1] At present only the following quotation from Mr. Nettleton's report need be appended: "The in-

---

[1] See farther on, p. 154.

vestigations do not show as great uniformity in the position of the upper watercourses or the main water-bearing rock as was first thought to exist, nor does there appear to be a general similarity in the character of the lower rocks."

Next to what is said in Mr. Nettleton's report about the Artesian wells of the Dakota basin come some statements of his assistant, Mr. Follett, in regard to the Red River Valley basin, north of Fargo, in North Dakota. The extent of the territory covered by this report is about 150 miles north and south, and thirty-five miles east and west: it lies very near the ninety-seventh meridian. The area over which Artesian water is found is on the river, and extends back from it for a distance of twelve or fifteen miles, having a very gentle and uniform descending grade from Fargo to Pembina, the difference of level between these two places, which are 150 miles apart, being only ninety-three feet, or six tenths of a foot to the mile.

The principal water-bearing stratum in this basin is a clean white sand or sandstone, lying at a depth of from 200 to 300 feet beneath the surface, and immediately overlain by red shale or cemented gravel, above which is "quicksand, some limestone in places, shale, clay with granite boulders, and clay, all belonging, apparently, to the superficial detrital formation, or drift." Above the main water-bearing bed there are two or three others of much less importance, and having but little continuity. The total number of wells in this basin is given as 436, nearly all having a 2-inch bore, and the aggregate flow is 4,585 gallons per minute. The quality of the water is somewhat variable;

but in much the larger number of cases it is very saline, that from some of the wells being described as "too rank for household use"; but stock, it is said, "will drink it greedily." Of one of the wells of Grafton, Walsh County, which is the "centre of the area giving large and free flows," the water is said to have 240 grains of salt to the gallon.

The Red River basin is described by Mr. Follett as being, of those the water of which comes from the drift, more extensive than any other yet discovered in the Dakotas; but there are basins of this character scattered over these two States, the water from some of which is thought to be superior in quality to that from the Red River Valley.

Mr. Nettleton is of opinion that there has been in the regions over which his investigations extended a "recurrence of wet and dry periods." In regard to this matter he writes as follows: "We have not been able to fix the probable returns of these periods, but they seem to follow each other quite regularly, with intervals of eleven to fourteen years." The evidence on which this statement is based seems very unsatisfactory. There is abundant proof that throughout this western region the lakes are diminishing in area, as is the case all over the world. Proofs of this decrease of the water surface can easily be obtained by examination of the terraces or benches by which the larger lakes are surrounded, which show that Great Salt Lake, for instance, has decreased from 350 miles in length to about sixty. That in the case of small shallow lakes — or, more properly, ponds — there have been fluctuations in the extent of the water surface, corresponding to the ordinary variations in the rainfall of successive seasons, there can be no doubt; but this is a phenomenon of extremely little importance compared with the fact of a general gradual desiccation which has been going on over a large part of the earth's surface and for an indefinite length of time.[1]

The third volume of the series of final reports now under consideration is that of Professor Hay, who was assisted in his work by Professor Culver in the Dakotas, Professor Hicks in Nebraska, and Professor Hill in Texas and New Mexico. The object of this investigation is said in Professor Hill's "Letter of Transmittal," to have been "the source, volume, and availability of the underground waters of most of the area of the Great Plains."[2]

Professor Hay's report begins with a sketch of the geology of the Plains, which is said to be, on the whole, simple, the chief difficulty being that over thousands of square miles certain later formations are spread "in great sheets," hiding the more regularly stratified formations below. The drift formation in the Dakotas and the Tertiary in the more southern region of the Plains are said to have much to do with

[1] See Appendix B for a fuller discussion of this subject.
[2] Each of these officials furnishes, in this volume, a special report, of which the titles are as follows: (1) "Artesian and Underflow Investigation between the Ninety-seventh Meridian and the Foothills of the Rocky Mountains," by Professor Hay; (2) "On the Occurrence of Artesian and other Underground Waters in Texas, Eastern New Mexico, and Indian Territory, West of the Ninety-seventh Meridian," by Professor Hill; (3) "The Underflow and Sheet Waters, Irrigable Lands, and Geological Structure of Nebraska, with its Effect upon the Water Supply," by Professor Hicks; (4) A report of fifteen pages only, and without a special title, by Professor Culver, Assistant Geologist for South Dakota.

the water supply," since "all the phreatic waters available without very deep borings are found in them." It is of importance, therefore, that their lithological and stratigraphical character be well understood, and in regard to these matters the following statements are made by Professor Hay: "In the Dakotas and Eastern Kansas and Nebraska there is a sandy marly formation known as the Loess, which in large areas overlies the drift and in others rests on bed rock of the district, Cretaceous or Carboniferous, as the case may be. In the plains from the White River of Nebraska to the Panhandle of Texas there is a similar formation, varying slightly in texture and substance, as sand, lime, or clay predominate, which makes the smooth surface and the deep subsoil of the prairie. The oldest parts are undoubtedly of tertiary age, but its formation lasted probably through the drift period, and its latest beds are probably contemporaneous with the Loess. We call it the plains' marl. Beneath the plains marl with occasional exceptions is a lower tertiary formation of Miocene age, which in this connection we shall call the tertiary grit. It has often been described, it is nowhere quite free from siliceous matter and mostly sand is present in quantity. In places it has become a gravel loosely held together, and again the material is more coherent, being a coarse gravel — some pebbles as large as the hand — but firmly cemented by lime and iron so as to form a firm conglomerate. Where the lime preponderates it looks when broken like chunks of hard mortar. Here it is known extensively as the 'mortar beds.' Sometimes there is scarcely any sand, and the lime gives it a white smoothness that makes it serviceable for plastering cellars. In the northern parts of the area it is known as 'plaster' and 'native lime,' and in the south it is the 'terra blanca,' or white earth of New Mexico and the Llano Estacado."[1]

From the above citations it will be seen that, as already noticed,[2] it is entirely impossible, over a large part of the Great Plains, to distinguish the Post-Tertiary from the Tertiary. There is no propriety in designating any part of the superficial formation occurring in this region by the name of "Loess," the use of which term by Western geologists can only tend to make the understanding of their superficial geology more difficult than it would otherwise be.

The "Tertiary grit," as here described, seems to be a formation varying greatly in lithological character, some parts being firmly cemented by lime and iron, while others contain scarcely any sand. In rocks of this character no regular "flow" could with any propriety be looked for. Still, it is said by Professor Hay to be very absorptive of the rainfall, when outcropping at the surface, and to be, for this reason, "the source of the phreatic waters which supply the wells of the level or gently sloping high prairies, which have for their surface the plains marl, whose less porous sheets cover much of the region." As a source of water-supply this grit takes the place of the drift gravels of the more northern part of the area under examination.

The Tertiary grit is considered by Professor Hay, on account of its porous nature and the impervious

---

[1] *Loc. cit.*, p. 10.   [2] See *ante*, pp. 119, 120.

character of the formations which lie immediately beneath it, as being a water-holder of great importance for a very extensive region. That it is actually so, he says, "is known by the wells that all over the plains have been dug or bored into it. The level region of the Texas Pan Handle has water from wells; the plain between the Cimarron and Arkansas has water; the divides between the Republican and Smoky have hundreds of wells; away up on the Niobrara the high prairie has wells. They vary in depth, but each divide has a uniform depth for long distances, or they increase gradually in a given direction. At Washburn, Texas, they are 150 feet deep; at Richfield, Kansas, and east thereof for seventy miles, they are eighty feet deep. North of the Frenchman, in Nebraska, they are over 200 feet deep on the Colorado line, increasing to over 300 feet forty miles east."

These wells are "considered inexhaustible," but, in point of fact, they have hitherto been almost exclusively used for watering stock.[1] That any considerable amount of irrigation can be effected by their aid seems, even to Professor Hay, hardly possible, for he remarks in regard to this point as follows: "Where a windmill already exists some few acres may be irrigated. A more powerful windmill pump and a small — one or two acres — reservoir would allow more water to be raised, and the farm redeemed at once from aridity and mortgage. It is not expected that any more than fifteen or twenty acres can be thus irrigated in any quarter section, and on large areas the average will not be more than ten acres; but the high divides and

[1] See *ante*, pp. 118, 119.

the body of the great plains must be thus irrigated if any large part of it is to be redeemed in the next quarter of a century."

The question of the importance as a source of water-supply of this formation is thus summed up by Professor Hay: "We have thus seen that the water in the Tertiary grit, buried from 50 to 300 feet below the plains and cropping on the sides of ravines in gushing springs, is the main reliance of the plains region; it is the sole reliance of the immense areas lying back from the valleys, the only reservoir on which these wells can draw to irrigate the land. We have seen that it is the source of the waters of the rivers of the plains, and adds to the volume of those whose origin is in the mountains. We have shown that its source is the rainfall of the region varying from eighteen or twenty inches on the one hundredth meridian to twelve or fourteen inches on the one hundred and fifth."[1]

The question whether this amount of rainfall is sufficient to replenish this reservoir (the Tertiary grit) with sufficient rapidity, and in sufficient quantity to allow of its being drawn upon to an extent sufficient to make it available for irrigation on a large scale, Professor Hay seems to think can be answered in the affirmative; but at the same time he admits that an approximately correct answer is "only partially possible at present," because "observations on the quantity of rainfall have only been made at comparatively few places widely separated, and no experiments at all have been made on evaporation as related to the absorptive character of the soil." In spite of this fact, however, he quotes

[1] *Loc. cit.*, p. 18.

with approval the opinions of Professor Van Diest that it is not an exaggerated estimate to suppose that half the rainfall in Eastern Colorado, and probably also in Eastern New Mexico, sinks into the ground. With special reference to Eastern Colorado it is thought that this would not be less than five inches over an area of 32,000 square miles, and if this "could all be redeemed from the subsoil it would be sufficient for the irrigation of 1,200,000 acres, or one seventeenth of the above-named area."

The present writer has already expressed the opinion that the amount of rainfall which percolates the soil in the region in question is much less than that here estimated by Professor Van Diest; and how, by any possibility, *all* that which actually does thus percolate could be "redeemed" — or, in other words, brought to the surface again — it is extremely difficult to understand: that more than a very small fraction of it could be made available for irrigational or other purposes seems quite clear.[1]

The volume of the rivers heading well up on the high valleys of the main range of the Rocky Mountains, which are largely fed by the melting snow is considerable, while that of the streams which head below the mountains, which Professor Hay calls "rivers of the plains," is comparatively insignificant, except in times of flood, as might be expected from the small average rainfall of this region.[2]

---

[1] See *ante*, pp. 105-121.

[2] See page 23 of Professor Hay's report, where the volume of some of these rivers is given, not, however, as the mean of any considerable length of time, but as the result of measurements made on one day only. All these rivers vary greatly in volume at different seasons, and even at

The meaning of the word "underflow," a term used in the act of Congress authorizing the investigation the results of which are here under discussion, the difficulty of defining which has already been suggested,[1] is a matter which receives some consideration on the part of Professor Hay, who endeavors to "indicate the right use of the term, as well as the extent of the thing itself."

In regard to the exaggerated ideas of the underflow current in the arid region, and *for which the officials connected with the irrigation investigation are largely responsible*, Professor Hay remarks as follows: "We have heard speakers dilating on the advantages of the semi-arid region refer to 'the mighty underflow of the plains.' In reference to particular valleys, we have met the statement that the 'underground Platte' and the 'underground Arkansas' are greater streams than the visible streams that bear those names. The underflow of the latter river is spoken of sometimes as being fifty miles wide, and sometimes the subterrene waters of the plains, both valleys and uplands, have been spoken of as one great underground ocean, with a general movement to the south of east.[2] ... The most extravagant form under which we have heard the underflow explained and defined is about as follows: There are heavy snows in the Rocky Mountains and subordinate ranges; these are melted every summer. There is a large body of water supplying wells on the plains

dates separated by intervals of only a few days. The liability of all these streams to "freshets"—that is, to very great and rapid increase of volume—is a matter of importance in reference to questions of irrigation, especially where control of the water-supply by means of dams is proposed, adding very greatly to the difficulty and expense of such operations.

[1] See *ante*, p. 101.   [2] See *ante*, p. 110.

in Wyoming, Nebraska, Colorado, Kansas, and Texas. There is a general slope of the country from the northwest to the southeast. There are immense springs in a line across the State of Texas. There are springs of fresh water rising on the bottom of the Gulf of Mexico. Therefore, there is a vast body of water under the plains, moving from the mountains toward the sea, capable of irrigating the whole country, and, as one person said, 'It is God Almighty's method for the redemption of the arid region.'"

Professor Hay thinks that most of the facts alleged in the above statement "are as stated." But, at the same time, he gives sufficient reasons for not adopting this widely spread belief in any underflow such as indicated above. The waters of the great Texan springs, he admits, "are fully accounted for without any recourse to the distant mountains"; the great volume of the Loup Rivers of Nebraska, and of the wells on the interfluvial upland "may be referred, without any possible contradiction, to the rainfall of the plains themselves." Moreover, "the great body of the area of the plains is cut off from contact with the mountains by deep river trenches, which make it impossible for them to receive any benefit from the melting of the mountain snows." Keeping these and other facts of a similar nature in mind, and realizing that the correct use of the term "underflow" has led to exaggerated and erroneous ideas of its quantity and its source, Professor Hay wishes to limit the use of this word "to the waters of the great valleys found in the alluvia under the beds of the streams, and to a limited extent under the fertile bottoms which bound the stream beds."

ARTESIAN BASINS OF GREAT PLAINS. 153

In regard to the fact that under and near the beds of the large streams of the Plains, water will be found in some quantity in the porous grounds and sands there accumulated, and to a considerable distance from the stream itself both laterally and vertically, there can be no doubt, while it may be questionable whether the use of the word "underflow" as descriptive of so universal a condition of things may be entirely justifiable, especially as its introduction and general application have heretofore had reference to something entirely different and which has been shown not to exist. That in most cases the origin of the water obtained in deep wells on the plains is the rainfall, either of the present or the past, is a fact in support of which it seems hardly necessary to offer farther evidence, and in regard to which sufficient has already been said.[1]

In regard to the proper "Artesian basins" of the Great Plains, Professor Hay remarks that their number had not been increased since the publication of the previous report, while, however, "important increments had been made to the areas of some of the principal. The Artesian regions having the largest wells and the most extensive areas are the James River basin, Dakota, and the Fort Worth-Waco basin, Texas.[2] The Dakota basin is said to have had many additional wells sunk and its area extended by the obtaining of water at Armour and Chamberlain. It is thought that the area of this basin will eventually be proved to extend on the west side of the Missouri toward the Black Hills, and "that the name James River basin must give way

---

[1] See *ante*, pp. 118–122, these pages being in type before the Final Report here under consideration had been received.

[2] See *ante*, pp. 113–116.

to the more extensive one of the Dakota Artesian basin." But it is suggested that "it will be wise to use the caution suggested by the wells at Denver and Fort Worth,[1] not to bore the wells too close together, no matter how large the underground reservoir may be, if it can be drained by persistent tapping."

In regard to the source of the Artesian water-supply of the Dakota or James River basin, it is said that "there is nothing yet learned to suggest any other origin than that given last year,[2] viz. the outcrops of the Dakota and other sandstones on the eastern foothills of the Rocky Mountains and subordinate ranges." The theory that the Missouri River is the source from which the water comes is considered untenable, because the pressure at the wells is too great.

The wells at Coolidge, in the Arkansas Valley,[3] are thought by Professor Hay to have their water also from the Dakota sandstone, but not from the mountains to the west, on the flanks of which these rocks crop out with upturned edges. The reason for this idea is, that at Oberlin, in Northern Kansas, a deep boring has penetrated these beds "without getting any supply of water that warrants the supposition of a mountain source." The explanation suggested for the failure to obtain water from the sandstone at that locality is, "that it is not in mountain uplift that we find the best sources of Artesian waters, but rather in the exposure of porous strata lying at comparatively low angles of bedding, giving wide areas in which to absorb rainfall and without breaks of continuity caused

---

[1] See *ante*, p. 116. [2] See *ante*, p. 113.
[3] See *ante*, p. 115.

by the faulting or folding of mountain structure."[1] It is suggested by Professor Hay that the water of the wells at Coolidge is forced upward, not by hydrostatic, but by gas pressure, and a little farther on in this report this agency as a cause of the rise of water to and above the surface, where there is no evidence of the existence of the necessary hydrostatic conditions is again alluded to, with the additional statement that "another cause exists for flowing wells which we call rock pressure."[2]

The report of Professor Hill, of which the title has already been given,[3] begins with a brief introduction in regard to the occurrence and availability of underground water, in which some interesting facts are given confirming a matter to which reference has already been made, namely, the extraordinary ideas on this subject held throughout the arid regions of the United States "by men of more than ordinary intelligence in other walks of life." The following quotation may be read as an illustration of this condition of things: "The most current of these erroneous ideas is that all underground water flows in streams 'like the circulatory system of the human body,' as an intelligent citizen once

---

[1] We find here a heavy blow administered to the theory most generally held by the advocates of the "underflow" of the Great Plains, and by Mr. Hinton as well as by Mr. Catlin, namely, that it is the rainfall upon the upturned edges of the formations cropping out at the base of the Rocky Mountains which feeds this moving mass of waters. (See *ante*, pp. 109, 110.)

[2] This subject of the cause of the rise of water to the surface in regions where there is no proof of the existence of the ordinary Artesian conditions, and where the facts seem to indicate that these are not at all likely to be present, will receive consideration farther on in the present volume.

[3] See *ante*, p. 145.

expressed it. The underground rivers are thought to supply every well and spring, and it is a curious sight to see the water witch or switch fakir plod over a farm with his forked stick trying to locate the 'current.' In the vast areas between the Rockies and the Mississippi the belief prevails that all the wells are supplied from precipitation upon the mountains, whose waters are supposed to disappear beneath the surface to rise again a thousand miles away along the coastal plain, (The Galveston News, November 7, 1891,) while beneath the vast intervening regions is an inexhaustible store of water, waiting for some intervention of man to bring it to the surface. The doctrine of the 'underflow,' as it is called, proved so contagious in Kansas a year ago that whole communities indulged in most exaggerated anticipations of its development."[1]

In view of these facts, Professor Hill considers that it is desirable to examine the simple laws controlling the distribution of underground waters, the source of which he admits to be the rainfall; but, he adds, "the underground supply in any region is not proportionate to the rainfall." The unequal distribution of water in the saturated portion of the earth's crust is thought to be "due to the difference in porous texture of the different rocks which compose it, their arrangement relative to one another, the amount of rainfall and surface evaporation and the relative altitude above or below the adjacent drainage level." If the strata are inclined at a high angle, as is the case in most mountainous regions, Artesian water will rarely be obtained by boring; but where the dip of the rocks is but slight,

[1] *Loc. cit.*, p. 49.

there the conditions are most favorable for success in undertakings of this kind. It is in the newer formations that the conditions determining the supply of water are most likely to be satisfactory. In illustration of these general principles various facts are cited, having more especially reference to the conditions prevailing in parts of Texas, and an ideal section from the Gulf Coast to the Rocky Mountains is given.

In concluding these general considerations in regard to water-supply it is said that "It is apparent that the best conditions for securing underground water are not in consolidated or mountain rocks, as shown by the futile experiments of the Government well borings under Capt. Pope in 1858, and the numerous failures of the Southern Pacific road — all of which were drilled with the idea that the water came from the mountains. But, on the other hand, the most sterile sandy upland plains, like the great Jornado Muerto, or filled-in-river valleys, like that of the Rio Grande, are the most favorable locations for imbibition and storage of underground water. By taking advantage of this law hundreds of wells, nonflowing it is true, have been obtained upon the greatest of our supposed waterless plains, such as the Llano Estacado and the Franklin-Huerco basin north of El Paso." It is candidly admitted, however, that the supply of underground water is sufficient to reclaim for agriculture by irrigation "only a very small fraction of our desert lands." Still it is believed that, "by applying these principles, thousands of wells can be obtained upon areas now absolutely waterless, which would be of great value to overland commerce and to herders, and would save large amounts of money now wasted in unprofitable experiments."[1]

Professor Hill next proceeds in the report here under examination to give a quite detailed account of what he designates as the "Texas – New Mexico Region."[2] This he describes as consisting topographically of "a series of extensive elongated parallel dip plains and plateaus, extending approximately in a north and south direction, and abruptly terminating at each end by a great mountain system, extending at right angles to them — an arrangement comparable to a wide stairway, in which the steps are represented by the plains and the walls by the inclosing mountains." This vast area he subdivides as follows: (1) The *Eastern Division*, a series of present and ancient coast deposits, occupying the eastern third of Texas and having a total area of no less than 172,800 square miles. The eastern half of this division is essentially similar to the adjacent lowlands of the Gulf States; the western half, including the Black and Grand Prairies is "uniquely Texan," and is the "chalk region of the United States." (2) The "*Central Denuded Region*," consisting of Palæozoic and Mesozoic rocks (the latter generally known as the "Red Beds"), which underlie unconformably the coast rocks of division (1), and are exposed by the erosion of that formation or by being upturned

---

[1] The conditions of water-supply as affected by the various circumstances indicated in this part of Professor Hill's report will be discussed farther on in the present work, in seeking to sum up our knowledge of this complicated and not yet thoroughly understood subject.

[2] Professor Hill had prepared himself for this task by his previous experience in the Geological Survey of Arkansas. See Annual Report of that Survey, Vol. II., 1888; and Bulletin No. 45 U. S. Geol. Survey (1887); also, The American Geologist, Vol. V. (1890), p. 9.

in the two great mountain systems which limit the region — the Ouachita on the north, and the basin ranges of the trans-Pecos country and Northern Mexico on the west. This division lies between the Eastern Division and the Llano Estacado, and is classed in three principal subdivisions, viz.: (*a*) the region of the Carboniferous coal measures, with the sandstones, clays, and limestones peculiar to that portion of the geological series; (*b*) a region of granite and metamorphic rocks and older limestones, called by Professor Hill the "Burnet-Mason Country"; (*c*) the Red Bed Region, including the peculiar red lands of the Concho, Abilene, Wichita, and Oklahoma regions. (3) The *Mountain Systems*, including, (*a*) the Ouachita system of Arkansas and the Indian Territory, older than the plains of the coastal system, which were laid down against it, and separating the Texas region from the Kansas; (*b*) the Basin Mountains, west of the Pecos and south of the Rocky Mountains proper, which end at Santa Fé. The so-called Basin Mountains are made up "of the uplifted, folded, and crumpled edges of the earlier of these plains, *i. e.* those formed of rocks of Cretaceous age." (4) *Remnental Plains*, either later than the Rocky Mountain uplift or allied in age to it. These plains are considered as being the continuation of the Plateau region of the West. In this division are included the Llano Estacado and Raton las Vegas plateau, which were once continuous with the Eastern Division, "but have been separated from it by the great denudation which laid bare the central denuded region." These plains occupy no less than 91,200 square miles of Northwestern Texas and New Mexico.

(5) The *Basin Plains* "which lie between the mountain blocks of the Trans-Pecos region, and are continuous in genesis and every physical aspect with the Great Basin region of Utah and Nevada, and the so-called High Plateau of Mexico." Each of these five grand divisions is said to have "its own peculiar features of topography, climate, geological structure, and water conditions," and each is discussed by Professor Hill at considerable length.

The Eastern Division, which comprises half of the State of Texas, lies east of a line drawn irregularly from the western edge of Cooke County, southward to the northeastern corner of Burnet County, and from there westward to the trans-Pecos Mountains. The stratigraphical character is very simple, so that there is not much difficulty in determining, so far as geological structure is concerned, its conditions with reference to an Artesian water-supply. There is, however, a remarkable difference in the amount of rain falling in various sections of this State. The isohyetal of twenty inches follows, in a general northwesterly direction, pretty nearly the course of the Rio Grande and its most important branch — the Rio Pecos — as far as the southeastern corner of New Mexico, while the curve of thirty-two inches, starting from Matamoras, at the mouth of the Rio Grande, and only about one degree east of that of twenty inches, follows the coast line, keeping at first at no great distance, but gradually receding from it and passing a little to the west of Austin. Thus the isohyetals, which are very closely crowded together at the southern extremity of the State, recede from each other rapidly in advan-

THE EASTERN DIVISION OF TEXAS.

cing toward the north. The northwestern part of Texas is, therefore, within the semi-arid and arid belt, while the eastern side of the State is a region of very abundant precipitation.

The Eastern Division of the State is underlain by a series of sedimentary deposits formed in and around the Gulf of Mexico as its surface was elevated or depressed, all dipping toward the coast at an angle which is very slight, but a little greater than that of the grade of the surface, so that in going westward, and ascending above the sea-level, older geological formations are being constantly encountered, and as these vary considerably in lithological character the consequence is that successive belts of country are crossed, each having its peculiar soil, rocks, and flora. If the underlying formation is a sandstone, the detrital material forming the surface is sandy, and covered with timber; if the underlying rock is marly or clayey, the soil will be "black, sticky, and treeless";[1] moreover, water will be obtained in abundance by sinking wells in the sandy rock, while this will not be the case if the underlying rock is not of this character. To quote Professor Hill: "Wherever the formation is sandy there are forests, as the east Texas pine woods and the lower and

---

[1] The fact that the distribution of the forests, in all countries and in all climates, is more or less dependent on the *texture* of the soil has been repeatedly insisted on by the present writer, and could have no better illustration than that presented by the conditions prevailing in Texas as described by Professor Hill, as also by others who have made a special study of the surface geology and botany of this State. See Geology of Iowa (1858), Vol. 1. p. 23; The American Naturalist for October and November, 1876; Science for All, Vol. V. p. 124; Names and Places (1888), pp. 174-177; The United States: Facts and Figures illustrating the Physical Geography of the Country and its Material Resources, 1889, pp. 212, 213.

upper cross timbers; wherever the country is an open prairie it is underlaid by compact formations with little sand, such as clays and chalks. The coastal prairie, the Fayette prairies, the Black prairie belt, the Eagle Ford prairie, the Grand prairie, and the red beds are all of this class. Each of these different strips of country has a soil radically different from that of the others, for the soil is the surface residuum of the underlying structures." The sheets of sand of the Coastal incline, being in a region of considerable rainfall, become receiving areas for water, which, where the conditions are favorable, will rise above the surface, so that, as Professor Hill asserts, throughout much of the area having this geological character Artesian wells can be obtained without difficulty.

Two great fault lines are also indicated by Professor Hill as being important features of the geology of the Grand and Black Prairie regions. One of these faults extends from near Dallas through Waco and Austin to Del Rio; this is a fault running in the line of strike of the formation, and having a downthrow to the east. The other is a dip fault, extending from Marietta, Indian Territory, to the south of Paris, Texas, with a downthrow toward the interior, "reducing the receiving area below the altitude of most of the Red River countries of Texas, where water would be most desired." This, as Professor Hill remarks, is the simple geological structure of the whole eastern half of Texas and of Southern Indian Territory, embracing an area of over 170,000 square miles, and including all the humid and semi-humid regions of the State. The above indicated topographical and geological conditions have developed five groups of Artesian water-bearing strata with corresponding Artesian areas, which are located by Professor Hill as follows, the geological age of the water-bearing stratum being appended in each case : —

1. Coastal wells of Galveston, Houston, Gonzales, etc. Fayette sands.
2. East Texas or timber belt wells of Marshall, Robertson, etc. Eolignitic and glauconite sands.
3. Dallas, Denison, and Pottsboro wells. Lower Cross Timber sands.
4. The Fort Worth–Waco system.
    a. Upper Division. Paluxy sands.
    b. Lower Division. Trinity sands and alternating beds.

Each of these systems is said to be of great importance economically, and a minute description of them follows in the report next under examination, of which the more important points will here be indicated.

As stated above, the wells in the vicinity of Galveston and Houston are supplied with water from the Fayette sands. The region of the "Coast Prairie," as this division of the State is called by Professor Hill, is said to extend from fifty to one hundred miles into the interior. It is a flat, timberless plain, and not elevated at its interior margin more than 200 feet above the Gulf. Its geological age is late Quaternary, and it is underlain by "several sheets of Artesian water-bearing strata, the same as those constituting the surface of the next regions inland, and from which Galveston, Houston, and many other places have secured

Artesian water." Furthermore it is said, "There are no doubt many of these water-bearing strata beneath the Coast Prairie, for there are several thousand feet of porous sands at slight intervals, of the Fayette sands and Eocene systems, and future experimentation will yield magnificent results as yet unattained."[1]

West of the Coast Prairies is another region designated as the "Washington County Black Prairies." This is characterized by a rich, black, sandy soil, derived from the disintegration of a friable sandstone, which is a water-bearing formation, and which supplies the cities of Galveston and Houston. This is the formation designated as the "Fayette sands," and it is thought to be of Miocene or Pliocene age. These porous strata are considered by Professor Hill as being able to supply the whole Coast Prairie region with water—a matter of great importance in the arid southwestern portion of the State.

Immediately west of the Coast and Washington County Prairies, north of the Colorado, is a region said to be very different in its geological and agricultural character from those previously described. It is designated as the "East Texas or timbered region," and is a continuation of the great "Atlantic Timber Belt," which marks the interior of the Coastal Plain from New Jersey to Texas, extending to a slight distance

---

[1] The water-supply from the Artesian wells of the cities of Galveston and Houston has already been noticed in the present volume, (see *ante*, pp. 84, 86,) the information there given having been taken from a work issued by the State Geological Survey of Texas, and bearing the date of June, 1893. The practical results of Artesian well boring in this part of the State as there described seem far less important than those predicted in Professor Hill's report, especially as concerns the quality of the water obtained from these borings.

beyond the Colorado. The soil of this region is said to be the same throughout its whole extent, consisting of loose sands and gravels, with some clay, and there is a great uniformity in its forest and shrubby vegetation. The increasing aridity of the climate toward the southwest prevents the farther development of this forested belt in that direction. The geological age of the formation underlying this belt of country is Early Tertiary: Professor Hill designates it as " Eolignitic or basal Tertiary." The strata, being made up chiefly of loose sand or gravel with alternations of clay, furnish all the conditions necessary for an ample supply of water, the precipitation being very considerable in this belt. "The water comes to the surface, as mineral springs, many to every square mile, while wells are always obtainable, if located with reasonable intelligence. Artesian wells have already been secured in many places from this formation, and can be secured throughout its extent."

Immediately west of the great Atlantic timber belt, of which the principal features have been noticed above, comes the region of the Cretaceous prairies, with which the so-called " Cross Timber" belts are included. This region is limited on the north by the Washita Mountains, and on the south by the Quaternary of the Rio Grande Valley; it extends westward " to the Coal Measures and Red Beds west of the Upper Cross Timbers, north of the Colorado River, the Trans-Pecos Mountains, and the basins west of that stream." The topographic features and the vegetation of this region are interesting and peculiar from various points of view. It covers an area of over 73,000 square miles, or more than one fourth of the whole State, and equals all New England in extent. This prairie region is the most fertile and densely populated part of Texas, for on it are situated most of the important inland towns. It is the "rich, black-waxy, and other calcareous soils" of this region to which this part of the State owes its prosperity. This district is "uniquely Texan, as far as the United States are concerned, constituting a distinct geographic region, which in every topographic, economic, and cultured aspect should not be compared with other portions of our country."

The Main Black Prairie Region, as Professor Hill calls the eastern edge of the Cretaceous Prairie division of the State, extends through the whole length of Texas, having in its widest part a breadth of over a hundred miles. It is a level plain, with a slope toward the east so small as to be almost imperceptible, and an elevation of from 400 to 600 feet. The streams by which it is intersected do not cut deep enough below the general level to destroy the characteristic flatness of the wide divides. Its surface is covered by a deep black clay soil, which when wet becomes excessively tenacious — so much so, in fact, that it is usually designated as "black-waxy."[1]

[1] Of this soil Professor Hill says, "It is rich in lime, which, acting upon the vegetation by complicated changes, causes the black color." This is an entire mistake, for there is no such reaction of lime on organic matter known. The real cause of this dark color is the fineness of the soil, by which the complete decomposition of the organic matter which it contains, and which has resulted from the growth of vegetation upon it, has been more or less hindered. Of this condition of things we see a most excellent illustration in the "Black Earth" of Southeastern Russia (the so-called *tschornozem*), which is of very dark color, rich in organic matter, and exceedingly fine in texture. The almost constant presence of organic matter in the bituminous shales of various geological

The geological formations underlying the Black Prairie region are all of Cretaceous age. The sands of its eastern edge are the outcrop of the extreme upper division of this series — the so-called "Arenaceous" or "Glauconitic." The Main Black Prairie division has at the surface the "chalky clays," belonging to the "*Ponderosa* marls."[1] The "White Rock escarpment," which is an outcrop of a chalky rock, forming a narrow strip, averaging two miles in width, which extends along a portion of the western border of the "black-waxy belt," in the northern division of the Black Prairie is the Austin-Dallas chalk, averaging about 300 feet in thickness, and lying immediately below the Ponderosa marls.

The belt called "the Lower Cross Timbers," which extends along the western and northern border of the northern division of the Black Prairie region, is a strip of country nearly 180 miles in length from north to south, and but seldom exceeding ten miles in width, but bending round to the northwest in the northern part of the State, and there having a development east and west of over one hundred miles. "The occurrence of this peculiar ribbon of upland timber between two vast stretches of prairie had long been a subject of inquiry until the writer, in 1887, investigated and published its geology, and showed that the cause of this forest growth was the sandy soil and substructure,

---

ages is a fact of similar import, while the formation of coal and lignite was unquestionably largely dependent on conditions which favored the burying of vegetation under fine detrital material by which the air was more or less completely excluded, while the process of decomposition was beginning. See "United States," etc., p. 212.

[1] So called from the characteristic fossil of the formation, *Exogyra ponderosa*.

which was the outcrop of a rock sheet marking the beginning of the Black Prairie series of rocks."[1]

That division of the State of Texas which Professor Hill calls the "Grand Prairie," and which adjoins the

[1] See an article by Professor Hill in the American Journal of Science, (3), Vol. XXXIII. pp. 291–303, entitled "The Topography and Geology of the Cross Timbers and surrounding Regions in Northern Texas." This article is accompanied by a sketch map of that State, on which its salient topographical features are indicated. On that map the Upper and Lower Cross Timbers are represented as running parallel with each other for a great distance, maintaining nearly the same width, but uniting toward the north and finally disappearing in that direction. Various theories previously held by writers on the peculiar botanic features of this region are mentioned in this article. One of these is, that they represent arms or inlets of the Tertiary Sea; another is, that they are the beds of extinct lakes; and a third, that they represent the channels of Quaternary rivers, the directions of which indicate the former general slope of the surface of the country. Professor Hill, after explaining that the soil of the Cross Timbers is the detritus of arenaceous strata occupying well-defined horizons in the geological series, gives the following as the reason why the timber confines itself to these arenaceous belts: "They afford a suitable matrix for the penetration of the roots of trees, and a constant reservoir for moisture, thus furnishing two of the greatest essentials to forest growth." The present writer's long-continued study of the conditions favoring the growth or absence of timber in general, and especially in the prairie region of the Mississippi Valley, had long ago led him to form conclusions in part similar to those here enunciated by Professor Hill (see references furnished on page 161 of this volume). That the question of the presence or absence of moisture is a matter of importance as bearing on this question cannot, however, be admitted, since abundant evidence can be furnished going to prove that over certain well-defined areas the fineness of the soil is the essential factor in causing the absence of the forests by which these treeless regions are surrounded, and that trees will grow in abundance on a soil which is not at all retentive of moisture, provided it is of so coarse a texture that the air can have easy access to their roots. Of course a certain amount of moisture is essential to the development of arboreal vegetation in general, but the question in regard to the growth of trees in the Cross Timbers is precisely similar to the "prairie question" in general, which is this: Why is there absolutely no forest growth over a certain area, when another adjacent area precisely similarly situated as to the amount of precipitation is heavily timbered, even when the soil in the latter case is evidently less retentive of moisture than is that of the adjacent prairie or treeless region?

Black Prairie on the west, is underlain by rocks belonging to the Lower Cretaceous, and it is said by him to differ from the Black Prairie region in nearly every physical feature. The strata of this division lie almost horizontally, dipping eastward at a slightly greater angle than the topographical slope. The eastern edge of the Grand Prairie is between 500 and 600 feet in altitude above the sea-level for a distance of 300 miles from its beginning in Indian Territory, while its western edge varies from 1,000 feet at Red River to 3,000 on the Rio Grande.

The "Comanche Series," as this division of the Lower Cretaceous is called by Professor Hill, consists of almost horizontal sheets of rock "of different degrees of hardness, endurance, and chemical composition, as well as different capacities for the imbibition and retention of water."

The Comanche series varies greatly in thickness, ranging from 500 feet at its northeastern outcrop to 3,000 at its southwestern. It is divided into three distinct and well-marked series: (1) the Washita or eastern and uppermost division; (2) the Middle Chalky, or Comanche Peak division; (3) the Trinity, or basal and western division. Of these the first two are impervious and the last constitutes the "great water-receiving formation of Texas," and is of the greatest importance with reference to the Artesian supply of the State. The above indicated geological divisions of the Grand Prairie region are described in great detail by Professor Hill, and the various topographical forms resulting from the disintegration and erosion of a series of rocks the subdivisions of which differ from one another so much in lithological character pointed out and discussed.[1]

In the present volume only some of the more important facts having reference to the water-supply of the region underlain by these Cretaceous rocks can be given. These "water-features," as Professor Hill designates this class of phenomena, are said by him to be "of three distinct classes: (1) the Grand Prairie drainage or river-system; (2) the Mammoth Springs of San Antonio, San Marcos system; (3) the Waco – Fort Worth and the Dallas-Pottsboro Artesian systems."

The river systems of the Grand and Black Prairies appear to present such peculiarities as would be expected in a region possessing the topographical and geological characters there displayed, coupled with a considerable but varying amount of rainfall. The valleys of the streams of the Edwards Plateau are said to be among the most beautiful and picturesque features of our country, and it is thought that a proper use of the waters of these streams "would increase the productivity of the region a thousand fold." The "Edwards Plateau" is that part of the Cretaceous region of Texas which lies north of the Rio Grande embayment, and south of the Central or Fort Worth division of the Grand Prairie, from which it is separated by the Colorado River. It is really the southeastern continuation of the Llano Estacado, and, like that, lies mostly in the arid region of the State. It is a vast rocky plain of hard limestone covered with a

---

[1] See not only the Report here under examination, but also various papers by Professor Hill and others in the Reports of the Arkansas and Texas Geological Surveys and in the American Journal of Science for January and February, 1890.

scrubby growth of mesquite, nopal (*Opuntia*), and "false laurel," and is said to be "good grazing ground for sheep." In spite of the aridity of its surface, and the small rainfall of the region in general, the Edwards Plateau is considered by Professor Hill as being a "great water reservoir of priceless value to the State of Texas," and it is said that "the time will soon come when it will be considered criminal to permit one drop of its valuable flow to reach the sea wasted."

The reason for the above extraordinary statement must be sought in the fact that the source of the spring waters which supply the streams running from this plateau is thought to be the "same as that which supplies the wonderful Artesian wells and the Mammoth Springs of the San Marcos–San Antonio system," which are described by Professor Hill in considerable detail. Following the boundary of the Grand and Black Prairie regions from Dallas to Del Rio, a distance of 400 miles, there is a series of most remarkable springs "which rise out of the ground and flow off as rivers. These springs are often of such magnitude and beauty that it is impossible to convey a proper conception of them. They do not break out from bluffs or fall in cascades, but appear as pools, often in the level prairie, filled with water of a beautiful blue color, which flows silently away by the outlet which drains them." The trend of the line along which these springs are developed coincides almost exactly with that of the great Austin–Del Rio strike fault which also follows the division between the Grand and Black Prairies. It is through the fissures formed along this fault line that the water finds its way to the surface. These springs are therefore considered by Professor Hill as being "natural Artesian wells."[1]

San Antonio, Del Rio, San Marcos, New Braunfels, and Austin are mentioned as possessing the most conspicuous of these springs, but there are "magnificent springs" at several other localities. The largest group is at the head of the San Antonio River, near the city of that name. The volume of these springs is said to be nearly 50,000,000 gallons per day, and this outflow forms a lake, from which the river San Antonio flows through the heart of the city, which has 48,000 inhabitants, and is from this source abundantly supplied with water, used not only for ordinary domestic purposes, but to a considerable extent for irrigation. The springs at Del Rio are next in importance to those at San Antonio. They break out at the edge of the Edwards Plateau, about two miles from the town and near the Rio Grande. The outflow of the Del Rio springs is not stated with exactness, but it is said to give rise to a "bold rushing stream" which excels the Rio Grande in volume. The outflow of the springs at San Marcos is said to be at least 20,000 gallons per minute. Those of Austin are beautifully situated, and are the favorite resort of the people of that city, being surrounded by "pleasing groves of pecan timber and picturesque rocks." Their outflow equals "many thousands of gallons per minute."

[1] This is a misnomer, for just as properly might all springs be called "natural Artesian wells" as these. The essential fact in an Artesian well is that it is artificial.

[2] Around this marvellous group of springs, and upon the banks of its outflow, were located the most ancient Indian settlements, or Pueblos, of Texas. These were six in number, with extensive surrounding farms and gardens.

An investigation of the waters and their temperatures rising along this remarkable line of springs, and comparisons of the facts thus obtained with those resulting from the examination of various Artesian wells in that region, prove that these are all of similar origin and nature, and that the source from which their outflow is derived is the Trinity division of the Comanche sands, which are the foundation of the Grand Prairie, and whose waters are absorbed on an outcrop at a higher altitude along its western edge.

We next reach the consideration of the Artesian well system of the Grand and Black Prairies, of which an extraordinary development has taken place within the past five years, so that Professor Hill feels justified in saying that in numerous places in that region " magnificent flows of water have been secured and what ten years ago was in many places a poorly watered district now abounds in magnificent Artesian wells, which supply water to cities and farms in quantity large enough to make many new industries possible, besides furnishing water to irrigate many thousands of acres." This Artesian area extends from Denton County, near Red River, to Del Rio, on the Rio Grande, a distance of about 448 miles, with an average breadth of forty miles.[1] Over this region the geological features possess great uniformity, but the wells vary greatly in depth and amount of flow. The beginning of this business

---

[1] These are dimensions of the Artesian area in question as given by Professor Hill, and it is added "that the area over which flowing wells may be obtained is about the size of Minnesota, Nebraska, or North or South Dakota." But the figures here quoted give as the area in question 17,920 square miles, while that of Minnesota is 83,365 square miles, and that of Nebraska 77,510.

seems to have been at Fort Worth, where, ten or twelve years ago, water was obtained from wells only 300 feet deep, but "not until the past year has Fort Worth discovered that her drills had not yet penetrated the lowest and greatest water-bearing strata." The success of these operations at Fort Worth led to "Artesian experiments" all through the Grand and Black Prairie region. A few wells were failures, but hundreds were successful, "and to-day most of the cities of the State which before this Artesian epoch were without good water are supplied with an abundance. . . . When it is considered that the first water was experimentally reached only twelve years ago, and the greater underlying sheets only four years ago, the future possibilities are beyond estimate."

The water-bearing formations which furnish the Artesian water of the Black and Grand Prairie region, of the extent of which and of whose presumed possibilities, according to the views of Professor Hill, an attempt has been made to give an idea in the preceding pages, are as follows, the enumeration being made from above downward: (1) the Lower Cross Timber, or Denison (in part) and Dakota sands; (2) the Paluxy sands; (3) portions of the Glen Rose beds; (4) the Trinity or Upper Cross Timber sands. These all incline to the eastward, as already mentioned, and at a slightly greater angle than the topographical slope, and these different water-bearing formations are separated by more or less impermeable or non-water-bearing strata, so that the farther east the borings are made the greater the depth which must be attained in order that any particular water-bearing formation be intersected in the bore-hole. Thus a drill on the western edge of the Black Prairie would begin in the Lower Cross Timber sands, while on its eastern edge the lowest water beds of the Trinity sands would not be reached until the bore-hole had penetrated to a depth of between 3,500 and 4,000 feet, since it would be necessary to bore through the entire thickness of the Cretaceous.

The Artesian wells of the Dallas-Pottsboro group of the Black Prairie region all have their origin in the Lower Cross Timber (or Dakota) sands. The wells of Pottsboro, Grayson County, at a depth of 250 feet, furnish 25,600 gallons of water per day. At Dallas several wells obtained Artesian water from the Lower Cross Timber sands, at depths varying from 672 to 800 feet. This formation crops out about twenty miles west of that city, and " furnishes, in most instances, an abundant supply." The Lower Cross Timber sands are said to have in this vicinity " several veins of water, owing to the fact that they have many clay beds alternating with them." At Denison the same sands are said to be porous and ferruginous, and to have a " great imbibing and transmitting capacity." Here a vertical well, twenty-five feet in diameter, has been sunk, and from it horizontal tunnels run, so as to increase the yield of water and at the same time form a reservoir, from which it is pumped and distributed through the city. The total area of the Lower Cross Timber sands in Texas is said to have been determined by accurate survey to be 794 square miles. The rainfall over this area is stated by Professor Hill at thirty-six inches, and it is thought by him that at least one half of this percolates the soil and becomes the source of Artesian water.[1]

Over a considerable part of the Lower Cross Timber area Artesian wells do not exist and are not to be expected from that formation: they can only be obtained at points to the eastward of its western outcrop, and at a lower altitude. But "negative or nonflowing" wells, in which the water rises nearly to the surface, can be had throughout the Black Prairie region, and from these the water can be raised by windmills or steam-engines, in quantity sufficient for domestic purposes, or even for garden irrigation. But there are other "great sheets of Artesian water" lying below the Lower Cross Timber sands of the Dallas-Pottsboro area which, when reached by the drill, are expected to furnish a much larger supply than that at present obtained, as has been the case at and near Fort Worth.

At the last-mentioned locality the first successful wells in the Grand Prairie region were drilled, the water from which came from the Paluxy sands. As this formation is of very moderate thickness, and consequently having but a limited receiving area, the wells being increased to over a hundred in number, the supply of water soon gave out, and in order to raise it to the surface pumping became necessary. The depth of various wells near Fort Worth obtaining water from the Paluxy sands is usually between 400 and 500 feet.

---

[1] No experiments seem to have been made anywhere in this or any other part of the United States to determine how much of the rainfall does actually penetrate the soil. The precipitation in the district under consideration in the text is so much larger than that in the arid region of the country in general, that a correspondingly larger percolation is to be expected. (See *ante*, pp. 105–108.)

At Waco, also, a flow of water is usually secured at a depth of about 1,100 feet, and this is supposed to come from the Paluxy sands. The importance of the wells from this formation in the Fort Worth – Waco region to the stock-raising industry is said to be "incalculable"; for irrigation it would appear not to be well adapted, since it is stated that an improper application of it — sprinkling the growing plants with water, namely, instead of soaking the soil — has created a strong prejudice against it. Professor Hill remarks, however, "that it would be improvident to stop a well in the Paluxy sands . . . since they are but the beginning of a much more abundant and valuable supply that everywhere underlies them."

Waco on the Brazos River, at an elevation of 431 to 500 feet above the sea-level, is the place where the first successful attempt was made to obtain water from the Trinity sands, the geological position of which water-bearing formation has already been indicated. The volume of the flow from this well is nowhere distinctly stated in the Report here under examination; it is said, however, that "it was so great (estimated at from 500,000 to 1,000,000 gallons per day) that it created great rejoicing and has been the cause of untold value in the development and improvement of the industrial and hygienic conditions of the city." Further, it is said that "the discovery of this flow immediately led to the drilling of other wells, flowing an aggregate of many million gallons per day, and supplying water not only for all public and domestic purposes, but power for various industries, such as clothing factories, wood-working machinery, and irrigation."

A statement from the Secretary of the Waco Board of Trade, dated July 7, 1891, is to the effect that there were at that time in and around Waco eleven overflowing wells and two approaching completion. The depth of these wells is given as being from 1,607 to 1,896 feet, nine of them being between 1,800 and 1,900 feet deep; the diameter of the bore is in most cases eight inches, and the temperature of the water is from 97° to 103°. The flow of these wells seems in no case to have been measured, but the estimate for the most copious one is 1,200,000 gallons per day, and for the least 300,000, while the flow of seven is estimated at 1,000,000 gallons or over. Professor Hill says the water of the Waco wells is "soft and tasteless." In the communication from the Waco Board of Trade it is said the water of the Bell well (one of those of which the statistics are furnished) was analyzed by the "leading chemist of Chicago," and that it was found to contain 53.8201 grains to the gallon of foreign matter, of which 23.9583 grains were "sodium potassium sulphates" and 20.6597 grains "sodium carbonate and bicarbonate." Furthermore, it is remarked that "there is no appreciable difference in the taste of the water of any of these wells; therefore we must assume that one analysis governs all."[1] From an examination of the records kept by the borer of one of the Waco Artesian wells (the "Padgett," 1,886 feet deep) Professor Hill concluded that the main flow was really from strata 876 feet below the horizon of the Paluxy

---

[1] The composition of this water, as stated above, is very remarkable, and it is desirable that the results of this analysis should be confirmed, if possible, by other analyses.

sands, and "especially the lowest ninety-eight feet of sands."

After these results had been attained at Waco — which was in 1890, — the City Council of Fort Worth determined to "fully test the possibilities of the Artesian water-supply for the city waterworks' use." For this purpose a boring was begun "at about the highest point in the city," and water struck at various levels: of these results it is said that "could all of these flows have been put together, then they would have discharged fully 500 gallons per minute, or 720,000 per day, and at a point 142 feet above the Trinity River." But the last flow (struck at 1,127 feet below the surface) not having sufficient pressure to carry it to a standpipe one hundred feet high, it was cased off, and the boring continued in search of a still stronger flow. At the time Professor Hill's report was handed in this experimental well had reached a depth of nearly 2,800 feet, and it was intended to continue the bore to a depth of 3,000, if an increased flow should not be obtained before that depth was reached.

Professor Hill's comments on this enterprise and his sanguine expectations with regard to its probable results may perhaps be best given in his own words: "This remarkable discovery has been farther demonstrated. First, the Texas Brewery, whose location is fifty feet lower than Tucker's Hill,[1] sank their well to the first or top Artesian vein, and obtained a flow of upwards of 240 gallons per minute, with a pressure which carries the water to the top of their immense building

---

[1] It was on this elevation that the City Council's experimental well, mentioned above, was bored.

ninety feet above the ground. Encouraged by this success, the packing-house company began a well at their house on the north side at a point 120 feet lower than the top of Tucker's Hill, and it has now been drilled through the first and second Artesian veins, and it is flowing at the rate of over 800,000 gallons in twenty-four hours. They will continue the well to and through the lower Artesian vein, when the flow will (if the Tucker Hill discoveries hold good for the north part of the city) be fully 1,500,000 gallons in twenty-four hours. The packing-house well is undoubtedly flowing more water in twenty-four hours than any other Artesian well in the State of Texas by at least one third, and when the third Artesian vein is reached it will be the 'Jumbo,' the geyser well of the State. The city experiment has demonstrated that Fort Worth has the Artesian water in quantities sufficient to supply a city of 1,000,000 people should occasion ever require it. Ten wells located down in the valley, above high-water mark, will supply over 10,000,000 gallons of pure Artesian water each twenty-four hours, and *the water is pure; there is no mineral of any kind in solution in it; it is as clear as a diamond, as pure as melted snow.*[1] Surely if there is an Artesian city in Texas it is Fort Worth."

Under the heading "The Limits of the Fort Worth —

---

[1] The water in regard to which these statements are made is water which had not been obtained at the time this paragraph (Italicized by the present writer) was written, so that no analysis of it could have been made. The water from the same geological position as that from which that of Fort Worth was expected to be obtained held in solution, according to the analysis of Chicago's "leading chemist," cited on page 178, fifty-three grains to the gallon of mineral matter.

Waco System" an attempt is made by Professor Hill to fix the position of the line in Texas beyond which the dip of the strata of the principal water-bearing formation of Texas will carry it to such a depth that it will be "beyond practical reach for economic use." From 2,500 to 3,000 feet seems to have been fixed upon as this depth, and this limit, it is said, will be found in the eastern belt of the Black Prairie region, between the great Atlantic Timber belt and the line of outcrop of the Austin-Dallas chalk. The only portion of the Grand and Black Prairie regions between the Colorado and the latitude of Denton where water cannot be made to flow is on the tops and slopes of the high mesas ("mountains" in local parlance) which form the high divides of the stream valleys of the western half of the Grand Prairie, and are higher in altitude than the receiving area of the Upper Cross Timbers.

The Black and Grand Prairie regions south of the Colorado are separated from those to the north of that river, in respect to their Artesian conditions, for two reasons. In the first place, the great fault which extends from north of Austin to beyond Del Rio breaks the continuity of the stratification, and, secondly, this fault is accompanied by a series of protrusions of basaltic rock, which appears in more than twenty places along the line of fracture. These conditions render it impossible to "predict the continuity of any area of flowing wells in the region, although the latter are numerous and abundant, while the great Artesian springs here attain their greatest development."

The mass of the Edwards Plateau is mostly composed of the "spongy strata of the Glen Rose and

Trinity beds, capped on the summits of the impervious Caprina limestone." The surface of this plateau is, therefore, dry and poorly adapted for agriculture, and the region has a very scanty population. The sides of this table-land are, however, deeply scored with ravines or "cañons," which usually have water and numerous springs, and constitute the agriculturally valuable portion of the region; but this is said to be "not more than one per cent of the vast area for which the springs might be available." It is along the eastern edge of the plateau, where the rainfall is considerable, that these so-called "Artesian springs" are numerous and of considerable volume. They all flow from the Trinity sands. On the surface of the Edwards Plateau water is obtained by means of wells which at a depth of from 300 to 500 feet penetrate the Trinity sands. "All experiments thus far have failed to reveal Artesian conditions on this Plateau."

In reference to the utilization of the Artesian waters of the Black and Grand Prairies, in general, it is said that the discovery of this source of supply has had an incalculable influence upon the material prosperity of an extensive region, to which it has given "new life." Not only are these waters remarkable for their purity, but some of them possess "superior medicinal virtues, resembling the celebrated Spas of Germany, which are found in somewhat similar rocks. . . . The hygienic aspect of these waters, both the pure and the medicinal, will also prove of great value to the live-stock interests." In reference to the utilization of these waters for irrigation Professor Hill remarks as follows: "It is not my intention to convey the idea that the

Black Prairie region is subject to drought; for crops of corn and cotton are often rich and abundant, but all admit that it has seasons of rain and drought, and that, if rich now, it could be made immensely richer by irrigation, and all the fruits and vegetables now imported from the irrigated lands of Utah and California could be produced at home." As no analyses or detailed statements of any kind are given with reference to the amount and character of the saline substances which these waters — some of which are confessedly "medicinal" — contain, it is difficult to form any idea of how extensively, or for how long a period, they are likely to be used for irrigation. Professor Hill's sanguine expectations of their future value for this purpose are, however, expressed in the following glowing terms: "Every drop of water from these springs and wells can be utilized for irrigation, and when the people of the region appreciate the fact that each gallon of water has a specific value in agriculture, as has a pound of coal in industrial enterprise, not one drop of this water will be allowed to escape unutilized, and the agricultural wealth will be enormously increased."

That part of Texas which is occupied by Carboniferous and older Palæozoic rocks lies to the east of the "Red Beds region," and it is said to have a "structure unfavorable for any large flow of water." In Burnet County "one or two small flows have been secured out of hundreds of borings made with the diamond drill by mineral prospectors."

The so-called "Red Beds region" is, both from a topographical and geological point of view, one of the most interesting parts of the Southwestern United

States, since the formation thus designated occupies fully 100,000 square miles of area in Oklahoma, Texas, and New Mexico. In Texas the Red Beds lie between the Carboniferous region and the Llano Estacado, beginning near San Angelo, and widening rapidly toward the north. The name by which this part of the State is known is derived from the fact that the "surface of the whole country underlain by these rocks is of conspicuous red colors, glaring vermilion, or deep-brown chocolate sometimes prevailing, varied only here and there by a bed of snow-white gypsum." It is in the Indian Territory that this peculiar formation is developed in its greatest width, occupying there and in Northwestern Texas a district 350 miles long from north to south, and with an average width of 150 miles, all an unbroken prairie, with the exception of "small areas occupied by the Wichita Mountains, and a few remnant buttes of the Grand Prairie and Llano Estacado formations which have been preserved to remind us of the vast erosion the region has undergone." The geological age of the Red Beds ranges from the Permian to the base of the Comanche series, thus representing or occupying the place in the geological series of the Permian and Triassic, and probably of the Jurassic. While thus comprehensive in their geological range, the Red Beds have everywhere the same remarkable characteristics of color and consolidation, and, according to Professor Hill, "are probably a single unbroken formation, representing the sediments of an ancient inland sea, which extended from the ninety-eighth meridian westward to the Sierras and from the Northern United States nearly to Mexico."

Although that part of the country occupied by the Red Beds is one of very scanty precipitation, yet "sudden and excessive rainfalls" do occur there during the summer months, at which times the streams which rise in or flow through this region "are all characterized by their phenomenal vermilion colored freshets known as 'red rises.'" These rivers have no permanent supply of water from the Red Beds themselves, but all are fed from the underground drainage of the Llano Estacado or from the adjacent mountains. This whole region presents very unfavorable conditions for water-supply, springs being few in number and wells "deep and scant," except along the less arid eastern border of the formation. Neither are there any known Artesian wells in the Red Bed area. It is thought, however, that water may be obtained from wells dug in certain lower areas, and an instance is cited of one twenty-five miles west of Eddy, on the Pecos, in New Mexico, from which 3,000 cattle are daily watered by a pump operated by horse-power. From the peculiar saline and gypsiferous character of the formation in question, it is to be expected that water, however obtained, will be very impure; and, as Professor Hill states, "all deep wells in the Red Beds strike salt."

The water conditions of the Llano Estacado are, in the Report under consideration, next discussed.[1] This

[1] Professor Hill remarks that "the name Staked Plains should be dropped from geographic nomenclature as the name for the great mesa to which it is applied." This remark is based on an entire misunderstanding of the meaning of the Spanish term Llano Estacado on the part of that author, who says that "a glance at the Spanish dictionary will show that it will be impossible to translate the word 'estacado' to mean a stake, but upon the contrary it means exactly the opposite, a palisade or wall, which is a most appropriate term for the Llano Estacado,

region is said by Professor Hill to be the "greatest continuous and least studied plateau of our country." It embraces an area of at least 50,000 square miles, and is practically so smooth " as to resemble the level of the ocean at a dead calm, and unbroken by trees or bushes or deep drained channels, and carpeted with a rich growth of gramma grass."

The Llano Estacado, once so remote and difficult of access, can now be easily reached by means of the Texas Pacific Railroad, which intersects it, crossing the Pecos River at the town of that name. The Den-

inasmuch as it alludes to the sharp declivity or face of the escarpment which in many places marks the edge of these plains." "Estaca" is the Spanish for "stake," and "estacado" is a participle, meaning "staked," while "estacada" is a "stockade," of which term the meaning is nearly the same as "palisade" ("palissade" in French). This last term is used in the plural in the United States, especially on the Hudson, and also in Nevada, as a topographical designation, with the meaning of a line of precipitous cliffs; but the present writer has not been able to obtain any evidence that the Spanish "estacada" or the French "palissade" has ever been used in this way. "Estocade" in French means a thrust with the point of a sword, and there is no use of this word in the language analogous to our "stockade," which is the exact equivalent of the Spanish "estacada." General Marcy, in his "Exploration of the Red River," says: "I was told in New Mexico that, many years since, the Mexicans marked out a route with stakes across this plain, where they found water; and hence the name by which it is known throughout Mexico of 'El Llano Estacado,' or the 'Staked Plain.'" General Marcy's graphic description of the Llano Estacado may here with propriety be quoted. He says: "The approximate elevation of this plain above the sea, as determined with the barometer, is 2,450 feet. It is much elevated above the surrounding country, very smooth and level, and spreads out in every direction as far as the eye can penetrate, without a tree, shrub, or any other herbage to intercept the vision. The traveller, in passing over it, sees nothing but one dreary and monotonous waste of barren solitude. It is an ocean of desert prairie, where the voice of man is seldom heard, and where no living being permanently resides. The almost total absence of water causes all animals to shun it: even the Indians do not venture to cross it, except at two or three points, where they find a few small ponds of water."

ver, Texas, and Fort Worth Railroad, also passes over a small arm of this great plain, crossing the Canadian River at Tascosa, and from there finding its way in a northwesterly direction to an intersection with the Atchison system at Trinidad, in Colorado. The Llano Estacado is bounded on the north by the Canadian River and on the west by the Pecos, both of which streams run in valleys sunk nearly a thousand feet below the level of its surface. Down its eastern edge flow in deep cañons, with almost vertical walls, various streams which are the head-waters of the Red, Brazos, and Colorado Rivers. The cañons at the head of the Red River, at the northeast corner of the Llano, are said by Professor Hill "to be excelled in beauty by only those of the Grand Cañon of the Colorado, which they much resemble in color and stratigraphy." Neither the Canadian nor the Pecos receives any surface drainage from the Llano Estacado.

The surface of the Llano is said by Professor Hill to be composed of unconsolidated porous sediments — water-worn sand, pebbly gravel, and the like — which average 200 feet in thickness throughout its whole extent, but which are thinnest toward the east. These sediments are thought by some to have been the deposit of a vast lake which occupied this region in late Tertiary times, but Professor Hill inclines to consider them as being marginal deposits of the Gulf of Mexico. This surface formation is believed once to have covered the whole of the Edwards Plateau, from which it has, however, been removed by erosion.[1]

---

[1] See *ante*, pp. 146, 147, for a description of these surface deposits, which are there shown to be widely spread over the region of the Plains.

These superficial deposits rest on a quite different series of rocks, which are of importance with reference to the question of water-supply. The rainfall in the Llano Estacado is estimated by Professor Hill at from twenty to twenty-five inches, and, as is the case over a large part of the semi-arid region, it almost all takes place during the summer months.[1] In spite of the somewhat large precipitation on the Llano there is no surface water to be found on it, unless it be in the form of small pools immediately after a heavy shower. The porosity of the surface deposits is considered by Professor Hill as the principal cause of the absence of water on the surface of this vast plain; but, in point of fact, the rapid evaporation which takes place under the climatic conditions there prevailing is a still more important agent in producing the phenomenon in question.[2]

According to the statements of Professor Hill and

---

[1] The statistics of rainfall on and near the Llano Estacado are by no means sufficient to justify any precise statement as to its amount.

[2] See *ante*, pp. 105-108. As already stated in the present volume, the amount of rainfall which actually percolates the surface detritus in the semi-arid and arid regions of the United States seems everywhere to be overstated by the engineers and geologists engaged in the irrigation surveys: this is the conclusion reached by the present writer after a study of the results of experiments made in other countries, such data being for the United States entirely wanting. The following statements in reference to the rainfall on the Llano Estacado are extracted from Mr. Roessler's Report (Ex. Doc. No. 222, 51st Congress, 1st Session, p. 291) on the Artesian Wells of Texas: "The rainfall of the Staked Plain varies between eighteen and thirty inches, falling mainly between the 21st of April and the 15th of September, apparently at the right time to perfectly mature crops. But this is not the case, as the rain comes in tremendous showers at comparatively long intervals and without regularity. Some locality will receive fine local showers at short intervals, while some other point not thirty miles distant will alternately have a deluge or a drought."

Mr. Roessler, water can be obtained over any part of the Llano Estacado by means of wells, from which it can be pumped with the aid of wind-mills, and this has been done in many localities and pasturage obtained for thousands of cattle. This water, as Professor Hill asserts, "is stored in the mortar beds and grits of the Llano Estacado, and is the most remarkable sheet of water in our land." This statement is said to be true for the northern and northwestern part of the Llano, where the "Llano formation" rests directly on the impervious "Red Beds," but farther south and southeast the well water and springs come from the Trinity sands, which are intercalated between these two formations.

While Artesian water has not yet been obtained on the Llano Estacado, Professor Hill is not without hopes that over some portions of its surface flowing wells may be secured. In regard to this point he remarks as follows: "Without committing myself to prophecy, it is my opinion that when the portion of the Llano along the Texas – New Mexican line is thoroughly prospected, somewhere in that region will be found an abundant Artesian supply from the underlying Dakota and Trinity sands which outcrop so abundantly at a higher altitude in the northwest escarpment."

The published statements in regard to the quality of the water obtained from the wells of the Llano Estacado, or from those of the adjacent region, are extremely imperfect and unsatisfactory.

Professor Hill, in the report here under consideration, passes next to a description of the water conditions of the "Trans-Pecos or Basin regions." That part of Texas and New Mexico which lies west of the Pecos River is topographically and climatologically a portion of the Basin region of the United States, and is continued to the south in the Mexican High Plateau or Table Land. The "Great Basin," as this term is generally used, comprises an area of about a quarter of a million of square miles, no portion of which has a drainage to the sea. As thus limited, the Basin has as its northern boundary the watershed of Snake River; as its eastern, that of Green River; as its southern, that of the Colorado; and as its western, the crest of the Sierra Nevada. From no part of this region does any river find its way to the sea, nor is it traversed by any stream while doing this, even if receiving no tributaries from the region through which it runs. The Great Basin is an elevated plateau, traversed by numerous ranges of mountains, which have a general north and south trend, and many of which are considerably elevated above the intervening valleys, each of which is, as a general rule, by itself an independent basin, having no drainage or water connection with any adjacent valley. The chief exceptions to this condition of things are the basins of Great Salt Lake and of the Humboldt River, of which the former receives the drainage of quite an extensive area, while the latter terminates in a lake or sink, into which flow, after a succession of unusually rainy winters, various streams originating on the eastern slope of the Sierra Nevada and generally sinking before reaching Humboldt Lake.[1] The bottoms of the valleys between

---

[1] The Humboldt River flows near the extreme northern edge of the Great Basin, in a break or depression extending along the southern edge

the numerous ranges of the Great Basin are usually themselves sinks, the lower portion of which are occupied by bodies of water which vary in size according as the preceding winter has been more or less dry, and of which many are hardly anything more than saline incrustations resting on a muddy bottom.[1]

Since the chief cause of the basin character of the area of which the outlines have thus been indicated is the small amount of the rainfall, it is evident that the adjacent areas which are similarly conditioned with regard to precipitation, but which are traversed by rivers heading in regions receiving a comparatively large rainfall, must partake to a certain extent of the characters of the Great Basin itself. Thus the country lying north of the Colorado, below the junction of the Green and the Grand, furnishes hardly any tributaries to that river, so that the southern boundary of the Basin must be drawn close to its right bank. The Colorado River, therefore, derives its water from the Rocky Mountains, its numerous affluents draining an extensive area of quite large precipitation on the western slope of that system of ranges, and thus collecting water sufficient to enable the main river, after their junction, to maintain itself as a powerful stream, al-

---

of the great northern volcanic plateau. It intersects the valleys of the Basin Ranges at right angles to their trend, and as the whole region rises in altitude toward the south, the Humboldt Valley is the natural recipient of the drainage of a very extensive area, the climatic conditions of which, however, are such as to cause the volume of this drainage to be very small, and extremely variable in amount. Carson Lake, the sink of the Carson River, is sometimes so united with the sink of the Humboldt that the two become in fact one continuous sheet of water.

[1] See "The United States," etc., pp. 82–89, in which the physical geography and geology of the Great Basin are briefly described.

though receiving no tributary of importance in a course of more than a thousand miles.

In the Great Basin proper, the ranges of mountains are so high and the valleys between them so narrow that the latter are the less conspicuous topographical features of the region; but as we leave this area which is strictly destitute of any drainage to the sea, and especially in advancing in a southerly and southwesterly direction, we come to a part of the country where the valleys broaden out and become relatively more important than the mountain ranges, these diminishing considerably in breadth and elevation, as well as in regularity of development. This is especially the case with the region which lies south and west of the great mass of the Rocky Mountains which extend through Colorado with such a breadth and with so much regularity of trend, but which is with difficulty traceable beyond Santa Fé, so that some have considered the eastern division of the Cordilleras as terminating at that point, the real condition of things being that this great system of ranges continues indefinitely to the southward into Mexico, while the individual masses of which it is made up become more and more broken and irregular, so that their connection is much less easily traced, especially as this want of continuity or absence of a dominating range is accompanied by a falling off in height, isolated volcanic masses more or less conical in outline beginning to form the highest summits.[1]

In New Mexico and Western Texas, as well as in

[1] The name "Rocky Mountains" is not in general use for any part of the Cordilleran system farther south than Santa Fé.

Southern Arizona, there is an immense development of this type of topography: the valleys become "mesas" or "basin-plains," and occupy extensive areas behind which the mountains seem almost to lose themselves. These wider and more table-like plains, however, differ but little from the valleys of the Great Basin itself, so far as climate is concerned; if there is any difference, it is that the former are still drier and hotter than the latter. The narrower the valley and the higher the mountains, the greater the chances of obtaining water from melting snow or from underground sources fed by precipitation, which is naturally greatest where the ranges are broadest and most elevated.

The region which lies south and southwest of El Paso, and which belongs to Northwestern Texas, Southern New Mexico, and Southern Arizona, is precisely that part of the United States of which the topography has been least studied, and where the names of the various mountain ranges are most uncertain. Professor Hill gives various details in regard to the geological structure of what he considers one of "the most extensive and characteristic of these great inner mountain basins," namely, the "Organ-Hueco Basin," as he calls it, and which lies between the Organ-Franklin and Hueco-Sacramento ranges, in extreme Western Texas and Southern New Mexico. This, he says, is a "vast expanse of dead level plain, extending from the Rio Grande, between El Paso and Fort Hancock, northward some 150 miles." It is ninety miles in width at its southern end, and narrows to less than forty at its northern, having a slope to the south sufficient to make a difference of 1,000 feet in the altitudes of its southern and northern ends. The soil of this "mesa," which is entirely unfurrowed by any drainage channel other than that of the Rio Grande itself, is a sandy loam, "resembling that of the Llano Estacado, and is the residuum of the substructure of stratified, alternating, or unconsolidated sands (grits), clays, and water-worn gravel, often cemented by the white chalky-looking material known in the region as tierra blanca, or white earth." These beds, like those of the Llano Estacado, are said to be "chiefly marked by excessive lack of consolidation, the sands, clays, and gravels being almost as loose as when first deposited." As in all the other valleys and basins of the region, this area is surrounded by numerous terraces — proofs of the former existence of a lake of large dimensions, but which has now become entirely dried up. The streams which flow down the slopes of the mountains by which this basin is irregularly surrounded all sink the moment they reach the porous materials which cover its floor; for, as Professor Hill observes, "they do not evaporate, as has been alleged, nor do they sink into caverns, as most people think, but they are imbibed, literally drunk up, by the soft sponge-like formation of the plain, and are stored below the line of saturation. The shedding of its rain waters by the impervious mountain rock and its imbibition by the spongy plains, is the key to the whole water question in the arid region."

West of the Organ-Franklin range is another extensive basin, called the Mesilla, through which runs the Rio Grande, on which are the towns of Mesilla and Las Cruces, "two of the most flourishing places in New Mexico," agriculture being carried on by irrigation from the river. The lake which once occupied the Mesilla was continuous with that of the Hueco-Franklin basin. The Jornada del Muerto is another of these mesas, extending parallel with the Rio Grande, but separated from it by a series of low ranges, and bounded on the east by the northern continuation of the Sierra de los Organos or Organ Range.

All these and many other similar basins appear to have nearly the same geological and climatic characteristics, and all, in the opinion of Professor Hill, are supplied with a great amount of underground water. The evidence on which this statement is based seems to be of a very unsatisfactory character. Thus it is stated that "Wherever upon this apparently sterile plain [the Franklin-Hueco basin] an experiment has been made, abundant water has been secured at depths below 232 feet, and windmills pump it for irrigation." Records of seven wells on the Lanoria Mesa,[1] furnished by B. D. Russell of El Paso, give the depth at which water has been obtained at that locality as varying from 210 to 621 feet, nothing being said as to its quantity or quality, but to this record is appended the statement by Professor Hill that "the success of these wells, together with their inexhaustible supply of water, demonstrates the fact that the capacity of the Franklin-Hueco basin formation for water is very great, notwithstanding the slight rainfall and excessive evaporation which has driven the line of visible moist-

[1] The position of the "Lanoria Mesa" is not given by Professor Hill, but as he uses the records furnished by Mr. Russell to justify the statement that there is a great amount of underground water in the Franklin-Hueco basin, it is to be presumed that it forms a part of that mesa.

ure nearly 150 feet below the surface." To this is added the remark, that, "relatively speaking, this basin is one of the great water-bearing areas of the West, where, if irrigation can be properly conducted by pumping, an agricultural community will eventually thrive. Already several large fruit farms are being irrigated in this basin, and if they prove profitable there is no reason to suppose but that much of this country, apparently a hopeless desert, will be made into a fertile region."

The Mesilla Basin, the Jornada del Muerto, part of the Pecos Valley, and various other "basins" of this region, are all considered by Professor Hill as being essentially alike in their water conditions, although but little definite information in regard to this matter is reported. Of the flowing wells at Pecos City, on the authority of Mr. Roessler, it is stated that their depth varies from 185 to 315 feet, that their flow is from "very light" to sixty gallons per minute, and that the water in all of these wells is slightly brackish, "some being better than others." On the same authority it is said of two wells at Toyah, 514 and 834 feet deep, that the shallower one yielded nine gallons per minute, and the deeper 310, the water from both being "white sulphur with a salty taste." It is added that "the wells of this subdistrict are as a rule very deep and the water in many of them is practically unfit for use."[1] In regard to Deming, the point of junction of the Atchison, the Southern Pacific, and the Silver City and Pacific Railroads, and near the eastern border of

---

[1] For information from another source in regard to the water conditions in the Pecos Valley, see *ante*, pp. 136-138.

Mimbres Basin, it is said that water can be obtained in inexhaustible quantity at about fifty feet in depth, the whole plain being covered with cattle ranches and windmills.[1]

In summing up in regard to the water conditions of these basins in general, Professor Hill remarks as follows: "These vast inter-mountain plains, or basins, or ancient lake valleys, have, until lately, been absolutely void of surface water, and so synonymous with sterility that they have been considered often the synonym of death, like Death's Valley in California, or the Jornado del Muerto of New Mexico.[2] That they should now be found to be underlain by an abundance of fresh water is a fact which is of the greatest value in the economic conditions of the arid region, where water is worth more than land, and where a drop to even quench the traveller's thirst is usually unobtainable, except in rare localities. The far greater extent of these basins than the mountains over New Mexico, Texas, and Mexico, seems to have been overlooked or considered unimportant by national surveys as well as its underground water conditions."

---

[1] This statement is made on the authority of Mr. Warren Bristol. See "Report of Special Committee," etc., Senate Document, Report 928, Part 4, 51st Congress, 1st Session, pp. 64, 65. Mr. Bristol declares "that as soon as forestry is systematically cultivated here [in the Mimbres Basin], and trees are planted so as to break the prevailing winds, it will be a wonderful country with water for productiveness."

[2] "Death Valley" was so named because a party of immigrants on their way to California, in 1849, perished there from want of water. "Jornada [*not* Jornado] del Muerto" (day's journey of the dead man) is a term not unfrequently given by the early Spanish settlers in the Cordilleran region, and having reference to the fact that a long day's march must be made without water, and of course not without difficulty and danger.

That similar sanguine expectations in regard to the future of the basin region of the Cordilleras are held by others, as well as by Professor Hill, will become evident on reading a statement made by a citizen of the driest part of the State of Nevada, who not only asserts that the water-supply of that region is "immense," but that the climate is undergoing a rapid change for the better: "In relation to the water supply beneath the surface, I believe it to be simply immense. Flowing wells can be found by boring a short distance in many of our valleys. . . . Nature is evidently preparing this section of country for great things in the near future. . . . Our great alkali flats, or dry lakes, are also being filled up to a level with the surrounding plains, and many of them are also being gradually covered with vegetation. . . . Cloud bursts and high winds are becoming less frequent, and many other things are looking favorable for a brighter future."[1]

The report of Professor Hicks, of which the title has been given on a preceding page,[2] begins with some general remarks on the geological structure of the State of Nebraska, and the relations of this structure to the problem of water-supply, as introductory to a somewhat detailed account of the results of a survey of the Loup Valley. Certain points in this report, which are worthy of notice as throwing light on some of the questions already raised in the present volume having reference to the climatic and irrigational con-

[1] From an article headed "Phreatic Waters in Nye County, Nevada, by George Nichols, Agent of the Nevada State Board of Trade," in Hinton's Report on Irrigation, Part I., 1891, pp. 210, 211.
[2] See *ante*, p. 145.

ditions of this part of the country, may next be taken up for examination.[1]

Two formations are said by Professor Hicks to "dominate the circulation of moisture, both on the surface and beneath it; these are the Cretaceous and the Tertiary, which lie in the form of a synclinal basin, the western rim of which is 3,000 feet higher than the eastern." These formations rest on rocks of Permo-Carboniferous age, but practically, with reference to the question of water-supply, this formation is of no importance, since the upper member of the Cretaceous is a shale "almost perfectly impervious or water tight." Above this shale is a series of porous Tertiary rocks — "grits, conglomerates, gravels, sands, vesicular limestones, and marls" — which fill this synclinal basin, forming the surface of the country, and having a general slope to the east of about ten feet to the mile. The formation designated by Professor Hicks as "Tertiary" in reality includes the Post-Tertiary or Quaternary deposits, or that which might properly be designated as "superficial detritus," since, as already remarked, the Tertiary and Quaternary cannot in this region be distinctly separated from each other.[2] Since the rainfall of a large part of Nebraska is considerable in amount, that of the eastern half of the State being between twenty and thirty inches,[3] it

[1] See *ante*, pp. 117-122 and 138-141.
[2] See *ante*, p. 119.
[3] On a map showing the "normal annual precipitation" in Nebraska, which is contained in a government publication bearing the date of 1890, (Executive Document No. 115, 51st Congress, 1st Session,) and entitled "Climate of Nebraska, particularly in Reference to the Temperature and Rainfall," the isohyetal of twenty inches runs from near the intersection of the 101st meridian with the south boundary of the State, in a nearly

is evident that under the geological conditions here existing, the Tertiary and superficial deposits being as a rule all porous, springs should be common at the junction of the overlying permeable with the underlying impermeable formation. These springs add to the volume of the rivers, "which sometimes become larger as followed downward, independently of the influx of tributaries." This is a matter of common occurrence in all well watered regions, and the greater the thickness of the superficial unconsolidated (and hence permeable) deposits, the more regular will be the flow of the streams and the less rapidly will they be affected by sudden changes in the amount of the precipitation. But, as Professor Hicks remarks, "in other parts of the Great Plains, however, not infrequently the result is precisely opposite; that is, the volume of the stream will be less at the lower point." This also is in regions of small rainfall a matter of common occurrence, many streams disappearing altogether during a part of the year — or sometimes even for several hours of the day at certain seasons of the year — and for considerable distances.

Professor Hicks considers that the rivers of Nebraska are now flowing in valleys "which were cut by older rivers, generally with a depth and breadth far greater than the present valley." These old valleys, he goes on to remark, "were silted up during the Pliocene submergence, which was the latest phase of the Ter-

northerly direction, but bending slightly to the eastward so as to cut the north boundary at its intersection with the 99th meridian. A part of the southeastern corner of Nebraska is comprised between the isohyetals of twenty-eight and thirty-four inches, and a small portion of its southwestern corner has less than sixteen inches of rainfall.

tiary age." This submergence he considers as having been the result of the formation of a "great inland lake," the disappearance of which was a very recent event — "so recent that the present rivers have not had time to restore their valleys to the former depth by washing out the sands, clays, and gravels deposited there." This accumulation of silt, or detrital material, will, he thinks, if sufficient time be given, be mastered by the rivers, which "will push or roll it along the bottom to a new resting place nearer the sea"; for, as he adds, "it requires a very strong volume of water to maintain a perennial current in such a silt-gorged valley. Even the regal strength of the North Platte is insufficient for these arduous conditions. Coming out of the mountains with a flow of over 10,000 cubic feet per second, it is often swallowed up in its own sands between North Platte and Columbus. The same thing happens to the Republican River in certain parts of its course. Many of the small streams entirely disappear after a course of a few miles, never reappearing."

The theories held by Professor Hicks in regard to the nature and epoch of the formation of the older deep and broad valleys in which the present diminished streams are running, and of the ability of these streams to carve out new valleys similar to those of a former age, if sufficient time be allowed, have no scientific basis on which to rest. The present streams do flow in valleys quite out of proportion, as regards dimensions, with the streams themselves. In other words, the volume of the rivers has diminished, while there is no proof that this change has been compensated, to any perceptible degree, by a change of grade in the region which they traverse. But this has nothing to do with the disappearance of any "great inland lake" formerly existing there as a feature of the Pliocene epoch. The diminution, or even entire disappearance, of many lakes, both large and small, and the general decrease in the volume of the rivers, are phenomena not limited to any special region or to any geological period, except that it may be said with truth, that if such events had been taking place during any period of indefinite length, and had also been continued during the present epoch, their effects would be more and more distinctly perceived in proportion as a nearer approach was made to our own times. Observations extended over a large part of the earth's surface demonstrate, beyond all possibility of doubt, that this phenomenon of the diminution of lakes and rivers is not peculiar to Nebraska, nor to the Cordilleran region in general, but that it has manifested itself all over the world, and that it had its beginning, not in Pliocene times, but earlier than that — how much earlier it is impossible to say — and that it is something which is still going on, or, in other words, that it belongs to the present or historic epoch as well as to the past, or to times of which there is no other record than the geological.[1] It is the small precipitation in the region drained by the rivers of Nebraska, the very slight grade of the surface over which these rivers run, and, finally, the fact that there has been, in later geological times, a general diminution in the

[1] See the present writer's "Climatic Changes of Later Geological Times," Chapter II.; also *ante*, pp. 133, 134.

amount of the rainfall in this as well as in other regions, which are the real causes of the condition of things which Professor Hicks describes: this will remain unaltered unless some orographic disturbance should take place by which the grade of the surface should be disturbed, or unless there be some change in the climatic conditions, accompanied by an increase or diminution in the amount of the rainfall, of which last two suggested events the latter is, so far as present evidence goes, the one most likely to happen, although any such climatic change cannot be expected to be rapid, or easily detected by instrumental observations.

Professor Hicks next proceeds to consider the subject of the "underflow," in regard to which so much has been said by other officials of the Irrigation Surveys, and which has already more than once been the subject of comment in the present work. The following quotation will illustrate the opinion held by the author of the report here under consideration with regard to the nature of the underflow: "The streams thus becoming entangled in the silt of their own valleys are indeed lost to view, but they are not really lost, they go to feed the underflow. No physical feature of the Great Plains is more impressive, when once fully realized, than the fact that a mighty invisible river accompanies each visible one. The underflow is vastly broader and deeper than the visible river, and it is always there, while the river in sight may cease to flow. The only point in which the river excels is velocity." In regard to the question what this velocity is, no definite evidence is offered, but it is stated that, in some places in the valley of the Platte, the underflow is so copious that when tapped at the distance of several miles from the channel "it responds to powerful pumps almost as freely as if the supply were drawn from a subterranean lake." The exact locality where this response takes place is, however, not specified, nor has the present writer been able to find in the statistics of the wells of this region any facts substantiating this statement.[1]

From the consideration of the "underflow," Professor Hicks proceeds to that of the "sheet waters," and it is evident that he makes no real distinction between the two; it is only when the "sheet waters" are considered from a theoretical point of view as *flowing*, that they become the "underflow."

The facts in regard to the region under discussion in Professor Hicks's report are simply as follows. The underlying rocks, which are of Cretaceous age, are impervious to water; over these is a covering of Tertiary and Quaternary, it being impossible to make any distinct line of separation between these two formations, and this superficial detrital material varies in thickness from being a "mere skin cover" to a thousand feet; moreover, it is as variable in its lithological character as it is in thickness, since its "texture runs from clays and tolerably compact marls to coarse gravels and conglomerates"; but, on the whole, the gravelly element seems to predominate, since the entire formation is described as being "a great mass of porous materials, forming the surface and filling the old

---

[1] See *ante*, p. 119, where it is stated in regard to the wells of Nebraska and the adjacent States that those yielding a considerable volume of water are *in the immediate vicinity of a river*.

valleys," and this it is in which "the waters are absorbed, hidden, drawn away from the surface out of sight, but not lost." These porous rocks " absorb and occlude " the rainfall, the deficiency of which is not so much the cause of the absence of surface drainage as are the peculiar geological conditions here existing, the consequence of which is that "a porous and uneven surface drinks up the waters that fall from the heavens"; but this is compensated by the fact that "the underflow and sheet waters are copious."

It is not necessary that any more space should here be given to the examination of the underflow question, since no new evidence of importance bearing on this subject is brought forward by Professor Hicks, who himself admits that the data are meagre. He does, however, draw some conclusions from a comparison of the time of the annual rise of the Loup Rivers, which he says is "slight but quite perceptible," and which generally takes place in September, with the seasonal distribution of the rainfall in the region drained by that stream.[1]

In the Loup Valley the annual precipitation is said to average 23.74 inches, but its seasonal distribution is very irregular. During the half-year beginning with October and ending with March the rainfall is less

---

[1] The Loup River system consists essentially of three streams of about the same length, which flow in channels which are nearly parallel with one another, and are from ten to twenty-five miles apart, having a length of from a hundred to a hundred and fifty miles. These streams, which are tributaries of the Platte, are known as the North, Middle, and South Loup Rivers, and they unite about fifty miles above their junction with the main river. Hence this system of parallel streams is sometimes designated as the "Loup River," but more frequently as the "Loup Rivers."

than a quarter of that of the whole year, the maximum being in June, July, and August, from the middle of which last named month the diminution is rapid and pretty regular to the time of the minimum in November. From these data Professor Hicks draws the inference that the rate of movement of the underflow is about one third of a mile per day. This result he obtains by estimating the distance through which the "subterranean waters" flow to be twenty miles, and the time occupied by this movement to be two months "from July to September." It is hardly necessary to point out how very unsatisfactory estimates based on such data must be. The maximum rainfall occurring in midsummer after a long period of almost drought, during which, as we are told, the rivers of the region in most years disappear entirely for months, the line of saturation must necessarily have descended very low in consequence of evaporation from the surface and draining of the porous rock to supply the springs which continue to flow for a considerable part of the year. After the rainfall increases to such an amount, and becomes so continuous, that percolation begins to exceed evaporation, the rocks which have become drained of their moisture must be again filled before the rivers can receive any farther supply of water than that which runs off the surface in the immediate vicinity of their channels. That there should be an interval of a few weeks between the period of maximum rainfall and that of the annual rise of the rivers is what would naturally be expected. That this rise should be gradual and unattended with disastrous freshets is the natural result of the combination of maximum rainfall occurring after a long period of what may almost be called drought, and a soil consisting of a very porous material developed to a very great thickness.

The seasonal distribution of the rainfall of Nebraska is admitted to be highly favorable to agriculture — to that carried on by the aid of irrigation as well as to that unassisted by it. It is acknowledged, however, by Professor Hicks, that practically the only irrigable lands of Nebraska are those lying in the valleys, and being thus adjacent to the rivers and nearly on the same level with them — in short, the river bottoms. Only very exceptionally can the higher lands between the river bottoms be irrigated, and that, so far as known, only by pumping from wells. Indeed it is quite doubtful whether the water of the rivers brought on to the valley lands by means of gravity ditches, will suffice to irrigate the whole area thus situated. An estimate is given of the number of acres occupied by the bottoms of the Platte, which are said to form the largest body of irrigable land in Nebraska. The length of the valley is taken at 441 miles, and the average breadth, not including the channel of the river, at five and a half miles, giving an acreage of one and a half millions. This, however, it is said, is "much beyond the capacity of the Platte to irrigate unless we count upon a very high duty of water." It is admitted that some of the valley lands are the poorest in the country, being both sandy and alkaline, "because the rivers seldom overflow their banks." It is thought, however, that a remedy may be found for this in "artificial flooding" — in other words, by diking the fields and keeping them covered by water during the non-growing season, by which means the alkali will be dissolved out and the sands covered with fertilizing mud for the next crop. How, and at what expense, this might be effected, is not explained. It is admitted, however, that the Platte "actually goes dry some two months almost every year at the very point where I [Professor Hicks] found it sweeping along like a moving sea. Hence it would appear that the changes in the volume of the Platte River, from season to season, are much more considerable than those of the Loup — one of its principal tributaries — for of this the annual rise is said, as has been stated above, to be but small in amount."[1]

A considerable part of Professor Hicks's report is devoted to a detailed description of the Loup Valley, of which a more careful survey was made than of the Platte and of the other large rivers of Nebraska. This was done because the Loup was considered as being "a typical river of the plains," in which it heads, and to which its entire course is confined; hence it naturally exhibits in the highest degree those peculiarities which characterize the drainage of the treeless belt. This valley is also of interest because it lies "in the debatable zone, the subhumid, where the question is forever recurring 'to irrigate, or not to irrigate'; where the rainfall is copious enough to encourage the farmer to plant, and in most seasons fills the land with plenty, but sometimes fails at the critical moment."

The Loup Valley has a well defined watershed on the south and east, but to the north and west the

---

[1] Professor Hicks remarks that "the main Loup is distinguished among the rivers of the treeless belt for the large and constant volume of water which it maintains throughout the year."

"drainage merges gradually into an undrained region of sand hills and lagoons where it is impossible to draw an exact boundary line." Of the whole Loup area, which equals a little over thirteen thousand square miles, about thirty-five per cent is without drainage, the surface being destitute of streams and even of dry channels of streams, but chiefly occupied by lagoons, sand-hills, and valleys of an old drainage system now filled with silt. These topographic forms are such as would naturally be found in a region very nearly level, having a decidedly moderate rainfall, and covered by a considerable but variable thickness of sandy detritus, the result of a long continued erosion and disintegration, in which both atmospheric and pluvial agencies have taken part. From this undrained area streams gather the moisture, at first almost imperceptibly, but after they have pursued their course for a sufficient distance they have gained in strength so that they are able to form regular channels, bordered by low bluffs, and having the ordinary cross-section of the valleys of those Western rivers which flow with varying volume and inconsiderable depth over a region which has a very slight but regular gradient and great uniformity of geological structure. In the higher and drier region the sands are more or less shifted by the wind, the action of which becomes, with the general gradually increasing desiccation of the region, sufficiently marked to give rise to topographical features which, in a country which is so nearly a dead level, may become of comparative importance.

In the valley of the Loup the region of sand-hills and table-lands is said to present unsurmountable obstacles to irrigation, but the bottoms lie near enough to the drainage level to be easily supplied with water by means of short ditches, and one eighth of the whole Loup area is believed to be capable of being irrigated in this way. With the usual sanguine expectations of the officials of the Irrigation Surveys, however, Professor Hicks has large views with regard to the future of what seems to inhabitants of a region more favored than the Loup Valley to have many and very decided disadvantages for settlers. "The occupation of the country," it is said, "and all the operations of agriculture will augment and intensify the excellent combinations of natural conditions in this valley. . . . Deep and frequent tillage of the table lands and hill slopes will secure more immediate and complete absorption and retention of the rainfall. Irrigation in the valleys will spread out the waters and retain them longer, permitting them to escape only by evaporation, which will increase the humidity of the air and promote precipitation, or by slow percolation through the soil and subsoil. Lastly foresting of the sand hills, if this shall ever be happily accomplished by combined and persistent efforts of individuals, or by a liberal policy on the part of the national or State government, will do more than all other artificial operations to ameliorate the climate."

The report of Professor Culver, which follows that of which an analysis has been given in the preceding pages,[1] is chiefly devoted to a recapitulation of the geological conditions of the Dakota Basin, in regard to which some information has already been given in the

[1] For the title of Professor Culver's report, see *ante*, p. 145.

present volume.¹ This basin consists of a low broad synclinal, of which the eastern edge is in the eastern part of the Dakotas, and the western near the foothills of the Rocky Mountains. The water-bearing formation of the Dakota Basin is the Dakota sandstone, which is exposed along the Big Sioux River in South Dakota, and farther south dips gently to the northwest, while the surface rises in the same direction. In the valleys of the Missouri, Big Sioux, James, and Vermilion the covering of this sandstone is so thin that the water escapes upward, giving rise to springs, which extend from Chamberlain, on the Missouri, to Sioux City, in Iowa, this causing, as is thought, a diminution in the pressure in the southeastern part of the basin. The eastern border of the Dakota Basin in South Dakota follows approximately the divide between the Big Sioux and James Rivers; farther north, in North Dakota, it is not clearly defined. Neither the Artesian wells of the Red River Valley nor the shallow wells of Southeastern South Dakota are connected with the Dakota Artesian basin. The region where the Dakota sandstone receives its supply of water is along the base of the Rocky Mountains, where this formation comes to the surface, or is so thinly covered that the rainfall finds its way into it. It has not yet been proved that the water from this formation will rise to the surface in the more elevated parts of the basin, the pressure in the best wells in the James Valley not being sufficient to cause it to reach an elevation greater than 2,000 feet above the sea level.²

[1] See *ante*, pp. 113, 114, 142.
[2] The hypsometric maps of this region are not sufficiently detailed to make it possible to fix with any approach to accuracy the limits of

In the southeastern part of the Dakota Basin the water-bearing sandstone lies directly on the Archæan or Azoic series; to the north and west the wells have rarely been drilled to a sufficient depth to prove the nature of the underlying rock. The uniformity of the stratification of the Cretaceous series in the Upper Missouri region is a very marked feature of its geology, the formation being not only continuous and developed with similar characters over a very wide area, but being also unbroken by faults, and only in the extreme western part of the area disturbed by the intrusion of volcanic masses, the effect of which on the water conditions is only local. This feature of the geology is considered as being highly favorable to Artesian development, removing much of the uncertainty which exists in many regions where this source of water-supply is sought to be introduced.

In regard to the quantity and quality of the water obtained in the Dakota Basin, the information given in Professor Culver's report is by no means as satisfactory as could be wished. As to quantity, the most satisfactory evidence is said to be that furnished by the wells themselves. The fact that many of these have been flowing for five years "points to an abundant supply, but does not prove it."

In concluding his report Professor Culver adds some remarks in regard to the geology and water condition

the Dakota Basin. On Mr. Gannett's latest map the 2,000-foot hypsometric curve follows pretty closely the right bank of the Missouri, and at no great distance from it, through South Dakota, in which State it does not appear on the eastern side of the river; but a considerable part of North Dakota, including all the area west of the Missouri, and a broad belt to the east of that river in the northern half of the State, lies above that curve.

of the Black Hills, of which a hasty reconnaissance was made. The central or axial area of this outlier of the Rocky Mountains consists of ancient schists (Archæan or Azoic), extending for a length of about sixty miles north and south, and having a width of from ten to twenty-five. These rocks have been very extensively eroded, and as a consequence are cut into ridges with prominent elevated peaks, and intersected by valleys, which are wooded in the northern part of the area, and are diversified with park-like openings toward the south. This older axial mass is surrounded by a series of rudely oval concentric valleys representing the various formations which encircle the nucleus, and which are made up of stratified rocks of Palæozoic, Triassic, Jurassic, and Cretaceous age. Next to the central Azoic peaks, the Red Valley (Triassic) and an outer wall of the Dakota sandstone (the lowest member of the Cretaceous) are the most prominent topographical features of the Black Hills. The drainage of this area is almost entirely toward the east, and the streams are all formed by springs which rise at the lower edge of the Azoic nucleus. Most of these sink on reaching the Carboniferous limestone, which forms the upper division of the Palæozoic. Several streams are mentioned which do not now sink, although they formerly did so, and this is believed to be the result of the active mining operations which have been going on for some years in the region above, and which have caused large quantities of sand and mud to be carried down the creeks. The area of the Black Hills region is about 5,000 square miles, and the average rainfall is said to be twenty inches, of which one seventh is supposed to fall on the Dakota sandstone, so that the drainage of this region must "contribute quite largely to the Artesian supply [of those districts in which the water is obtained from this formation (?)]; and the Black Hills in this relation may be considered as an outlier of the Rocky Mountains."

Professor Culver, in closing his report, suggests that there are several districts which need more careful examination, and in which "test wells" are desirable. The region between the James River district and the Missouri River is said to have been only hastily examined, and two wells here would settle the question whether water will rise to the surface or not for a large area. Two test wells are also recommended for South Dakota west of the Missouri, and one for the region lying between the forks of the Cheyenne and the Black Hills. A fourth district needing examination is found in Western North Dakota and Montana, the question here being whether there is a higher water-bearing rock than the Dakota sandstone, in regard to which it is said that "it is not to be expected that flows like those of the James River district will be found, but water sufficient for domestic and stock use may be in the sands of the Laramie."

The question of the adequacy of the supply is said to be "one of prime importance," but to which particular region this remark is specially applicable is not stated. It may, however, be presumed that it relates to the water-supply of the Great Plains in general, or — as perhaps is more probable — to that of the Dakota Artesian Basin, the special subject of Professor Culver's report. A twelve-inch well is mentioned as being in progress of construction at Yankton, in South Dakota, and appended to this statement is the remark "that no basin has yet been found in which a limit to the number of wells it would furnish was not soon reached; the Dakota basin has a limit, and if it is possible to determine approximately what that limit is, no better work can be done than that."

The fourth part of the Final Report here under consideration is comparatively brief, and but a limited amount of space needs here to be devoted to it.[1] Here again we find the subject of the underflow — or, as it is here called, the "underwaters"— of the Great Plains the principal topic discussed. In fact Mr. Gregory the author, with the title of Special Agent, after stating the boundaries[2] of his field of work — which, as he remarks, "contains more than 200,000 square miles and about 130,000,000 acres of territory" — proceeds to explain that "the subject of investigation is the subterranean water resources of the division."

As introductory to this discussion the "surface characteristics" of the region are described, which is said to consist, " in general terms, of a broad, treeless plain"; but this when examined in detail is found to be made up of alternating shallow valleys and low divides, extending from the mountains eastward, with a gradual downward slope in the same direction. This slope on

[1] This document occupies sixty-one pages. For its title and contents see *ante*, p. 123.

[2] These boundaries are, substantially, the thirty-sixth and forty-third parallels of latitude, and the ninety-seventh and one hundred and fourth meridians of longitude. The region thus enclosed embraces nearly all of Nebraska, the western two-thirds of Kansas, the eastern third of Colorado, and a narrow strip along the northern border of the Indian Territory and Texas.

the 100th meridian is about seven feet per mile, but it increases gradually westward, so that on the 104th meridian it is about fifteen feet per mile. As a rule its divides are broad, and the valleys narrow and shallow. The rise from valley to upland is gradual, and the highest portions of the divides are from 200 to 500 feet above the nearest streams or valleys. "Rough country" and sand-hills occur, but constitute only a small portion of the whole area. "Except a small spot, here and there, containing a few square feet or rods, at rare intervals, in river bottoms, there are no swamp lands in the division."[1] The soil of this region is described as being "a tertiary marl, of great average depth and extraordinary fertility, of fine and even texture, and containing few or no bowlders." This marl is said to be "laid down in vast beds forming almost unbroken areas thousands of square miles in extent"; its depth varies from three or four feet to upward of a hundred, but "a depth of forty or fifty feet is not above the average."[2]

The Special Agent next turns his attention to the climate of the region which forms the subject of his report. This he describes as being "equable, sunny, healthful, and invigorating," while the winters are "dry and mild." It is said to be a winter of rare severity when farm-ploughing cannot be done in each month of it, at least as far west as the 102d meridian.

[1] But compare what Professor Hicks says of the swamps on the head-waters of the rivers of the Loup region. See *ante*, pp. 209, 210.

[2] This is the "plains marl" of Professor Hay, a description of which, as given by him, will be found in preceding pages (*ante*, pp. 146-148) This formation is there described as being underlain by the "Tertiary grit," which rock is considered as being of great importance over an extensive area as a source of water-supply.

The only thing needed "to make this region both densely populous and wonderfully rich and productive . . . is a sufficiency of moisture to mature crops."[1]

[1] Mr. Gregory here introduces some remarks in regard to the propriety of the designation of "Great American Desert" by which, he says, this region for decades was known, adding that it had been pronounced by well informed persons to be unfit for the habitation of civilized people; but, he proceeds to remark, "it was afterwards thrown open to settlement as agricultural land and actually settled as such by home-seekers upon the invitation of the General Government. There must have been, therefore, misjudgment on one side or the other." In point of fact, the name "Great American Desert" was originally given to the unexplored region lying beyond the Mississippi without any special designation of its limits. Later, and as early as 1840-45, after some knowledge of this part of the country had been acquired, the use of the word "desert" began to be limited to what we now call the Great Basin, which is frequently spoken of by Fremont in his reports as "the Desert," and sometimes as the "Great Desert Basin." During the past twenty years or more the name Great American Desert has been limited to the tract of country lying south and west of Great Salt Lake which was covered by its waters at the time of their greatest extension. This region is with propriety so named, since it is not only uninhabited but entirely uninhabitable. The meaning of the word "desert" has undergone a change since it was first introduced into the English language. Properly, according to its etymology (*deserere*, to abandon), it does not mean an *uninhabitable* but an *uninhabited* place, or a locality abandoned or deserted, either permanently or temporarily, by its inhabitants. But since the most extensive and best known regions which are very scantily populated are in this condition because of the lack of water, it is natural that the word "desert," in the ordinary acceptation of the term, should have become specialized with the meaning which it has when the Desert of Sahara and the Arabian Desert are spoken of, these being regions very thinly populated, nearly destitute of vegetation, and scantily supplied with water. As bearing on this question the following quotation from Fremont's "Geographical Memoir upon Upper California" (p. 13) may be appended: "Such is the Great Basin, heretofore characterized as a desert, and in some respects meriting that appellation; but already demanding the qualification of great exceptions, and deserving the full examination of a thorough exploration." Areas over which a low temperature, rather than the lack of moisture, is the prime cause of the scanty development of an arboreal vegetation, are rarely designated as "deserts." They are called in North America "barrens," or "barren lands," and in Northern Europe and Asia "tundras." Both barrens and tundras are very thinly inhabited.

Mr. Gregory next proceeds to give some statistics of the rainfall of his district, from which it appears that he considers himself justified in drawing the conclusion "that this region has enough and to spare under average conditions." This subject has already received attention in this volume;[1] but as the form in which he arranges his statistics is different from that adopted by the present writer it will be worth while to give an abstract of Mr. Gregory's results.[2]

The following table, compiled by Mr. Gregory, shows the mean annual precipitation along the various meridians from the 99th to the 104th, as also the amount of rainfall from April to September inclusive, and the percentage of the summer rainfall.

Meridian.	Mean Annual Precipitation.	Rainfall from April 1 to September 1, inclusive.	
	Inches.	Inches.	Percentage.
99th	25.48	18.57	73
100th	21.45	15.33	72
101st	17.85	14.42	81
102d	17.30	12.97	75
103d	16.40	12.61	76
104th	14.85	11.06	73

The average annual precipitation of the whole district is said to be 18.89 inches, of which three fourths fall in the summer, or from April to September, inclusive.

[1] See *ante*, pp. 37, 38.

[2] One important difference between the results presented on a preceding page of this volume and those contained in Mr. Gregory's report is, that the former depend exclusively on observations made at stations during a period of at least ten years, while the latter embrace many localities where observations were continued for only a little more than twelve months.

Here follows a discussion as to the minimum amount of rainfall necessary for the successful pursuit of agriculture, and the opinion of A. W. Greely, Chief Signal Officer, published in 1889, is quoted in support of the idea that the "arid region limit" should be fixed at fifteen inches, and not at twenty, as had been previously done by the Director of the United States Geological Survey; for, as Mr. Greely observes in support of this idea, "the fact that wheat can be grown without irrigation where the annual rainfall is less than twenty inches is evidenced by official statistics from Dakota, which show that wheat is grown by tens of millions of bushels yearly in sections where the rainfall ranges from twenty inches downward. To this statement is added another, quoted from a report made by the same official, to the effect that "regions where the annual rainfall ranges from thirty to fifty inches have been visited by the most serious and protracted droughts," and this is adduced as a reason why the arid region limit should be reduced from twenty to fifteen inches. Furthermore the Chief Signal Officer "does not hesitate to express the opinion that the trans-Mississippi and trans-Missouri rainfall is slightly increasing as a whole, though in certain localities it may be slightly decreasing." [1]

In the report here under examination the subject of the "need of irrigation" is next taken up for consideration, and various statements are made with reference to this matter, having for their object to prove that irrigation is not an absolute necessity in the region

---

[1] Quoted from a report on "Rainfall in Washington, Oregon," etc., p. 15. This matter will receive attention in Appendix B.

under consideration. Various localities are mentioned where "timber-culture experiments" have been carried on without irrigation, and with success, and one is specified near Denver, where also, except for a short time at the very beginning, without irrigation, "there is to-day a magnificent young orchard of bearing fruit trees at the one hundred and fifth meridian, upon the western extreme of the 'Great American Desert,' where the annual average rainfall for a period of eighteen years has been but 14.6 inches."

What might have taken place in the arid and semi-arid region of the United States, if the resources of the region had been developed by settlers *in a manner such as it is only possible that they should have been in a region favored by an abundant precipitation* is thus fancifully depicted by Mr. Gregory, who says: "If it could have been brought about that the whole of this region [the Great Plains] could have been settled in a single season, or two or three, by a class of people each one of whom should have been possessed of the discernment, training, natural aptitude, and knowledge of what he wished to do, which characterize the superintendent of the forestry station referred to, each able and willing to practice the industry and frugality of the Germans of the Thurman Colony, each having the surplus means with which to provide all needful buildings, seeds, plants, and farming tools to emulate the Kentucky settlers in Stevens County, and to enable them to continue work three or four years, if need be, at large expense, before any returns could begin, as in the case of the nursery-men who have grown the unirrigated orchards at Denver, then there can be little doubt that the sudden cessation of prairie fires, the wide-spread planting of groves and orchards and belts of timber as windbreaks, the upturning and thorough cultivation of a large proportion of the surface soil on every habitable quarter section, and the covering of millions of acres of land, theretofore almost as bare as a slate roof, with green, luxuriant, and succulent vegetation would have worked an almost miraculous change; the desert would have blossomed and borne fruit often enough, without the aid of irrigation, to make the Plains as a whole habitable after a fashion." That, however, the wealth and intellect of the country should have been concentrated for years on the task of making a region which was distant, not easily accessible, destitute of timber for fuel or building, and poorly supplied with water, "as a whole habitable after a fashion," was something hardly to be expected. On the contrary, the natural result of these adverse conditions has been entirely different, and what has really happened can best be described in Mr. Gregory's own graphic words: "The semi-arid region has been, and unless proper efforts shall be made to prevent will still be, an absorbent of wealth and energy; a famine-breeding, heart-breaking zone; a mirage to tempt men to ruin; and the question is asked whether it should not be made certainly habitable or settlement there, under ordinary conditions, prevented."

The manner in which the settlement of the semi-arid region could be prevented by the General Government is not indicated by Mr. Gregory, neither is the possibility of such a thing being done even hinted at by him, any further than it is done in the paragraph quoted above. On the contrary, that author proceeds at once to assert that "all of the arable land of the Great Plains may be, and ultimately undoubtedly will be, reclaimed and made habitable": not only, however, does he make this assertion, but he adds that "an exceptionally dense and prosperous population may be supported thereon."

That this extraordinary development of the agricultural capacity of the Great Plains will take place is a theory said to be based on three facts: 1st, the great retentiveness of moisture by the marly soil of that region; 2d, the large proportion of the annual rainfall which occurs during the growing season, or from the beginning of May to the end of August; 3d, the existence of "stores of accessible water underlying and overflowing the entire Plains region." The means by which the semi-arid lands may be reclaimed are classified as follows: "1st, the recovery of underground water by gravity, by mechanical means, and by Artesian wells; 2d, the storage and conservation of other waters; this involves not only the construction of reservoirs, but the protection and extension of forests; 3d, the greatest economy and care in the use of the water supplies." The methods suggested by means of which this economy may be put in practice are the gradual saturation of the soil, experience in the application of water to the soil, and the adoption of the most highly economical methods of its use, the growing of crops best adapted to the climate, and largely increased thoroughness of cultivation. The prevention of prairie fires is looked upon, in this connection, as a most important element in the work of reclamation, but no method is suggested by which this can be accomplished. It is admitted that "working people with families to support and educate — and others with accumulations of debt instead of surplus property — are not prepared to await for years the changes which are necessary to convert desert lands into farms."

Finally, the Special Agent falls back on the opinion so generally held by the settlers on the Plains, that it is the duty of the General Government to interfere in their behalf, and the following statement to that effect is made: "The opinion prevails among the common people throughout the division that the Government should cause a few practical demonstrations of the existence, availability, and economical conservation of water supplies, so that private capital may be induced to invest in the work of development to the fullest extent and upon an assured footing. This opinion is founded upon the fact that not only have the settlers upon such lands paid for the same, into the United States Treasury, very large sums of money — this alone constituting, as they believe, a sufficient reason for the active intervention of the Government in matters of irrigation development for their benefit — but, further, such action upon the part of the General Government as would take the lead in the provision of general systems of irrigation works would confirm to the National Government, fully and unquestionably, the right to make such regulations for their use as will inure most largely to the benefit of the people. And such are the intermingling, interdependent interests of individuals, communities, and States in the general development of the means of irrigation upon the Great

Plains, that the regulation of such works and the settlement of the grave questions arising from the use of the same may proceed, it is believed, only from the National Government; that there is no other possible source of such regulation."

After this somewhat introductory matter, Mr. Gregory proceeds to take up in some detail the subjects of Artesian wells and the underflow in his district. It is candidly admitted, at the outset, that Artesian wells, "must, in the nature of things, remain an insignificant factor in the problem of arid land reclamation so far as concerns this division." Various small Artesian areas are enumerated, one of which (in Meade County, Kansas[1]) irrigates at present about 1,200 acres of land; another (in Stevens County, Kansas), will "probably be developed"; and seven more in the same State[2] have "a flow too weak to render them of appreciable value for irrigation." To this enumeration of actual results is added the statement that "there is, at present, nothing to indicate that the supply of water from such sources, considering the cost of procuring the same, will be of appreciable value to the general irrigation of the lands of the district.[3]

In regard to a subject which has already more than once been brought up in the present volume for discussion — the underflow, namely — Mr. Gregory has much to say, and with the consideration of this phenomenon his report is chiefly occupied. "Since the begin-

---

[1] See *ante*, p. 116.

[2] See *ante*, pp. 154, 155.

[3] Yet a few pages earlier in this report Artesian wells are specified as one of the important means by which the semi-arid lands are to be reclaimed.

ning of settlement of the Plains," it is said, "people have been familiar with the fact that, throughout the whole region, excepting in isolated cases and in certain small areas, wells obtain their supply from what is popularly known as 'sheet water,' and that this has proven a copious and inexhaustible supply." Two diagrams are furnished illustrating the mode of occurrences of this "sheet water"; in one it is represented as saturating sand or gravel, or both, which occupies large depressions scooped out in the underlying impervious strata, these sand-filled cavities having little or no apparent communication with one another; the other diagram shows the water-bearing strata as forming a continuous mass underlain by impervious rocks and overlain by soil, and this latter condition is thought to obtain "at least locally," because "all the larger streams and most of the small ones traversing the Plains from west to east flow over beds of water-bearing grit, ranging from a few feet to hundreds of feet in depth, and of unknown lateral extent." That there must be a current throughout large portions of these same beds is said "to be evident upon the most cursory examination of the facts." In contradiction to what has been asserted by other irrigation officials in regard to the difficulty of establishing the fact of the existence of such a current, and especially of determining its rate of flow,[1] Mr. Gregory maintains that "in some cases the flow of the water may be plainly seen, while in others the existence of a current is indicated only by the fact that bits of wood, paper, straw, etc., blown into the wells, gather closely against

[1] See *ante*, pp. 140, 141.

the eastern wall in the course of a few hours." Various other statements are made, based on information obtained from residents of Kansas and Nebraska, in regard to the ease with which artificial ponds can be formed "by scraping away the surface soil, and enough of the underlying sand to make basins for the sub-water." No less than thirty citizens of the semi-arid region furnish statements, the general character of which may be inferred from the perusal of one of them, which is here given in full, and which reads as follows: "We are located on an ocean of water, which can easily be made to flow to the surface perpetually in sufficient quantities to flood the whole country at any and all times." This is from C. H. Longstreth, of Lakin, Kearney County, Kansas. In addition to this testimony that of twelve other residents of Kansas and Nebraska is furnished, to the effect that, when water is struck in the wells of this region, it rises to a considerable height above the bottom of the bore-hole.

More remarkable still is the statement by Mr. Gregory that there are "known to be many and large subterranean streams throughout the region of country to the southeastward, even to the Atlantic coast, and interesting stories are told of immense fresh water springs off the South Atlantic coast and in the Gulf of Mexico, which send up from beneath such floods of water that it may be dipped up fresh and drinkable from the midst of the sea." In corroboration of this statement a letter is inserted from the Superintendent of the United States Coast Survey from which it appears that there is a spring "actually furnishing fresh water, about three miles off the coast abreast of St. Augustine," and that there are rumors of a similar spring near the mouth of the Mississippi River, "but our surveying parties have never happened to find it." The connection of a submarine spring of fresh water near the Atlantic coast, entirely to the east of the Gulf of Mexico, with the drainage of the Rocky Mountains, as "evidence of the existence of great stores of subterranean waters in the region of the Great Plains," as is done by Mr. Gregory farther on in his report seems to imply the possession on his part of an extremely vivid imagination. That, in spite of the denial by the Coast Survey authorities of there being any proof of the existence of such springs off the Gulf Coast, they should also be used in a similar way to support the theory of the underflow in its most exaggerated and extravagant form, is a fact in regard to which comment is unnecessary. Only Mr. Catlin has gone one step farther in the same direction, and utilized this subterranean current for the formation of the Gulf Stream.[1]

Among the various methods for utilizing the "sheet waters" of the Plains, that depending on the use of mechanical means (hoisting machinery driven by steam, wind, or horse power) needs no explanation; the method "by force of gravity," to use the term employed by Mr. Gregory, is somewhat peculiar, and is worthy of notice.

This "recovery of under water by gravity" is said to be "up to the present time that which is attracting attention and to which experimentation has been

[1] See, for Mr. Catlin's theory of the origin of the Gulf Stream, *ante*, p. 110; and for Professor Hay's remarks on the exaggerated ideas of the underflow current in the arid region, *ante*, pp. 151-153.

confined." It is called by Mr. Gregory "the fountain method";[1] and is said to consist "of simply drifting from the surface of the ground into the water-bearing strata by means of an open-cut or 'fountain,' having a less rate of inclination than has the surface of the ground, and of the water-bearing stratum penetrated." This method of securing water from the underflow is said to be under test in a number of places. Dodge City, Kansas, on the Arkansas River, is mentioned as being the first place where this method of obtaining water was tried, and the main canal served by this fountain is thirty-five miles long, carrying about one hundred cubic feet per second, a quantity considered sufficient to irrigate 15,000 acres. On the opposite side of the river is the so-called Eureka Canal system, which has a length of ninety-six miles and has cost about $2,000,000. The "fountain" to supply this canal was, at the time Mr. Gregory's report was made, in process of construction, a cutting twenty feet wide, 500 feet long, and eighty feet deep having been made, from which water was to be pumped into the canal by centrifugal pumps.

It does not appear that the construction of these sub-canals has been attempted anywhere except in the immediate vicinity of a considerable river, with the course of which they are parallel, the object seeming to be to obtain a permanent flow of water from the saturated sand and gravel even when the river bed itself is entirely dry owing to the greater evaporation

---

[1] To a description of this method in Mr. Gregory's report the following note is appended: "The word 'fountain' was adopted and is used by Mr. Gregory; the 'investigation' decided on the word 'sub-canals,' and has used it everywhere else in the reports."

THE FOUNTAIN METHOD.

of the shallow stream when not concentrated in a deep channel.[1]

Several cities are said by Mr. Gregory to pursue essentially the same plan in securing their water supply, "but generally in such cases, the open fountain is replaced by sub-canal or pipe line piercing the under water. Denver, Colorado, and Cheyenne, Wyoming, have systems of this sort. Such works are necessarily expensive and could rarely be profitably employed for irrigation purposes."[2]

It has been generally held by climatologists and others, that water raised from below and spread out

---

[1] Thus, in a statement by the engineer of a system of canals belonging to the Southwestern Irrigating Company, having its headquarters at Garden City, Kansas, it is mentioned that when this work was begun the Arkansas River was dry. At the highest stage of water in the river, it was from seven to nine feet higher than the water in the ditch for a period of two months, during which time the latter increased in flow about one third, as would naturally be expected since the ditch and river ran parallel with each other for a distance of 1,000 feet, and were only one hundred feet apart. Yet the engineer considers this a proof that the water in the ditch is substantially obtained from the underflow. The method of obtaining water for city use by excavating filter chambers in the gravelly bed of a river not far distant from the river itself is not uncommon in the Eastern States, but this seepage has never there been called an "underflow," nor considered part of a great sheet of water running from the crest of the Rocky Mountains to the Atlantic Ocean.

[2] This method of water-supply is somewhat like one extensively employed in Persia. In that country, which so much resembles the American Great Basin in topographical character and climate, subterranean canals are cut often for considerable distances (Elphinstone speaks of one thirty-six miles in length) in the limestone gravels. These conduits are often at great depths beneath the surface, and are reached by large wells, down which a descent is made by steps. The skill with which by this method water is brought from the mountains in such a way as to insure a minimum of evaporation is indeed wonderful, and has been the object of comment on the part of travellers and historians from Polybius down to the most modern times. These subterranean canals or conduits are called by the Persians *Kanáts* or *Konáts*.

upon the surface for irrigational purposes was in this manner brought under favorable conditions for rapid evaporation, and that consequently a large part of it would be lost; hence, as Mr. Gregory remarks, there has been some apprehension expressed by people in the lower part of the Arkansas and Platte valleys "that the use of the underflow for irrigation in the regions west of them may deplete their supply of water for domestic use." This fear, the Special Agent thinks, is groundless. On the contrary, "the widest possible utilization of the underflow, gradually brought about, will largely add to the subterranean waters instead of exhausting them." How this reversal of the conditions prevailing in other parts of the world is to be effected for the benefit of the people of the Plains is not mentioned; it is simply stated as a fact, that "a fountain may produce water sufficient to irrigate 50,000 acres of land, which may be utilized within a distance of fifty miles, and the water, spread out over the ground and percolating through the soil back into the underflow, be ready for use upon the next fifty-mile stretch below." It is admitted, however, that there will be losses of the water "by evaporation, saturation, and diversion, but these have their compensations." Of what nature these compensations are, it is said, "there is not now time to discuss." All the practical information given in regard to these points is comprised in the statement that the elements entering into the development and constant renewal of such water supplies are: "the recovery of phreatic waters, storage, the growth of trees and other vegetation, irrigation, and the gradual saturation of the soil."

Furthermore, this recovery of the sub-waters, accomplished "by gravity through the 'fountain method,' by sunk dams, by sub-canals, and by driving or laying perforated or other permeable pipes and conduits; by pumping and hoisting by steam, wind, and water power, the last eventually employing electricity as an important auxiliary" will have certain results which are enumerated, and among which the following may be considered as being the most surprising: "Very great power for use in manufacturing, etc., may be developed"; the now bare and arid plains may be made to enter largely into the growth of timber and the production of fish; and, finally, "the Great Plains region developed and utilized to the fullest extent may become in an economic sense, as well as geographically, the centre and heart of the nation, such breadth and depth of fertile soil supplied with water for irrigation being a steadfast safeguard against famine; and it will be, or can be made, a region impenetrable by any foreign foe and capable of sustaining the entire nation throughout the duration of any probable foreign war."[1]

A publication of the United States census of 1890, bearing the date of September 9, 1892, and edited by F. H. Newell, has come to hand since the preceding pages were written, and, although it gives statistics for no later period than that embraced within the year ending May 31, 1890, it really contains the latest accessible general information in regard to the actual results of irrigation for the country at large, — that is for that part of the country in which irrigation is

---

[1] See farther on (pp. 242-244) for the latest opinions of the officials of the U. S. Geological Survey in regard to the importance of the underflow.

employed in agriculture to an important extent, and considered a matter of State or national importance.[1]

In this Bulletin it is said that there were irrigated in the Census Year ending May 31, 1890, within the arid and subhumid region on the western half of the United States 3,631,381 acres, or 5,674.03 square miles, which is approximately four tenths of one per cent of the total land area west of the 100th meridian. Of this irrigated area 61.31 per cent was devoted to the raising of various kinds of forage. The following table gives the more important items of the irrigation business for each State and Territory in which this was carried on, as also for the States "lying largely within the subhumid region to the east," the statistics for these being grouped under the designation of "subhumid region."

States and Territories.	Area Irrigated.		Percentage Character of Irrigated Crops.	
	Acres.	Per cent of entire Land Surface.	Forage.	Cereals.
Arizona	65,821	0.09	65.82	34.18
California	1,004,233	1.01	47.22	52.78
Colorado	890,735	1.84	70.25	29.75
Idaho	217,005	0.40	70.97	29.03
Montana	350,582	0.38	78.61	21.39
Nevada	224,403	0.32	93.32	6.68
New Mexico	91,745	0.12	36.78	63.22
Oregon	177,944	0.39	69.99	30.01
Utah	263,473	0.50	56.35	43.65
Washington	48,799	0.23	57.99	42.01
Wyoming	229,676	0.37	91.73	8.27
Subhumid Region	66,965			

[1] This is called an "Extra Census Bulletin, No. 23," and, although bearing the date of September 9, 1892, it appears not to have been given to the public much, if any, before the end of 1893. The statistical information

In discussing the attempts of the General Government to throw light on the irrigation problem in the United States, it was mentioned in previous pages that, with this end in view, various appropriations had been made by Congress, the expenditure of which was intrusted to the Geological Survey.[1] Three reports of this department of the Irrigation Survey are there enumerated, and a synopsis given of their contents, and from this an idea can be had of what had been accomplished in this work up to that time. Since those pages were in type, a fourth report of this survey has been received, and it will be next in order to state what additions have been made in this volume to that which had been previously published,[2] this being, so far as known to the present writer, the latest official publication relating to the subject of irrigation in the United States.

The report here to be examined consists of three parts: the first of these, by F. H. Newell, is entitled

embodied in this Bulletin appears to be essentially the same as that which is contained in the House Executive Document No. 1, Part 5, 52d Congress, 2d Session, 1892, which also will form a part of the Thirteenth Annual Report of the U. S. Geological Survey, and having the sub-title "Water Supply for Irrigation," also by Mr. F. H. Newell.

[1] See *ante*, pp. 29–31.

[2] This *fourth* of the series of Irrigation Reports issued by the United States Geological Survey is contained in the "Report of the Secretary of the Interior, communicated to the two Houses of Congress at the Beginning of the Second Session of the Fifty-second Congress," of which it forms Volume IV. Part 3, bearing the date of 1892. Following the precedent already set in this matter, this report will, it is supposed, form Part II. of the Thirteenth Annual Report of the U. S. Geological Survey. The volume of the report of the Secretary of the Interior was obtained by purchase at Washington in April of the current year. The *Twelfth* Annual Report of the U. S. Geological Survey was received at the Museum of Comparative Zoölogy about the same time.

"Water Supply for Irrigation"; the second, by Herbert M. Wilson, is devoted to "American Irrigation Engineering," and to the "Engineering Results of Irrigation Survey"; the third, by A. H. Thompson, to the "Construction of Topographic Maps, and the Selection and Survey of Reservoir Sites in the Hydrographic Basin of the Arkansas River," and "Location and Survey of Reservoir Sites during the fiscal year ending June 30, 1892."

Mr. Newell has already been mentioned as being the author of "Extra Census Bulletin, No. 23," which relates to Agriculture and Irrigation, and brief extracts from the document have been given. In the present report, some general remarks on various subjects connected with irrigation and water-supply form an introduction to a more detailed description, from the hydrographic and irrigational point of view, of the basins of the Missouri, Yellowstone, and Platte rivers. At the outset the same statement is made which appears in the Extra Census Bulletin, namely, that the area on which crops were raised by irrigation, during the year ending May 31, 1890, was 5,674.03 square miles, this being approximately four tenths of one per cent of the total land surface of the United States west of the 100th meridian. "In other words, for every acre from which crops were obtained by irrigation there were nearly 250 acres of land most of which was not utilized in any way except for pasturage." The area of land surface west of the 100th meridian, not including thirty-six counties of western Oregon and Washington, is given as being 1,371,960 square miles, and this is divided with reference to the amount of moisture received or the water supply available, as shown principally by the character of the vegetation, as follows:—

	Square Miles.	Per Cent.
Desert	100,000	7.3
Pasture	961,960	70.1
Firewood	180,000	13.1
Timber	130,000	9.5

The term "desert land" is defined by saying that "it is that within which the water supply is so small that the cattle cannot obtain sufficient for drinking purposes, and the vegetation is too scanty to be of value for pasturage." It hardly needs to be suggested that, where water cannot be obtained even for drinking purposes, there vegetation must necessarily be scanty; and that, however luxuriant it might be, it would be of no use. The land designated as "firewood" is mainly that fringing the streams; and that classed as "timber" includes the forested areas upon the high mountains. A large part of this "timber" has been burned over at different times, so that much of its original value has been lost; while but a very small part of it would in its natural condition bear any comparison, as to value, with the timber lands of the well watered part of the country, most of it being soft wood, and the individual trees usually quite small, and very rarely large. The arboreal vegetation along the streams is mostly wood of a very inferior character, and only scantily covering the soil.[1] As most of the

[1] For a somewhat detailed description of the nature and distribution of the forests over the area included between the two heavily timbered regions of the country — the Appalachian and the Pacific Coast — see the present writer's "United States," etc., pp. 201-213.

area coming under the designation of "firewood" is too low and sandy, and too much exposed to be swept by freshets, and as a large part of the timber land is too rough and rocky for cultivation, it is evident that the irrigated and irrigable lands are mainly included within those divisions which in their natural state are classed as "desert" and "pasture," any sharply drawn distinction between these two classes of land being manifestly impossible.

The proportion of the desert or pasture land which can be brought under irrigation in the future is next discussed by Mr. Newell in the report under consideration, and it is remarked that "it is obvious at the outset, that this proportion must be small, probably under three per cent, but its exact amount can be determined only when the available waters of the region have been accurately measured."

The method in which Mr. Newell endeavors to arrive at an approximate idea of this amount, which by no possibility could be *exactly* determined, is not easily explained, and is in absolute conflict with the views which in the preceding pages have been shown to be held by most of the officials of the Irrigation Surveys. The greater part of the available water supply is said by him to come from the high mountains with precipitous slopes, this including the greater part of the areas covered by timber and firewood, while from the remaining land, namely, the pasture and the desert, there is very little water available for irrigation, "for although there is a large amount of water falling on these tracts, yet the conditions are such that streams valuable to agriculture are seldom formed, for the greater part of the moisture sinks into the ground, and is subsequently lost by evaporation, or, when coming in heavy showers, flows off in the streams whose beds are nearly or quite dry for the rest of the year, and thus is plentiful only at times when there is no need of irrigation."

The total area considered, in accordance with these views, as furnishing water available for irrigation, is said to have been ascertained to be 360,000 square miles, and on this the average amount of water, taking one year with another, is said to be seldom greater than one second-foot per square mile. This figure was obtained by determining the average run-off of twenty-three streams, said to be "well distributed through the mountainous area of the arid region," and on that account "fairly representative of the discharge from the higher mountains of the West." This gives 360,000 second-feet as the whole amount of water available for irrigational purposes in the arid region, and it is said that the area which can be irrigated by it "can be approximately ascertained by assuming a standard duty of water." What may fairly be taken as a standard duty is, however, not stated: it is simply suggested that, if one second-foot will irrigate one hundred acres, the total irrigable area will be about 36,000,000 acres, or about ten times that on which crops were raised by irrigation, in the census year, and if the duty of one second-foot be taken as 150 acres "the area irrigable will be 54,000,000 acres, and so on, according to the duty of water assumed." These computations do not appear to throw any light on the main question of how large a portion of the arid region of the country can really be irrigated.

The matter is an exceedingly complicated one, and it is doubtful whether it can ever be ascertained in any other way than by actual experiment.

The subject of the fluctuation of rivers and lakes comes up next for discussion, and here again the uncertainties are great, and it is candidly admitted that "the quantity of water flowing in a river is the resultant of so many variables, that it is impossible to predict with any degree of certainty what will be the amount flowing in the stream during the next crop season." Two classes of fluctuations in rivers and lakes are briefly considered by Mr. Newell. The first is the periodic or seasonal oscillation, which, in the case of a river, depends mainly on the climate, and secondarily on the topography of the region through which the river runs: in the case of a lake, especially if it be one of large size, these seasonal oscillations are in general much less strongly marked than they are in rivers, and in very large lakes are almost or quite imperceptible. Hence, a comparison of the periodic oscillations of lakes and rivers such as that furnished by Mr. Newell is of no value, since we have here results given for lakes of closed basins as well as those having free drainage, and for rivers differing from one another as far as possible in reference both to the climate and topography of the region which they drain. Thus, in the diagram furnished, Great Salt Lake and Lake Champlain, and the Missouri and the Savannah rivers, figure together.

Much more important from the point of view of both the engineer and the irrigator, as well as that of the climatologist, are the non-periodic oscillations both of lakes and rivers, but especially of the former, since these can be much more easily and satisfactorily registered and studied than those of the latter. Some interesting facts selected from various sources, and bearing on this question, are brought together by Mr. Newell, but the data at present available do not appear to furnish a satisfactory basis for any conclusions which would be of value as helping to solve the irrigational problem. A diagram showing the discharge in second-feet of the Cache la Poudre and Arkansas rivers for several consecutive years ending in 1891, and the height of Great Salt Lake from 1876 to 1891 and of Utah Lake from 1884 to 1891, is said to indicate that, "taking the country as a whole, there was an extraordinary amount of precipitation during 1884." To this is added the statement, that "about this time the great increase in rainfall was noticed and popularly attributed to the effects of cultivation and to other causes under the control of man. That these fluctuations are widespread, and wholly remote from human influence even in the slightest degree hardly needs discussion at present."[1]

[1] The subject of the extent and causes of the secular changes in the areas of lakes and the volume of the rivers of the globe is one which has excited much attention, and which has been investigated more or less thoroughly by various climatologists during the past few years. An elaborate discussion of the climatic fluctuations (Klimaschwankungen) which have taken place since the year 1700 was published by Professor Eduard Brückner, of the University of Bern, in 1890, and a reference is made to this work by Mr. Newell, who does not, however, give any of Professor Brückner's results, or draw from them any general conclusions. The present writer has also devoted much time to an investigation somewhat similar in character to that of the Professor of Geography at Bern (see *ante*, pp. 122, 132, and 202, for the title of a work published by him on this subject, and references to its contents). Professor Brückner's conclusions

Again we are told by Mr. Newell, in connection with his discussion of this subject that "the principal fact taught by the examination of the fluctuations of the rivers and lakes of not only the arid regions, but of the United States as a whole, is that these are due to climatic forces, not only continental, but even world-wide in extent.... These matters cannot be regulated or affected, except perhaps in a very slight degree, by any action on the part of mankind. There is an idea widely current that the removal of the forest cover at the head waters of a stream acts injuriously in many ways and causes greater fluctuations in the quantity discharged, especially in times of flood. This is a matter, however, exceedingly difficult to prove on account of this enormous variation in volume which takes place in every stream, whether in a forested country or not, the fluctuation due to climatic changes being enormously greater than that which can be attributed in any way to the result of forest destruction."

The subject of the underflow, so often mentioned in the present volume, is discussed by Mr. Newell under the heading of "Subsurface Waters." The statistics of

may be briefly summed up in his own words (translated from the German) as follows: "We have enumerated since the year 1020 twenty-five complete oscillations, and computed from these a mean duration of 34.8 ± 0.7 years. In the last two centuries the years 1700, 1740, 1780, 1815, 1850, and 1880 appear as centres of cold and moist periods, and 1720, 1760, 1795, 1830, and 1860 as centres of warm and dry periods." How little these results apply to the secular changes of climate which have taken place in this country will be made evident by a study of the curves of secular oscillations, and of the other data presented in the work here cited. The present writer's investigations have led him to conclusions very different from those of Professor Brückner, as may be inferred from what has been said in regard to this subject in the present volume.

Artesian wells given by him in the report here under discussion are essentially the same as those already abstracted from the Census Bulletin No. 193, issued June 11, 1892.[1] Only on 1.43 per cent of the total area irrigated in the United States during the census year was the water used obtained from Artesian wells. To this statement is added the remark, that "no statistics have been obtained concerning the ordinary wells from which water is pumped or drawn by various means, but there is found in nearly every locality water saturating porous rocks near the surface in all places except on desert areas. On the Great Plains, for example, in Western Nebraska and Kansas, it is sometimes necessary to go to depths of from 100 to 300 feet or more before water-bearing strata are reached, but throughout the arid region as a rule wells are successfully dug to a less depth."[2] The theory of an underflow, as upheld by various officials whose opinions have been set forth and criticised in the preceding pages of the present volume, meets with no favor on the part of Mr. Newell, who remarks as follows in regard to this matter: "The widespread occurrence of water in pervious layers of the earth's crust, and sometimes in such quantities as to appear almost inexhaustible, has given rise to the notion that it flows in great channels very much as do the rivers of the surface, but covered from sight by rocks and soils. There are a few instances where underground watercourses actually occur, but these are extremely rare and are extraordinary in their nature, being found only in the great limestone deposits or among the lava flows of recently extinct

[1] See *ante*, p. 91. [2] See *ante*, pp. 117–121, 145–153.

volcanic regions." In the majority of cases the subsurface water is said to be "merely moisture saturating the rocks," but the behavior of this water is admitted to be "still a matter of inquiry, and is not clearly understood."

That this "subsurface water" is a matter of importance over a very extensive region, as furnishing the only means of obtaining a more or less permanent and satisfactory water-supply, cannot be denied. All that part of the Great Plains not in the immediate vicinity of a river must remain dependent on water obtained from wells sunk to the water-bearing rock; but this matter, in regard to which so much has been said by most of the irrigation officials, is passed over by Mr. Newell almost in silence. A "leading question" in regard to the subsurface waters is admitted to be: Are they stationary, or do they flow freely from place to place? To this no more definite answer is given than that "it is probable that to a certain degree both these conditions are found in nature." In short, it is admitted that we are here confronted by a problem of which a satisfactory solution cannot be given, only experience in each locality can determine the rate with which the moisture beneath the surface will move to take the place of that removed by the stroke of the pump. This will depend on the nature of the rock in the immediate vicinity and for some distance away, and on the extent and manner in which its homogeneity is interrupted by bars of clay, faults filled with that or some other impervious material, and on a variety of similar conditions of which nothing definite can be known until after an actual trial has been made by boring or well-sinking. Furthermore, there is another all-important question: How much of the moisture drawn from a great depth beneath the surface will be replaced by water derived from the rainfall of the present, and how much of it is that which has been stored up in the depths during a former period of more copious precipitation than that which now prevails in the arid and semi-arid regions, and will therefore not be replaced after it has once been raised to the surface and become exposed to evaporation?[1] In regard to this important point Mr. Newell is silent.

As respects the "fountain method" of obtaining water, considered by Mr. Gregory to be of so much importance, and of the nature and application of which some details have been furnished in the preceding pages,[2] Mr. Newell is very outspoken. The following quotation will sufficiently set forth his opinions in reference both to the underflow and the method of making it available by sub-canals or "fountains": "The somewhat misleading and indefinite term 'underflow' has been applied to these waters [the subsurface or underground waters], and many persons awakening for the first time to a realization of their presence have received exaggerated impressions, or have magnified the importance of phenomena previously known to engineers and geologists. Extravagant reports have been made as to the results of rude experiments, and many persons have been induced to believe that it was practicable to irrigate large portions of the subhumid

---

[1] See, in regard to this point, *ante*, pp. 120–122.
[2] See *ante*, pp. 227–229.

region by means of the ground waters conducted to the surface of the gently sloping plains through long tunnels or open channels. Acting on this belief, thousands or even hundreds of thousands of dollars were expended, mainly in the years 1890 and 1891, in the construction of such projects, principally along or in the valleys of the Platte and Arkansas rivers. So far as can be ascertained by examination and measurement, none of these projects can be said to be successful, although in a number of cases small quantities of water are obtained from the long deep channels which penetrate the pervious beds of sand and gravel. . . . The projectors of these irrigating schemes often failed to appreciate not only the fact that ground waters must in their very nature move slowly, but also that even in comparatively humid countries large volumes of water are necessary to conduct irrigation on an extended scale."

The following figures are given by Mr. Newell, under the head of "Cost and Value of Water Supply." The average first cost of water for irrigation throughout Western United States is at the rate of $8.15 per acre, while its value, wherever the rights can be transferred without the land, is $26. Applying these figures to the total acreage, as ascertained by the last census, the total cost of irrigating the lands from which crops were obtained in 1889 was $29,611,000, and the total value of the water rights $94,412,000, the increase of value being $64,801,000, or 218.84 per cent of the investment. The average annual expense of maintaining the water supply was $1.07 per acre, or an aggregate of $3,794,000, this being the amount expended in keeping the canals and ditches in repair and free from sediment. The estimated first cost of lands from which crops were obtained in 1889 was $77,490,000, and their present value, including improvements, $296,850,000, showing an increased value of $219,360,000, or 233.08 per cent of the investment in the land, not taking into consideration the water. The average value of the crops raised was $14.80 per acre, or a total of $53,057,000. These figures have been introduced to exhibit the cost and value of irrigation in the arid regions. The value of the unutilized water supply can scarcely be estimated until more accurate information is obtained concerning the total amount of water and the acreage that it can be made to cover. By making certain assumptions, however, a rough estimate can be arrived at.

Taking the average first cost of water at $8.15 per acre, and its present value at $26 per acre, the difference, $17.85, may be assumed as the value of the water as it flows in the stream. If one cubic foot per second will water one hundred acres, then the value of one second-foot is $1,785. As previously stated,[1] the total quantity of water probably available is 360,000 second-feet, and the total value of this water would thus be $642,000,000. These figures, as Mr. Newell remarks, "have no claim to accuracy, but merely indicate that, calculated on the most conservative basis, the water supply of the arid country must be ranked among the most important of its undeveloped mineral resources." It is hardly necessary to point out, in addition to what has been already said on this subject, how many sources of error there are in these computations. One of the

[1] See *ante*, p. 237.

most important ones is this: that the data employed must have been almost exclusively obtained from the statements of parties interested to magnify the success of their operations, and especially to place the value of both irrigated land and crops at as high a figure as possible. The estimate which Mr. Newell makes of the total quantity of water probably available for irrigation seems to the present writer not to have any really sound basis of fact on which to rest. Indeed, the only entirely reliable statistics which can ever be obtained which will — to a certain extent at least — throw light on the real success of the irrigational undertakings in the arid and semi-arid regions will be their actual population and products as shown by the various censuses of the United States, — or of the individual States, if such should ever be made.

The remainder of Mr. Newell's report is devoted to a discussion of the principal drainage basins of the insufficently watered portions of the country. The Missouri, Yellowstone, and Platte River basins are taken up in order, and various items of information concerning them are given, especially such as bear more particularly on the irrigation business. The material here gathered together forms an important beginning of a more accurate knowledge of the hydrography of the Cordilleran region.

This report ends with a tabular statement of the mean monthly and annual discharge of the principal streams gauged by the Irrigation Survey. The most striking feature of this table is the extraordinary difference in the case of almost all the rivers measured between their maximum and minimum daily discharge.

Thus, for the Rio Grande at El Paso the maximum daily discharge for the year ending December, 1891, was 16,620; for 1892 it was 10,050 second-feet; the minimum daily discharge for both these years was 0. For Salt River the maximum for the year ending December, 1890, was 143,288; the minimum for the same time was 397 second-feet. The difficulties which such conditions present to the hydraulic engineer need not be enlarged on.

The second division of the report here under discussion was furnished by Mr. H. M. Wilson, and consists of two parts. The first of these is a technical discussion of the methods of American irrigation engineering, and is illustrated by a large number of plates, showing, more or less fully, various engineering constructions existing in the Cordilleran States. Of these works, Mr. Wilson says: "There are under construction to-day, or already completed, a number of great irrigation systems in the West which, while costing much less than those of equal magnitude in Europe or in India, are the equals of these in the quality and excellence of their workmanship and design. These works embody all the peculiar characteristics which distinguish American works from those of Europeans." The literature of irrigation from the general legislative and economic side is said to have become voluminous within the last few years, but "nothing worthy of note has as yet been written descriptive of the engineering features of our works. It is to fill this want that this report has been prepared."

In the introduction to his report Mr. Wilson touches briefly on various matters connected with the subject of irrigation. It is said, he remarks, to be now generally agreed that the recent experiments to produce rain artificially will not result in any benefit to the arid regions. Artesian wells for irrigation are disposed of in a few words: "Much useful information bearing upon the extent and distribution of the various Artesian belts has been written, and numerous wells have been sunk as a consequence, but the discharge and value of these is relatively insignificant. It is doubtful if a hundred thousand acres over and above the area already irrigated by Artesian wells will be supplied from this source for many years to come. The average well is capable of irrigating but a comparatively small acreage, and until water becomes more scarce than it is at present, their chief value will be for domestic purposes and for watering cattle."

The subject of the underflow is handled with equal brevity by Mr. Wilson, who defines it as being "the seepage or ground water which is at a short depth beneath the surface, and which is tapped by the common well. It is claimed that the volume of this underflow water, especially on the great plains sloping eastward from the Rocky Mountains, is such as to render irrigable in the near future vast tracts of the region. But it has been discovered by experiment and investigation that the discharge from such sources is extremely limited." Of the "fountain method" it is said, "Tunnels and trenches of sufficient depth may be sunk into the ground and run along it for great distances to intercept this water of percolation, though the volume obtained by them is very limited, and their multiplication impossible, as each work of this kind materially affects the output of any similar work which may lie below it." Pumping by means of windmills or steam is looked upon with more favor by Mr. Wilson, and it is admitted that this method will ultimately be largely resorted to, and it is believed that the areas thus irrigated "will be enormously increased as the country becomes more settled. There are cases, however, in which ground water is a matter of considerable importance, and this statement is said to be especially true in regard to the dry beds of certain streams in California and Colorado, under which tunnels have been run, or dams resting on impervious foundations built across their channels, by which means subterranean reservoirs have been created, supplying water enough for purposes of irrigation. Similar works are now being constructed in a few of the gulches on the eastern slopes of the Rocky Mountains, the most notable of which is for the water supply of the city of Denver."

The source from which water is to be obtained in sufficient quantity for irrigation, in the opinion of Mr. Wilson, is the utilization of the great rivers, such as the Columbia, Sacramento, Colorado, and Rio Grande. The smaller streams are now almost all utilized, and on many of those of the larger, but not of the largest size, irrigation works are either being planned or are in actual process of construction. The time will soon arrive, he thinks, when the waters of the great rivers will be diverted, and when that is attempted "the engineering problems which their utilization will raise will far surpass in magnitude anything of the kind yet undertaken in America." Moreover, much of the water collected in the smaller streams in the mountains is lost by seepage and evaporation shortly after it reaches the plains, while the greater portion of that which flows throughout the year is not utilized during the long period from August to April when irrigation is not practised. But this is the time of the year when the rivers carry the largest volume of water, which can only be saved by the construction of extensive storage reservoirs. Such works, it is said, "will add enormously to the volume of water available for irrigation." It is thought also that the duty of the water, or, in other words, the area which a given volume of water will irrigate, will be constantly increased as the proper methods of handling it become better understood, and as the dry earth becomes saturated by successive seasons of irrigation. In this way Mr. Wilson conceives that the value of the present available sources of supply "may become nearly doubled, and the area irrigable from these sources be correspondingly increased." No proofs of the correctness of this statement are offered, but it appears to be of the same character as that of various other generalizations of the officials of the Irrigation Survey. It does not seem as yet to have been discovered, in other countries where irrigation is practised, that with the more thorough cultivation of the soil, there arises less need of water, although this may in some cases be the result of the introduction of more expensive irrigational methods.[1]

[1] Further on in his report, under the heading "Duty of Water," Mr. Wilson discusses this subject more at length. He admits that "the duty of water as at present accepted in the various portions of the West is a matter of extreme variability and doubt," but he thinks that during the last ten years it has nearly doubled in Colorado, and more than quadrupled in portions of California. The duty of water flowing from wells in Utah, according to Mr. Newell, as reported in the Census Bulletin, is 80.3 acres

IRRIGATION IN INDIA. 251

The subject of irrigation in India is briefly touched upon by Mr. Wilson, and, while admitting that there are difficulties in the way of deciding what can be successfully undertaken in the United States by reference to experience gathered in another country of which the prevailing conditions are so different, yet on the whole he makes light of these difficulties.[1]

The striking contrast between the density of the population of the arid region of the United States and that of the irrigated districts of India is recognized, and it is said that, "in the central Western States, it is not the feasibility of a project from a theoretically financial point of view that stands in the way of its construction; it is the lack of people to inhabit and cultivate the lands served by the project, for this forces a large proportion of the water furnished to remain uncalled for. The great problem to be confronted by most irrigation projectors at present is immigration, not irrigation. If but a few good projects were started in the entire West, sufficient settlers could probably be found to make these interest-paying, but as there are many projects on foot, they divide up the number of

per second-foot; but Mr. Wilson, immediately after citing this statement, adds, "There is little doubt, however, that the duty of water in Utah averages about one hundred acres." Under special conditions the duty of water may be made very high, as in some localities in California, where it is taken to the land in wooden flumes and allowed to run over it from holes in their sides, or where in some orchards each tree is supplied from a separate outlet pipe. In this manner a duty as high as 1,000 acres has been realized. Professor Carpenter, of the State Agricultural College of Colorado, on the other hand, says fifty-five acres is the duty ordinarily taken in that State, and is "the safer guide."

[1] See *ante*, pp. 34-46, where this matter is discussed, and facts presented showing how entirely different the conditions prevailing in the two countries are.

settlers to such an extent that many must prove financial failures for many years to come, and until valuable lands become more scarce and settlement more dense."

Another most important matter, namely, the difference in the relations of the government to the people, the land, and the irrigation enterprises in the two countries, is not stated by Mr. Wilson in a sufficiently explicit manner. It is true that he admits that " in India all land and all water belong to the government, and the irrigation works are designed, constructed, maintained and operated by the government," and that, in consequence of this, " the legal questions involved are comparatively simple." Hence " the question of profit is not always paramount, and, while the direct money return is often small, the indirect return to the government is always large, in enhanced revenues from the rental of the land, in immunity from famine, and the consequent heavy drain on the treasury for relief and charity, and in the general benefit to the people resulting from increased government resources and exports." Then again, in the United States, as the lands are all private property, and the water the property of the public until appropriated, the constructors do not benefit by the enhanced value of the land consequent on irrigation unless they purchase and own it. This matter of the ownership of the water sought to be appropriated by an irrigation company is admitted to have given rise "to some of the most troublesome and expensive legal complications with which the Western people have had to deal." In general, to be successful in this country in an irrigation enterprise, the managers must begin by purchasing the land, then construct the works and provide that land with water, and finally sell, in greater or less quantities, as occasion offers, the tracts to which they by their operations have given an enhanced value. If such sales are made to intending settlers, as a rule the land will have to be sold on mortgage, with often a necessarily great delay in the final receipt of the money.

How different in this respect the whole condition of things in India! There the government has the power to plan and to carry out any irrigational enterprise it may deem to be for the best interests of the region to be more especially benefited, while not disregarding the welfare of the country as a whole. When finished, the work will be properly taken care of and kept in repair, and the water equitably distributed, so far as it is in the power of disinterested and skilful engineers to bring this about. The interest on the investment, or such part of it as the government may see fit to provide for in this way, will be paid in the form of an increased rental of the land irrigated, and this charge cannot be evaded. The country is densely inhabited, and the people cannot migrate from one district to another with the hope of bettering their condition, as is so commonly done in the United States.

But besides the difference between India and the Cordilleran States in the density of the population, the climatic conditions, and the relations of the government to irrigational enterprises, there is another important matter which must not be left out of account in comparing the two countries. This is the formation of an alkaline deposit, or "reh" as it is called in

India,[1] on and within the soil as a result of long-continued irrigation. In regard to this much debated subject, Mr. Wilson makes the following remarks: "There is no doubt that irrigation, if practiced ignorantly and carelessly, may result in the production of a film of alkaline salts on the surface of the ground, though it is equally certain not only that the intelligent practice of irrigation need not be accompanied by these results, but that lands which were originally alkaline may be made arable. With an increased knowledge of the necessity of natural or artificial drainage as an adjunct to any well-planned irrigation project, and a better understanding of the proper method of locating and constructing canals so as to produce a minimum rise of the subsurface water level, the production of alkali may be reduced to a minimum or wholly stopped."

A comparison of this statement with what has been said in previous pages of the present volume, in which the experience of the irrigation engineers of India is cited in reference to the alarming condition of things in that country, will show at once how incorrect and imperfect Mr. Wilson's treatment of the "reh" question is. It is not true that any method has as yet been discovered by which "the production of alkali may be reduced to a minimum or wholly stopped." It has not yet been proved possible to continue irrigation for a great length of time without filling the soil with alkaline or earthy salts to such an extent as eventually to render it unfit for cultivation, unless it be in certain highly favored regions. Where the average precipi-

[1] See *ante*, pp. 39-46.

tation is large, and there are occasional seasons of very heavy and long-continued rains, there the excess of alkali is washed out of the soil, at least to a considerable extent; and here it is that the "remedying of defective water circulation" may be of importance.[1] Under such climatic conditions, if every facility is offered for the cleansing of the soil by the passage through it of the superfluous water, carrying with it the alkaline particles with which the soil is saturated, the evil will be entirely overcome, or at least greatly lessened. This seems to be the condition of things over a considerable portion of irrigated India. Where, on the other hand, the average precipitation is very small, and seasons of over-abundant rainfall are either very few or even entirely wanting, then it is difficult to see how the accumulation of alkali in an irrigated soil can be prevented by any kind of artificial drainage. Here, however, comes in another question. If perfectly pure water were used in irrigating, there would be no alkaline or other matter left from its evaporation, and the nearer the approach to absolute purity in the water the longer the time would be delayed before the evil effects of over-irrigation began to be felt. That irrigation has been practiced along the borders of the Nile for an indefinite length of time without injurious results would seem to be due — in large part, at least — to the extraordinary purity of the water used, which, even as low down as Cairo, contains only about five or six grains of foreign matter to the gallon. The beneficial effect of the water covering the low lands of the Nile Valley, as a consequence of the annual rise of the

[1] See *ante*, p. 45.

river, is due in part to the deposit of sediment which is formed. This, coming in large part from the decomposition and erosion of granitic rocks, acts as a fertilizer, and neutralizes — to a certain extent, at least — any injurious effect which might otherwise result from long-continued irrigation.

When, therefore, Mr. Wilson says that "neglect and ignorance of the principles governing the production of alkali have been most serious, and in a few portions of the San Joaquin Valley in California, and in India, it has cost millions of dollars in the loss of lands and in the diminished demand for water," he evidently misunderstands the nature of the problem, representing it as one easily solved, which is by no means the case, as will become evident from the consideration of what has been attempted to be done in India, and of how little has been accomplished toward diminishing the evil of the "reh."

Mr. Wilson himself recognizes the fact that "there are some classes of water which it is not advisable to use for purposes of irrigation." Yet he seems to consider this condition of things as exceptional, and as being one which can be easily remedied. This is far from being true, and some of the methods proposed by him would aggravate the difficulty rather than diminish it.

From what has been stated in the preceding pages, it will be evident that we are as yet much in the dark as regards the composition of the water obtained from the various wells and rivers of the Cordilleran region, which are already to some extent employed for irrigation, and of which it is proposed and expected that a far larger use will be made in the future. That much of this water is of a quality such that it cannot be expected to benefit the soil to which it is applied, seems already to have been clearly demonstrated. That animals can sustain life on an exceedingly impure water, and that some crops can be raised where the soil is irrigated with a strong solution of various mineral salts, is a well known fact, as witness the thriving of the date-palms in the water procured by means of the Artesian borings in the Sahara, as well as the willingness of the camel to drink it. But to what extent very impure water can be used for irrigation in general agriculture, or how long animals will thrive under conditions which seem so abnormal to those who are accustomed to see stock watered with a fluid holding in solution not more than ten or twenty grains of solid matter to the gallon, remains as yet to be ascertained by actual experiment.[1]

Under the head of "History and Legislation," Mr. Wilson gives a brief historical sketch of the introduction of irrigation into this country. Several valleys in Arizona are said to show unmistakable signs of former cultivation. "In nearly every portion of the Salt and Gila river valleys the close observer will find traces of early habitation and of systems of irrigation, by means

[1] The subject of the composition of the water obtained from the various wells, springs, rivers, and lakes of the western part of this country is one of great scientific as well as practical importance. In the reports of the officials of the Irrigation Survey this matter seems to have been by far too much neglected. From some of the State Geological Reports more satisfactory information may be obtained, as has been seen in the preceding pages. Some of the analyses which these reports contain, however, are manifestly unreliable, and the whole body of information on this subject is of too uncertain a character to make it worth while to attempt to enter into any generalization with regard to the quality of the water furnished under different geological conditions throughout the Cordilleran region.

of which the broad plains and mesas were brought to the highest state of productiveness." This development of the agricultural resources of a region now so dry and thinly inhabited [1] dates back to a period long antecedent to the arrival of the Spaniards in Mexico; but when these irrigation works were constructed is entirely a matter of conjecture. Mr. Wilson seems to think that it was solely owing to the skill with which this region was irrigated and cultivated by the early inhabitants that its former productiveness was brought about, the natural inference being that this condition of things may be restored by a return to the ancient practices, improved, it may be, in certain respects by modern methods. This is doubtful, for there is abundant evidence that the climate of this part of the country has been changed for the worse within a not very remote period. The topographical features of the Colorado River and its tributaries prove unmistakably that these streams once flowed with much larger volume than they do at the present time, and the same is true of the western slope of the Sierra Nevada, where there is ample geological evidence that this desiccation was begun at least as early as the later Tertiary epoch, the gravels deposited by the once much larger rivers of that region containing abundant fossils of Miocene and Pliocene age.

The founders of the missions of California were the first persons historically known to have practiced irrigation within the limits of the United States, and this they were led to do by knowledge of the business

---

[1] See *ante*, p. 89, for statistics of the area at present under irrigation, and of the density of the population of Arizona.

brought from Mexico and even from Spain. Mr. Wilson considers that the old mission of San Juan Capistrano, near San Diego, was "the site of probably the oldest irrigation development by civilized people in this country." The Mormons, immediately after their settlement in Salt Lake Valley, became aware of the necessity of irrigation in that region, and the practice of bringing water from the mountains above for use in gold-washing led the miners along the western base of the Sierra Nevada to similar results in that region, the ditches first constructed for mining purposes being soon utilized, to a greater or less extent, for irrigation.[1] Very much the same condition of things occurred in Colorado, where more than twenty-five years ago those who began by mining for gold and failed of success were led to take up agriculture, and soon found out that they could not succeed without obtaining an artificial supply of water.

The statistics given on a preceding page[2] show that it is only in California and Colorado that more than one per cent of the entire land surface is irrigated, while Utah stands third in the list, these three being the only States or Territories of which the irrigated area amounts to as much as half of one per cent of the whole. The great superiority of the States of California and Colorado with respect to the development of agriculture by means of irrigation is easily accounted for. In both mining is and has been actively and successfully pursued, and a home market thus secured; both are favorably situated for the establishment of extensive and successful irrigational works, since both

---

[1] See *ante*, p. 28.   [2] See *ante*, p. 232.

include broad and lofty ranges of mountains on which snow falls in large quantity, and from which flow perennial streams of pure water. California, however, possesses an additional advantage in that its irrigable lands do not lie at a high elevation above the sea level, as is the case in Colorado, so that they are more favorably situated with regard to climate, and especially well suited to the raising of fruit, large quantities of which are shipped to the Eastern States to supply a region where semi-tropical products cannot be raised, so that in this way a very extensive business has been developed, which the early settlers in California could not have foreseen. The less favorable conditions of Utah in these respects are manifested in the diminished area of that territory cultivated by the help of irrigation, this being about one fourth of that thus cultivated in California and one third of that in Colorado.

Under the head of "Legislation and Administration" Mr. Wilson next proceeds to give a brief sketch of what has been done in this direction by State legislatures and by Congress. In California and Colorado, and more notably in Wyoming, it appears that "legislation has been enacted which covers many important features calling for attention," while the government of the United States is said "to have enacted little legislation for the protection of irrigators or of corporations intending constructions." To this, however, is added the statement, that "government has in recent years done a great deal for the encouragement of irrigation by directing investigations in various channels, and making provisions for surveys and experiments on the more important abstract questions relating to irrigation." The work of the Agricultural Department, of which considerable has been said in the preceding pages of the present volume, is also alluded to, as well as the investigations ordered to be made by the United States Geological Survey, the nature of which has already been indicated.[1]

In regard to the present status of the work executed under the direction of the United States Geological Survey, and the action of Congress in that connection, the following statement is offered by Mr. Wilson: " Appropriations were made for the fiscal years ending in June, 1889 and 1890, and the work prosecuted with vigor. The following Congress, however, failed to make appropriations for the continuance of this work, and little has been done since beyond the completion of reports and the segregation of reservoir sites by the topographic field parties of the Geological Survey. The clause contained in the bill above cited, which provided for the segregation and withdrawal from sale or occupation of irrigable lands, was repealed by act of Congress passed in the spring of 1891. A further act, however, passed during the same Congress and approved March 3, 1891, made some regulations and provisions regarding the mode of obtaining and settling on public lands, which, while it does not go as far as the act segregating irrigable lands, prevents the wholesale occupation of the same by corporations or speculators."

As the law seems to stand at present, no one settler can acquire a title to more than 320 acres, the amount having been reduced from 1,120 acres, which it would

---

[1] See *ante*, pp. 29–31.

seem that a settler previous to that change could have acquired by means of an ordinary pre-emption act and the so-called "timber-culture act." The present enactments make it possible for settlers to obtain title to reservoir sites and right of way for irrigation works over government lands without payment for the same, and by merely filing on the land and fulfilling the requirements of the law, of which the most important seems to be the expenditure of three dollars per acre, or one dollar per year for three successive years, on each acre claimed.

Following the above more general considerations in regard to irrigation comes a detailed description of various irrigation works, such having been selected for this purpose as embody all the principal features distinguishing American irrigation engineering. Under the head of "Perennial Canals," illustrations of works of this class are furnished from California, Colorado, Arizona, Wyoming, New Mexico, Utah, and Idaho. Most of the works described are intended for irrigation, but a few furnish water for mining also, and one has been built to supply power for the state prison at Folsom, in California. These latter works are described by Mr. Wilson as being "the most substantial and elaborate of their kind that have been constructed, either in this country, Europe, or India." Furnishing water-power for the prison is the main object of this canal, but it is also intended that the water shall be used for irrigation and for hydraulic mining. Some of the difficulties of this enterprise may be inferred from the facts reported by Mr. Wilson, that a depth of thirty-one feet of water has passed over the crest of the weir, on the occasion of one high spring flood, and that in this same year a depth of thirty feet of wet silt was deposited in the reservoir.[1]

Following the chapter devoted to perennial canals in Mr. Wilson's report comes one in which certain technical details connected with their construction are discussed, under the heads of "Headworks," "Weirs," "Diversion Dams," "Regulators," "Escapes," "Falls and Rapids," and "Drainage Works, Flumes, Siphons, etc." Next comes a chapter the several sections of which are entitled, "Distribution and Measurement of Water," "Application of Water," and "Maintenance and Supervision."

This matter is purely technical, and its discussion does not fall within the province of the present volume, neither could its results be epitomized in such a manner as to be intelligible and useful.

The chapter next to those cited above, which is entitled "Water Storage," presents interesting features, some of which may here be indicated, especially as this department of irrigation engineering is that in which falls most of the work done under the direction of the United States Geological Survey, and which is evidently considered by its officials as being much more important than any other. Storage reservoirs are constructions with which Eastern engineers are familiar, since it is by them that many of the largest cities at the East are supplied with water, although this is not there used for irrigational purposes.

[1] How irrigation works of any kind can be built which will stand such a freshet as that of the year 1861-62, which extended over the whole Sacramento Valley, the present writer confesses himself not able to understand.

In regard to this matter Mr. Wilson makes the following remarks: "Since the passage of the Act of Congress signed October 2, 1888, providing for the survey by government engineers and the withdrawal from occupation of lands included within reservoir sites, and since the passage of a subsequent act, approved March 3, 1891, regulating the methods of disposal of these reserved storage sites, the growth of the popular interest in the subject of water storage in the West has led to the development of a great number of storage projects, a few of which are already under construction. Many of these are within themselves excellent and feasible projects, and will some day be undertaken, while a large proportion will in the course of time prove impracticable and be abandoned."[1]

Mr. Wilson next proceeds to give descriptions, with considerable engineering detail, of various reservoir projects which have already been more or less completely carried out. There are seven of these. The first mentioned is the reservoir and canal system of the "San Diego Flume Company," which is said to contain nearly all of the typical features of a combined storage and irrigation system. It consists of a storage reservoir situated high up in the Coast Ranges of California, and of the bed of the San Diego River, down which the storage waters flow for some distance, and are then diverted to a wooden flume, which conducts them to the irrigable lands. The reservoir is about seventy

---

[1] See *ante*, p. 31, where the location of the sites for reservoirs selected by the Geological Survey is indicated, and various other particulars mentioned in regard to them.

miles east of San Diego, and is situated at an altitude of 5,500 feet. It has a capacity of 11,500 acre-feet. There are in all about thirty-six miles of wooden flume and trestle-work, the number of trestles being 315, and there are eight tunnels, the longest of which is nearly 2,000 feet long. The total cost of the work, to the end of the year 1888, is stated at $958,790. The water-supply as yet provided for it is said by Mr. Wilson to be insufficient; but an enlargement of the works by the diversion of the head-waters of other streams and the construction of additional storage reservoirs is contemplated.

The next project mentioned is the "Merced Reservoir," which consists of a temporary diversion weir on the Merced River, about twenty-five miles above the city of Merced, in California, and a canal twenty-seven miles long, which leads to the distributing canals and pipes through which the town and the irrigable lands are supplied. The reservoir has a surface area of 500 acres, and is closed by a dam 4,000 feet in length and fifty-four in maximum height, which is constructed entirely of earth. The total expenditure has been about $1,500,000; but this includes the cost of most of the land owned by the company, amounting in all to about 60,000 acres. The irrigable lands commanded by this canal system are said to be well adapted to raising fruit and vegetables.

"Long Valley Reservoir," the third of Mr. Wilson's projects, is in Honey Valley, in Northern California. The plan, which seems as yet to exist only on paper, includes a storage reservoir having an area of 1,080 acres, and closed by an earthen dam ninety-six feet in maximum height and 950 feet in length. The cost is estimated at about $100,000.

The "Walnut Grove Reservoir," on the Hassayampa River, in Arizona, is the next project discussed by Mr. Wilson. The locality is about thirty miles south of Prescott, and the object of the storage reservoir formed there was to furnish water for mining gravel in the bed of the river, and for irrigating the land in the valley below. This dam is described in considerable detail, the object being apparently to illustrate its defective construction, since it was carried away by a cloudburst with great loss of life in 1890. It was of the type known as the "rock-filled dam," which is said to be "essentially the product of Western engineering."

The "Castlewood Reservoir," of which a description follows next in Mr. Wilson's report, is said to be a very interesting scheme which combines two different systems of water storage. The system comprises a main storage reservoir known as Castlewood Lake, situated on Cherry Creek, Colorado, at a narrow point in the cañon, about thirty miles southeast of the city of Denver, and of a diversion weir a mile and a half lower down on the creek which receives the water that has been turned into it from the reservoir, and passes it into a canal which heads at the weir and by which it is conveyed to the irrigable land lying southeast of Denver. There are also four secondary reservoirs, situated in different parts of the tract to be irrigated, and these are natural depressions in the surface. The design of the dam is said to be peculiar, and to have been the cause of alarm to the people living below it, so that it was not allowed to be filled, and a heavy earth embankment has been planned to be placed above for its reinforcement, and this is said by Mr. Wilson to be "under construction and now nearly completed." The capital of the company is $2,500,000, and from the proceeds of a portion of the stock sold land has been purchased, and about $425,000 spent on the dam.

"Bear Valley Reservoir" is situated in the San Bernardino Mountains, a little east and north of the town of that name, its purpose being to irrigate the land in that vicinity. Bear Valley itself is a large basin in the heart of the mountains, at an altitude of about 6,200 feet, where the rainfall is very large.[1] The lands to be irrigated are said to have shown such a remarkable development, and the value of water for irrigation to have increased so rapidly within the past few years, that the company has extended its scope and operations, and is constructing a new and larger dam to replace the existing one, which, as Mr. Wilson remarks, "has been frequently described because of the peculiarly bold cross section given to it."[2] The new dam is to be a much larger and more substantial struc-

---

[1] According to observations made in the year 1883-84, the rainfall amounted to 93.3 inches, and in the months of February and March it was respectively twenty-four and thirty-five inches. That year was an exceptional one, and the annual average is presumably less than this. In February, 1890, a fall of nineteen inches in twenty-four hours was measured at the dam site.

[2] This dam, built of rough ashlar masonry on both faces, filled with coursed rubble masonry in the interior, laid in uniform beds of Portland cement, is 3.2 feet wide at the top, the lower face being vertical for forty-eight feet, while the upper face has such a batter that at a depth of forty-eight feet from the crest it is only eight and a half feet in thickness, while the foundation is twenty-feet thick only. The total height of the dam is sixty-four feet.

ture than the old one. It will be about 120 feet in extreme height, fifteen feet wide at the top, and seventy-three and a half at the bottom, and built of the best granite masonry throughout.

The "Sweetwater Reservoir" is a storage reservoir for the waters of a creek of that name about twenty-five miles east of San Diego, in the suburbs of which town, as well as for irrigation in the vicinity, these waters are used. The dam is ninety-four feet high, forty-six feet thick at the base, and twelve feet at the top, the extreme length being 380 feet. This dam, like some others in this region, is arched up stream, and Mr. Wilson says of it that its cross section is "much lighter than theory would call for in a structure expected to stand by gravity alone," but "great reliance has been placed on its curved plan and the shortness of the radius of this curvature."

Various other reservoir projects are now briefly described by Mr. Wilson, among which that of the Lake Hemet Water Company may be mentioned, since of this it is said that when completed "the reservoir will form one of the largest of its kind, while the dam closing it will be nearly the highest and probably the best constructed ever built." The water is to be used for irrigating land in the San Jacinto Valley, California. The height of the proposed dam is 150 feet; its length on top at 120 feet will be 220 feet, and at 160 feet 400 feet; the top width is ten feet, and the thickness at bottom 100 feet. The dam is arched up stream, with a radius of 300 feet, and is constructed throughout of the largest uncoursed rubble masonry. The estimated capacity of the reservoir at a depth of 150 feet will be

26,000 acre-feet, and with a depth of 160 feet 32,500 acre-feet, sufficient for a constant discharge for 180 days of about 100 second-feet. The cost of the dam is estimated at $250,000, and the pipes, flumes, and distribution system will cost $250,000 more.

Another somewhat similar work, now in process of construction, is "Reservoir No. 1 of the Arrowhead Reservoir Company," which is to gather the head waters of the Mohave River on the northern slope of the San Bernardino Range, to be used for irrigation in the valley of that name. On this work will be six tunnels aggregating three miles in length, and about sixty miles of conduits. The dam will be 150 feet high, arched in plan, with a radius of 575 feet. "Its cross section will be unusually slight, its length on top being 680 feet, and its width at top ten feet and at the base only forty-seven and a half feet." Its total capacity is expected to be about 68,000 acre-feet, and its catchment area is seventy-five square miles, on which the annual precipitation is about forty inches. The estimated cost of the entire work is $1,500,000.

Under the head of "Water Storage," Mr. Wilson next proceeds to describe the great reservoir for the storage of water to be used chiefly for the supply of the city of Denver, although it is expected that a small portion of it will be taken for irrigation in and about that city. The water is to be collected in "subsurface gathering galleries" under the South Platte River,[1] and two storage reservoirs are to be constructed, closed by "mammoth earth dams," one below the other, built across two valleys near Wheatland, a few miles above

[1] See *ante*, p. 229.

Denver. As the catchment area of the reservoirs is relatively small, the water to fill them is to be brought from nineteen miles farther up the river in a wooden pipe line thirty inches in diameter. The upper reservoir will have a surface area of 322 acres, with a mean depth of fifty-seven feet and a capacity of 23,000 acre-feet; the lower will have a surface area of 157 acres, and a capacity of 12,000 acre-feet. The upper dam, which at the time of Mr. Wilson's writing, was in process of construction, is 705 feet long on the crest, and 261 feet in maximum height; its width at the top being thirty feet, and at the base 986 feet. The lower dam will be similar to the upper one in construction, and not very different from it in dimensions, its width at the base being 989 feet.

The next subject taken up by Mr. Wilson in his report is "Subsurface Sources of Supply," under which designation he includes "all those sources of water-supply which are obtained by mining, digging, or boring." It is a well-known fact, he says, that in many regions the subsurface water level rises very nearly to the surface, while nearly everywhere water is to be found at some greater or less depth. This ground water in some cases may be nearly inexhaustible; in others, of very limited amount. In regard to the "underflow," Mr. Wilson remarks as follows: "Where there is a sufficient slope, as in the plains east of the Rocky Mountains, this ground water is so well distributed and so great in amount that it is frequently, though incorrectly, spoken of as the 'underflow.' This is not an accurate description, as the water does not flow under the soil, though there is a slow and constant creeping motion along the general slopes, due chiefly to capillary attraction, and to a much less extent to the action of gravity."

Passing rapidly over this branch of his subject, with the remark that "wells from which water must be raised by pumping are as yet employed in this country to such an extremely limited extent as to deserve no more than a passing mention," Mr. Wilson proceeds to speak of the subsurface waters which flow under the dry beds of the mountain torrents and streams of the southern arid region; these, he thinks, "will in the future furnish a moderate supply for irrigation," and are extremely interesting "because of the engineering devices employed in rendering them available." The development of the ground water under stream beds, the hillsides, or the prairie slopes in California, Colorado, and similar regions, is said to offer "the greatest field for engineering ingenuity."

To this class of undertakings may be referred the building of submerged dams, with the object of cutting off the subterranean flow and bringing the water to the surface. As a specimen of this source of supply, the works of the American Water Company of Denver are described. These consist of a submerged open crib dam in the gravel and sand bed of Cherry Creek, resting on solid rock, which is about seventy-three feet below the bed of the stream. Its total width, across the channel of the stream, is 700 feet, which is less than half the width of that channel. The dam is ten feet wide at its crest, and seventeen feet at the bottom. A pump pit or well is sunk from the hill to nearly the same level as the bottom of the dam, and the water is to be pumped to a storage reservoir located on a hill near by.

The most interesting submerged dam yet constructed is said to be that of the San Fernando Land and Water Company on Pacoima Creek, in Southern California. The object of this dam is to develop the water which is known to flow under the dry gravel bed of the stream during most of the irrigating season. For this purpose the dam is built in a straight line in such manner that it completely shuts off the flow of subterranean water, and forms a submerged reservoir in the gravel about half a mile in width and several miles in length, averaging thirty feet deep. The subsurface water is gathered by means of cement pipes, which lead it into two wells of masonry forming part of the structure of the dam, and from these it runs under ground to the towns of Pacoima and San Bernardino, furnishing a supply for irrigation as well as for domestic use.

Various methods of raising the subsurface water by means of pumps are next described by Mr. Wilson; but, as he remarks, the percentage of irrigation which is effected in this way is "so small as to be scarcely appreciable when compared with gravity supplies." Still he thinks "there is little doubt that the employment of pumps and other lift apparatus will steadily and rapidly increase."

The concluding portion of Mr. Wilson's report, entitled "Engineering Results of Irrigation Survey," begins with a brief description of the methods by which that work was conducted, the principal factors of which are said to be: "(1) the delineations and segregations of the irrigable lands within each basin; (2) the study of the sources of supply and hydrography of the basins from which these lands should be watered; (3) detailed surveys indicating the methods by which the best use should be made of this water supply for the irrigation of the land." After a summary of what had been accomplished in each of these departments up to the date of closing his report, Mr. Wilson proceeds as follows: " It is a matter deeply to be regretted that in no case was the work of these various branches completed, owing to the discontinuance of the appropriations for continuing the work. The topographic work is still being carried on under appropriations for that purpose, and valuable preliminary information is being collected and published as rapidly as obtained. This work is complete within itself as far as it goes. A certain amount of hydrographic work, consisting chiefly of stream gaugings and the discussion and study of them, is still being conducted, and this work already furnishes us with a great deal of information relative to the hydrography of the arid region and the various hydrographic basins contained therein. This work will in the course of a series of observations extending over a period of years be complete within itself so far as it goes, though many correlated studies, especially those relating to evaporation, seepage, and the duty of water, and similar problems, should be investigated before the study of the hydrographic basins approaches absolute completion."

Finally, after enumerating all the factors required to be known before the engineering work of the Irrigation Survey could be considered as being complete, (and this department is said in particular to have suffered from lack of appropriation,) five of the drainage basins, in which "all these factors have been obtained in a preliminary and incomplete manner," are reported on, and a statement given in regard to each, with accompanying diagrams and sections, so that the exact condition of the work may be clearly understood.

These surveys are grouped in the description under the following heads: (1) Arkansas Basin, Colorado; (2) Sun River system, Montana; (3) Truckee and Carson River systems, Nevada; (4) California Division, including seven reservoirs in the High Sierra, and a survey of Clear Lake in the Coast Ranges; (5) El Paso Reservoir; (6) Pocatello Canal, Idaho.

Having in the preceding pages passed over in review the more important publications of the various irrigation surveys, and given a synopsis of the opinions held and theories advocated by the officials who have, under government authority, been employed in the different departments of the work, a few general remarks bearing on some of the problems which have presented themselves will properly be here appended.

It cannot fail to have been noticed how much the views of those who have written about the water-supply of the arid region differ in many important points, and how far the present writer is from agreeing with some of the authors whose opinions he has subjected to criticism. It will also have been seen that with the progress of the irrigational investigation some of those employed in the work have themselves been led to adopt much less exaggerated ideas of the possibilities of irrigation than they were inclined to hold at the time of beginning their labors. The present writer in the earlier pages of this volume (the later works reviewed by him not having then appeared or come into his possession) occupied more space in controverting some of the views then generally advocated by the government officials than would be necessary at the present time, because the earlier exaggerations have in a measure been relinquished, and a more sober mental condition has begun to prevail. This is especially the case with the later contributions of the irrigational department of the United States Geological Survey. The views of those employed in that work do not differ very essentially in reference to the most important points from those advocated by the present writer.

It is not necessary to enter into any long discussion of the matter in order that it may be made clear that an inadequate supply of water must necessarily be a great drawback to the prosperity of a region laboring under this disadvantage. The density of the population of that part of the earth which is not uninhabitable on account of extreme cold is more affected by this cause than by any other. There is no nation which holds a commanding position in respect to population, wealth, and political influence which is not occupying — in large part, at least — a region of adequate precipitation. All the drier portions of the earth's surface are thinly populated, and the very dry regions are almost uninhabitable. That this may not always have been the case in former times must, however, be admitted, for the countries bordering on the Eastern Mediterranean, where was once the focus of enlightenment, were probably somewhat scantily supplied with water when at the height of their power. That this region is now, or could easily be, entirely controlled by nations occupying areas of abundant rainfall is not a matter of accident: there is good reason for believing that this more favorable climatic condition is a powerful factor in these changed relations of intellectual development and political power.

It is safe to say that the part of the United States which is inadequately supplied with moisture will never compare in density of population with that more favorably situated in this respect. There are portions of the arid region, however, which are important on account of the deposits of the metals and their ores which they possess. This is especially the case with that region of small precipitation, but of large mineral resources, which lies between the Rocky Mountains and the Sierra Nevada, and embraces a large part of both those great mountain systems. The metallic treasures which the Cordilleran region contains, however, are not inexhaustible, and the prosperity of a region dependent on their development will not be of indefinite continuance. The energy, or even recklessness, with which these mineral resources of the Western United States have been and are likely to continue to be developed forbids the idea of their long duration. The statistics which have been presented in the preceding pages of this volume show plainly how great the contrast is between the well watered and the arid portions of the United States, although the mines of the drier metal-producing region have been in process of development for nearly half a century.

The region which lies east of the base of the Rocky Mountains, and is not metalliferous, belongs in part to the arid and in part to the semi-arid belt. Under the name of the "Great Plains," much has been said of its topographical character and its conditions of water-supply in the preceding pages. In spite of the sanguine expectations of some of its inhabitants, backed by the opinions of various irrigation officials, it may confidently be asserted that it will remain as it is — a thinly inhabited pastoral region, in which the water-supply will chiefly be drawn from deep wells, by the aid of steam in some cases, but mostly by means of windmills. The use of this water for irrigation will be very limited, and what is raised for that purpose will be for small gardens. It is impossible that people never seeing a river or a lake, or water running except from the spout of a pump, never seeing a mountain or a ledge of solid rock, never seeing what with any propriety could be called a forest — it is impossible that those living deprived of all these natural advantages can ever rise to even a moderately high plane of civilization. Whether the population of this part of the country will ever become so dense as materially to affect the supply of water is a question which cannot be easily answered. The difficulties which may arise, as respects the quantity and quality of the water obtained from the deep wells on the Plains, have already been alluded to in the preceding pages, and more need not be added in regard to them. That the "fountain method" of utilizing "subsurface water" will ever be of importance in irrigation seems hardly probable, although in certain cases some of the ingenious engineering works constructed for this purpose, and which have been described in the preceding pages, may be successful in providing water for use in those favorably situated towns which are natural centres of travel or of mining development.

The importance of Artesian wells, not only in general, but especially with reference to their use in irrigation, has been much exaggerated. Only on four tenths of one per cent of the total land area west of the 100th meridian were crops raised by the help of irrigation at the time the last census was taken, and only on 1.43 per cent of the irrigated area was Artesian water used. In the well-watered part of the country Artesian wells are never used for irrigation, and of the many deep-bored wells on the Atlantic coast and in the Mississippi Valley the water of very few is of value for any purpose, unless it be medicinal. The regions in which Artesian water can be obtained are few in number, and of small dimensions as compared with the total area of the country. Much the most important of these seems to be that of the Grand and Black Prairie region of Texas; but in regard to the composition of the water which there comes to the surface in such large quantity more information is much to be desired.

There does not seem to be anywhere in the United States an Artesian area possessing the ideal basin structure which is so typically presented by the wells in and near Paris, which draw their supply from the Lower Greensand. In the Artesian districts of the Atlantic coast and of Texas the assemblage of strata has a uniform dip toward the sea, and is made up of alternating permeable and impermeable beds. The necessary pressure, which in the case of a complete basin is furnished by the water seeking to descend from all sides toward the centre, is, when only one leg or one side of the synclinal is present, derived from the inability of the water to find any escape below. This condition is due, in most cases, to the fact that the pervious beds which hold the water become less and less capable of allowing it to pass through them, because their particles are finer and more clayey material is mixed with them, in proportion to the distance over which the sediment of which the rocks are formed has been carried from the place where it originated. In a somewhat similar manner, Artesian conditions may be produced by a fault or fissure which has become filled with clay, or by a dike of impermeable volcanic material which intersects the basin, the function of this being to intercept the passage of the water to a lower level at which it might escape in the form of springs, but where, if no opportunity for its discharge in this way is offered, it must accumulate under pressure, which will cause it to rise whenever the stratum in which it is thus confined is penetrated by the borer.

The theory which has been sometimes advocated by geologists, that, where an examination of the stratigraphical character of the region fails to reveal the existence of the requisites for an Artesian flow, but where, notwithstanding this, water does rise to the surface when a water-bearing stratum has been reached by the drill, there the pressure of the rock is the cause of this anomalous condition of things, cannot be accepted as being a satisfactory solution of the problem. When examined in the light of our knowledge of the physical characters of rocks, this theory is found to have no basis of truth. Neither gas, oil, nor water can escape from the strata in which they are confined without some other cause than the simple gravity of the particles between which they are enclosed. Gas, however, does escape under great pressure, and this is often accompanied by oil and water, either mixed or separately. That the pressure which this gas exerts is the result of the manner of its formation is generally admitted. Generated under conditions which are not clearly understood, but which result from the transformation of organic matter, the gaseous particles are held imprisoned between formations through which they are unable to pass, until a chance of escape is offered through the hole made by the drill. But of course the gas may exert its pressure, and force either oil or water to rise to the surface without being itself able to escape, its exit being prevented by interposed accumulations of either or both of these substances. Oil, water, brine, and gas are all products of various wells sunk in the pretroleum-producing regions of the country, and it is necessary to admit that there may be areas over which the pressure of gas is exerted to raise water to the surface without itself appearing in any considerable quantity. Most of the localities where water rises above the surface, but where the ordinary Artesian conditions seem to be wanting, are at no great distance from gas or petroleum producing regions.

The subject of water-supply for irrigational purposes by means of storage reservoirs, which has been the chief field in which the officials of the United States Geological Survey have labored, is a difficult one. There can be no doubt that water can be obtained in large quantity by this method; and as there are localities where it is already in use, so others will be found where it may properly and profitably be introduced. But these appear to be regions where the conditions are exceptionally favorable. That the construction of storage reservoirs is a kind of improvement which demands very large capital cannot be denied, and the responsibility and expenditure by no means end with the completion of the necessary dams and reservoirs: these must be kept in order and constantly watched with a vigilant eye, the more so because over much of the area where works of this nature have been projected the irregularities of the precipitation are extraordinarily great, while the disastrous effects of such events as cloud-bursts can only with difficulty be guarded against, even with the exercise of the greatest engineering skill in the original construction, and of constant vigilance after the delivery of the water has begun.

Up to the present time there does not seem to have been any serious attempt made to turn over the business of building dams and reservoirs for water-supply of the arid region to the General Government, as has been done, to a certain extent, with reference to supposed improvement of the navigation of certain rivers.[1] That something of this kind may eventually be asked for by the settlers in the Cordilleran States is by no means impossible. An idea of the amount of expenditure which such a policy would necessarily involve can be formed by investigating the history of the water-supply of the large cities at the East; as, for instance, New York and Boston, which depend on storage reservoirs, in the construction of which (in-

[1] See *ante*, pp. 32, 33.

cluding the necessary mains and service pipes) many millions have been expended.[1]

[1] The cost of land taken for the enlargement of the Croton Reservoir and for the new dam building at Quaker Bridge to hold back the water which this artificial lake will contain, has been estimated at from $8,000,000 to $10,000,000.

SUPPLEMENTARY NOTE. — Since the preceding pages were in type, an article has been received entitled "Artesian Well Prospects in Eastern Virginia, Maryland, and Delaware," by N. H. Darton. (See "Transactions of the American Institute of Mining Engineers," Virginia Beach Meeting, February, 1894.) In this article it is said that "the success of a number of wells, scattered widely over the middle Atlantic coastal plain region, indicates in itself the strong probability of the existence of subterranean waters throughout the region." Considerable information is given by Mr. Darton with reference to the geological character of the coastal plain on which these wells have been bored, the conditions being somewhat similar to those which have been described in the present volume as characterizing the Southern Atlantic and Gulf Coast. There are beds of sand and gravel, alternating with clays, which are of various ages, from Cretaceous to Recent, and these rest on a floor of granitic and gneissic rocks, which has a gentle slope to the east. A few of the Artesian wells which have been bored are described as affording abundant water, "but their number at present is very limited." There is great need, it is said, all over the coastal region, of purer and more abundant supplies of water. Reference may also be made to the New Jersey Geological Reports for the years 1889 to 1892, in each of which there is information given in regard to wells of various kinds in that State, where the subject of water-supply from this source seems to have begun, within the past few years, to excite considerable attention. In general, the details which are given in regard to the quantity and the quality of the water which these wells furnish are very meagre. As might be expected from the geological conditions of the region, the volume of water is never very large, and in most cases the wells are not what could properly be called "Artesian," pumping being necessary.

APPENDIX.

APPENDIX.

A.

LATEST STATISTICS OF IMMIGRATION, WITH ADDITIONAL REMARKS ON IMMIGRATION IN GENERAL, AND ON THE PRESENT STATUS OF THE CHINESE IN THE UNITED STATES.

THE tabular statement on the following page is a continuation of that on a preceding one,[1] and brings the statistics of immigration into the United States down to the middle of the year 1894, with a detailed statement of the various nationalities represented; and to make this more complete, the figures are given for each month of the current year.

The number of immigrants arriving on our shores during the year 1893 was large, as will be seen, although somewhat less than in the year 1892; but it was much less than it was in the year 1882, when the figures reached a maximum of 788,992, although more than it was in 1885, 1886, 1887, 1889, or 1890.

The reasons for these very considerable fluctuations in the number of immigrants cannot usually be stated in a very satisfactory manner: they depend on varying conditions in the countries from which the immigrants come, as well as in that to which they are attracted and where they hope to make a new home. In the case of the present year the very considerable falling off in the immigration indicated by the figures of the first half of the year, which sum up only a little more than one fourth of those of the year 1893, and only about one fifth of those for the year 1892, must without doubt be regarded as the result of the unfavorable condition of things in this country, into the nature and causes of which it is not necessary here to inquire. The movement of immigrants from a foreign land is influenced largely by the more or less favorable reports of friends or relatives who have already established themselves in the country toward which their thoughts are in-

[1] See *ante*, p. 18.

TABLE SHOWING THE NUMBER AND NATIONALITY OF IMMIGRANTS INTO THE UNITED STATES IN 1893 AND THE FIRST HALF OF 1894.

Countries.	Calendar year 1893.	1894.						Total for six months, 1894.
		January.	February.	March.	April.	May.	June.	
England and Wales	44,567	821	1,017	1,806	1,990	2,425	2,161	10,220
Scotland	11,865	141	183	416	591	478	681	2,490
Ireland	50,102	239	379	1,154	4,931	6,438	3,964	17,105
Total, United Kingdom	106,534	1,201	1,579	3,376	7,512	9,341	6,806	29,815
Denmark	8,490	87	145	532	850	659	400	2,673
France	5,260	178	171	227	312	229	223	1,340
Germany	89,690	1,560	1,709	3,482	5,406	5,216	3,564	20,937
Italy	69,269	1,639	2,306	3,594	9,092	7,562	3,621	27,814
Netherlands	7,757	67	66	272	287	358	99	1,149
Austria-Hungary	65,881	1,416	1,356	2,238	2,406	2,576	1,835	11,827
Russia	57,923	1,901	1,153	2,339	4,408	2,791	2,943	15,540
Sweden and Norway	52,058	179	410	2,043	2,586	2,705	2,299	10,222
Switzerland	4,808	71	124	435	440	279	171	1,520
All other countries	27,360	906	583	930	2,800	1,561	1,421	8,201
Total	495,030	9,208	9,602	19,468	36,099	33,277	23,384	131,038

clined. Any important change in the amount of demand for labor, or any other circumstance likely to affect the success of new-comers, is quickly made known at the home of the intending emigrant, who, thus advised, either relinquishes his plan altogether, or postpones his departure for a time. In the case of the present year, at all events, there has been no change of any importance in the condition of things likely to influence emigration in the countries from which our immigrants come, so that it seems to be only causes originating here which have reduced the figures to so considerable an extent as is shown in the table given above.

The character of the immigration, so far as it relates to the nationalities represented, did not differ much in 1893 from what it had been in the years 1890 and 1891, so that the remarks heretofore made [1] still hold good. The immigration from the United Kingdom on the whole is slowly decreasing; that from Ireland, however, remained at very nearly the same figure during the years 1890 to 1893; while a falling off in the number from Germany in 1893, as compared with 1892, is quite marked. Italy furnished about the same number in 1893 as in the previous year, while from Russia came only half as many. The figures for the first half of 1894, making allowance for their diminished number, as already noticed, do not indicate any considerable change in the nationality of the immigration as having occurred during that short interval.

The question of Chinese immigration has been before Congress repeatedly since the passage of the act excluding them entirely (with few exceptions, and under certain strict regulations, as previously stated [2]), but up to the present time no essential change has been made in their status.

The history of legislation and of judicial action relating to the question of the exclusion of the Chinese from the United States is briefly as follows. The Congressional acts of 1888 aimed at entirely excluding the Chinese from this country, although those who were already here when those acts were passed were allowed to remain. The number in the country, however, did not appear to diminish rapidly enough to suit the views of the opponents of Chinese immigration, and it was assumed (there being no positive information on the subject available) that the places of those who had died or who had returned to China in consequence of the manifest dislike of their race on the part of the majority of the citizens of those States where Chinamen are chiefly located, had been surrepti-

---

[1] See *ante*, pp. 18, 19.   [2] See *ante*, p. 23.

tiously taken by others of their race who had obtained an entrance into the country in spite of the laws by which this had been prohibited.[1]

Agitation was therefore begun in Congress, and, in spite of very strong opposition from the Eastern States, a law was passed, and approved May 5, 1892, which is generally known as the Geary law. Under the provisions of this Act, which is entitled "An Act to prohibit the coming of Chinese into the United States," every "Chinese person or person of Chinese descent convicted and adjudged to be not lawfully entitled to be or remain in the United States shall be imprisoned at hard labor for a period of not exceeding one year and thereafter removed from the United States." Moreover, every Chinaman in the country is required to prove that he is lawfully entitled to remain here, that is, that he was here prior to the passage of the acts of 1888, and to take out a certificate of residence to that effect: those found here without this certificate after the expiration of one year from the passage of the act of 1892 were to be adjudged unlawfully in the country, and to be imprisoned and deported accordingly.

Many friends of the Chinese, however, relying on the treaties existing between China and the United States, believed the Geary law to be unconstitutional, and, encouraged by these and by the managers of the immigration business at San Francisco, the Chinese in this country very generally refused compliance with the law requiring registration. In consequence of this, and in view of the fact that Congress had made only a very insufficient appropriation to carry out the project of deporting the Chinese, the authorities at Washington assumed the responsibility of neglecting the provision of the Geary law, or at least of delaying action until the constitutionality of that law had been investigated by the Supreme Court. A case was, however, very speedily made up and submitted to that tribunal, by which it was decided, May 15, 1893, that the law was constitutional. The difficulty with regard to the provid-

---

[1] Mr. Geary, author of the "Geary law," made the following statement (in an article in the North American Review for July, 1893, Vol. CLVII., p. 60): "It is claimed that the Act of 1892 was unnecessary, because more Chinese were leaving the country than entered it, and the number entering and leaving the port of San Francisco is cited to show that 48,000 more Chinese left the United States than entered it during the past decade. But the census shows the falseness of this argument. In 1880 there were 105,000 Chinese in the United States; in 1890 there were 106,000, or instead of decreasing 48,000 the number had actually increased. The only conclusion deducible is that 49,000 entered in defiance of our laws."

ing of the funds necessary to pay the expenses of deportation, however, had not been overcome, and the Chinese still remained in this country. Meantime Congress passed another act, which was approved November 3, 1893, by which certain not specially important changes were made in the act of 1892, and the limit of time after which deportation was to take place was fixed at six months after the passage of this new amendatory act.[1]

The time of enforcing the Geary law, as thus prolonged, has already arrived, and a considerable number of Chinese have complied with its provisions, but it does not appear that the business of deportation has begun. In the absence of official information in regard to this matter, it may be assumed that lack of funds applicable to this special purpose stands in the way of the fulfilment of the requirements of the Geary law.

In the mean time, however, a new treaty has been negotiated between China and the United States, which, after being several months before the Senate, was confirmed August 13, 1894. According to the provisions of this treaty, the coming to the United States of Chinese laborers is absolutely prohibited for a period of ten years from the time of the ratification of the treaty. The exceptions of this absolute prohibition are chiefly that it shall not apply to the return to the United States of any "registered Chinese laborer who has a lawful wife, child, or parent" in this country, or "property therein of the value of $1,000 or debts of like amount due him and pending settlement." The provisions of the treaty, moreover, "shall not affect the rights at present enjoyed by Chinese subjects being officials, teachers, students, merchants, or travellers for curiosity or pleasure, but not laborers, coming to the United States, and residing therein." Furthermore, it is agreed by the terms of the treaty, "that Chinese laborers, or Chinese of any other class, either permanently or temporarily residing in the United States, shall have for the protection of their persons and property all rights that are given by the laws of the United States to citizens of the most favored nations, excepting the right to become naturalized citizens." And the government of the United States affirms its obligations to exert all its power to secure protection to the persons and property of all Chinese subjects in the United States.

---

[1] While the provision of the Geary law authorizing the imprisonment of the Chinese for the crime of being in this country was not formally repealed by the amendatory act, no mention is made of anything else than deportation in it.

B.

BRIEF DISCUSSION OF THE QUESTION WHETHER CHANGES OF CLIMATE CAN BE BROUGHT ABOUT BY THE AGENCY OF MAN, AND ON SECULAR CLIMATIC CHANGES IN GENERAL, WITH SPECIAL REFERENCE TO THE ARID REGION OF THE UNITED STATES.

OF the various phases which the discussion of the irrigation question in the Far West during the past few years has assumed, one of the most interesting is the belief very generally felt and expressed throughout that part of the country where the rainfall is insufficient, that the climate of that region is undergoing a change for the better as regards this most serious defect. This idea is not only very generally advocated by the settlers themselves, but it has received support not only from government irrigation officials, but also from those who from their connection with educational and scientific institutions might naturally be supposed to be qualified to speak with authority in regard to this matter. It requires, however, but a very limited amount of study of climatic questions to become convinced that there is no subject in regard to which the public is more easily deceived, or more willing to allow itself to be deceived, than that of the ability of man to control climate. There are certainly few if any subjects which have been so much discussed, and about which such positive statements have been made and theories advocated by those who were not in possession of any facts on which to base them, as this very question of the possibility of the modification of the climatic conditions of a greater or less extent of the earth's surface through the agency of its inhabitants.

As an illustration of the desire to generalize on this subject with absolutely no knowledge of that which would give to such generalizations any value, Gibbon's remarks on the changes which have taken place in the climate of Northern Europe within the historical period, and on the causes of the difference in the temperature of regions on the same parallel of latitude on the two sides of the Atlantic, may be cited. This painstaking and ordinarily so accurate writer on historical subjects in general had absolutely no

DISCUSSION OF CHANGES OF CLIMATE. 291

knowledge of the real causes of the difference between the climates of Europe and Eastern North America. His ideas on this subject will become apparent on reading the following quotation from what he says when discussing the influence of the climate of ancient Germany over the minds and bodies of the natives : "In the time of Cæsar, the reindeer, as well as the elk and wild bull, was a native of the Hercynian forest, which then overshadowed a great part of Germany and Poland, but at present he cannot subsist, much less multiply, in any country south of the Baltic. The modern improvements sufficiently explain the causes of the diminution of the cold. These immense woods have been gradually cleared, which intercepted from the earth the rays of the sun. The morasses have been drained, and, in proportion as the soil has been cultivated, the air has become more temperate. Canada, at this day, is an exact picture of ancient Germany. Although situated in the same parallel with the finest provinces of France and England, that country experiences the most rigorous cold. The reindeer are very numerous, the ground is covered with deep and lasting snow, and the great river of St. Lawrence is regularly frozen, in a season when the waters of the Seine and the Thames are usually free from ice."[1]

Not long after the last volume of Gibbon's "Decline and Fall of the Roman Empire" had been issued, the climate of the United States began to be written about with some detail, for that which had been published prior to the appearance of Volney's im-

---

[1] See "Decline and Fall of the Roman Empire," Vol. I. Chap. IX. The order of the sentences has been slightly changed in the quotation for the sake of clearness. The problem as stated by Gibbon involves two considerations of a very different order. The difference between the climates of the two countries on the opposite sides of the North Atlantic depends on various natural causes easily understood, and these must have always been in operation, or, at least, they have not essentially changed in character since the continental land masses occupied the same position and had the same area which they now have. (See the present writer's work, "The United States," etc., pp. 137-139.) The former existence of various arctic mammals, among which the reindeer is included, over a part of Central Europe, and even as far south as Southern France, is a problem of another order, the solution of which connects itself with the complicated conditions of the so-called "Glacial Epoch," the precise character and causes of which have not yet been satisfactorily made out. That man was in existence at the time of the spread of the reindeer over Northern Germany is not denied, but no geologist, at the present time, claims that human agency had any share in bringing about that change of the climate of Northern Europe which led to the disappearance or retreat to the North of the reindeer, arctic fox, and various other species, which are now only met with in high northern latitudes.

portant work[1] was exceedingly fragmentary and imperfect. There seems to have been a striking unanimity of opinion among these earlier writers, however, in regard to the condition of things in this country as respects the changing character of its climate. It was almost universally believed that the winters were becoming less severe, the summers warmer, and the climate in general more variable, but on the whole decidedly more favorable, than it was when the country first began to be settled by the whites. The current ideas on this subject are well exemplified in the following quotation from Jefferson's Virginia:[2] "A change in our climate is taking place very sensibly. Both heats and colds are becoming much more moderate within the memory even of the middle-aged. Snows are less frequent and less deep. . . . The elderly inform me that the earth used to be covered with snow about three months every year. The rivers, which then seldom failed to freeze over in the course of the winter, scarcely ever do so now." Volney himself tells the same story: "Everywhere, throughout the entire extent of my journey, whether on the Atlantic coast, or in the West, I collected testimony to the same effect, everywhere I heard the same story; longer summers, later setting in of autumn, harvest similarly delayed; winter shorter, snows not so deep, nor lasting so long, but cold spells not less severe; and in all the new settlements they have described these changes not as being gradual and progressive, but rapid and almost instantaneous, in proportion as the country is cleared [proportionnés à l'étendue des déboisements]." Equally certain were various writers on the climate of this country that the rainfall was diminishing. Mease, in his "Geological Account of the United States," says: "Within a few years the quantity of rain has certainly diminished." And a little farther on he adds: "It is highly probable that our climate is undergoing a change in regard to the quantity of rain."

That these presumed climatic changes had been brought about chiefly, if not solely, by cutting down the forests, seems to have been generally admitted by those who attempted to offer any explanation of this most remarkable phenomenon.

Views very similar to those adopted by Volney were, just a

[1] "Tableau du Climat et du Sol des Etats-Unis," a work containing observations made by the author during a three years' residence in this country, from 1795 to 1798.

[2] Written, as the author states, in 1781, and somewhat enlarged and modified in the winter of 1782; but the edition from which the quotation here offered was taken bears the date of 1787.

century ago, advocated by Samuel Williams in his History of Vermont, from which indeed the former obtained a considerable portion of the information contained in his work on the climate of the United States.[1] Mr. Williams maintained that, although it could not be determined, for want of meteorological observations, whether there have been any alteration in the annual quantity of rain in any part of America, yet a change had been manifested "in the apparent decrease of the snow in all the ancient cultivated parts of the United States." "Snows," he says, "are neither so frequent, deep, or of so long continuance, as they were formerly: And they are yet declining very fast in their number, quantity, and duration." He further considers it proved that "the east winds, which half a century ago seldom reached farther than thirty or forty miles from the sea shore, have now advanced as far as the mountains, which are generally eighty or a hundred miles from the ocean." That these changes of climate are "much connected with and greatly accelerated by the cultivation of the country cannot be doubted." "But," he wisely adds, "whether this cause is sufficient to account for all the phenomena which have attended the change of climate in the various parts of the earth seems to be uncertain."

The above citations from works published at the time when the climate of this country first began to be written about are given that it may be distinctly seen at how early a period positive assertions began to be made in regard to the changes which were

[1] Williams's "Natural and Civil History of Vermont" was published at Walpole, N. H., in 1794, and a second edition in two volumes appeared in 1809, which was printed at Burlington, Vt. This later and larger edition contains, in an Appendix, "Observations on the Change of Climate in Europe and other Places." In this discussion Mr. Williams endeavors to show that the climate "in the course of several centuries has remarkably changed at Palestine, in Italy, around the Euxine Sea, at the Alps, and throughout all Germany." Furthermore, he feels justified in fixing with some approach to exactness the amount of the change of temperature which has taken place in that part of the world, for he proceeds to state that "through all this vast extent of country the climate has now become sixteen or seventeen degrees warmer than it was eighteen centuries ago." After discussing and commenting on this statement, for proof of the truth of which he mainly relies on the authority of Gibbon, supported by that of Moses, whom he regards as having been the author of the Book of Job, as also by that of David the Psalmist, he inquires "Whether cultivation is sufficient to account for these changes?" To this question he furnishes no answer, but adds: "For whatever the cause may be, the fact seems to be certain, the heat of all that part of the earth, of which we have any exact accounts, has been increasing from the earliest ages."

believed to have taken place, although but an extremely small portion of our vast territory had been invaded by the white man, while even in the most densely populated areas meteorological observations were almost entirely wanting. This tendency to generalize without any sufficient basis of fact was, however, by no means peculiar to this country. In Europe many years ago speculations on climatic changes began to assume a character which, to a large extent, they have maintained up to the present time. The removal of the forests has, during the past half-century, again and again been declared to have wrought unutterable woe over a large part of the earth's surface. The undeniable fact that during the historic period there has been a considerable diminution in the amount of water flowing in rivers or standing in lakes in many countries, and notably in Central Asia and Northern Africa, as well as in various parts of both North and South America, has been repeatedly commented on, and, almost without exception, the cause of this condition of things has been declared in the most positive manner to have been the destruction of the forests.[1]

Within a very few years, however, the opinions of scientific investigators of climate have undergone a change. Few, if any, of those who have made a thorough study of this subject will now be found maintaining that the phenomena of desiccation can be explained by appealing to deforestation as their cause.[2] The newspapers and popular writers in general, however, almost unanimously remain advocates of the idea that man can exert a powerful influence as a controller of climate, and that this nation is rapidly advancing toward ruin through "forest devastation."[3]

---

[1] See the present writer's "Climatic Changes," in which this subject is discussed at considerable length, and a large amount of evidence brought forward showing the fallacy of this idea, and proving that this general desiccation began in geological times before the human race made its appearance, and has been and is being continued during the historic period, and most certainly without any reason to believe that it has been brought about by the agency of man.

[2] See, for instance, the views of Mr. Newell in regard to the cause of the non-periodic oscillations of lakes and rivers, noticed on a previous page (*ante*, p. 239.)

[3] As an illustration of this, the following may be quoted from a popular periodical, published during the present year: "The results of Canadian woodchopping made themselves felt in the Middle and Eastern States many years ago, and now the evil is sweeping across the ocean. Has Great Britain the same climate that she had not many years ago, before forest denudation in Canada had denuded the surface of the province and given increased violence to the storms which crossed the Atlantic? The shores of Europe have, during the past season, shown the effects of this improvident work."

The form which the idea of man's ability to control climate has taken of late years in the arid region of the United States is that which concerns us most in connection with the present work; but before making an investigation of this it will be convenient to give a rapid sketch of the development of systematic meteorological work in this country, and to inquire what light this has thrown on the question of secular changes of climate in the region over which observations of this kind have extended.

A really serviceable thermometer did not exist until Fahrenheit invented his in 1714; but, in point of fact, thermometric observations made prior to about the year 1822 are of no value for use in any investigation such as that of a secular change of the climate at any specified locality.[1] Observations of rainfall, of the real accuracy of which we have little knowledge, but which we cannot so summarily reject as we can the earlier thermometric ones, seem to have been begun at Charleston, S. C., as early as 1738, and there is a continuous series from that year to 1759, from which time on there is a break lasting until 1840. The longest consecutive series of rainfall observations in this country is that taken at New Bedford, Mass., beginning in 1813. At New Haven, Conn., there was a continuous record from 1804 to 1829, and at Brunswick, Me., from 1808 to 1818; also at Philadelphia from 1824 on. At Boston, Mass., and at Marietta, Ohio, the record is nearly continuous from 1818 on. This list comprises nearly all the stations for which a long continuous record of the rainfall is available, either for the later years of the past century or the earlier of the present.

In 1825 the first regular systematic series of meteorological observations in any part of the United States began to be taken: this work was under the supervision of the New York State University. In 1836 the system of meteorological observations at the United States military posts, under the direction of the Medical Department of the Army, was begun. In 1849 the system of observations by volunteers, planned and directed by the Smithsonian Institution, was inaugurated. In 1870 the system of meteorological observations and of storm warnings, forming a part of the

---

[1] "It was in 1822 that Bellani, a Milanese observer, recognized the fact that all thermometers are liable to a change exactly such as would result if the bulb began to grow smaller soon after it was blown, and continued to do so for a long time. Of course observations made previous to this discovery, and indeed all observations made without special examination, from time to time, of the accuracy of the zero-point, are of no value for use in any such inquiry as that now before us." (Climatic Changes, p. 224.)

work of the Signal Service of the United States was organized, and at the present time this is the source from which most of our statistics of temperature, rainfall, and of climatic conditions in general are derived. But there is, in addition, a small amount of information to be obtained in various other ways.

The meteorological material thus available for an investigation of the kind here contemplated is far from being homogeneous, or of the same degree of accuracy throughout. Observations taken at the great astronomical observatories by the assistants, who are usually practiced observers, are likely to be trustworthy, but these are few in number and of short duration. Observations, especially of rainfall, made in connection with the various sources of water-supply for our principal cities may perhaps be considered the most valuable of all, since in these localities such records are of the greatest practical importance, and are likely, therefore, to be most carefully attended to. This will in time become a source of information of great value; but at present series of this kind are short and not numerous.

The observations at the United States military posts seem to the present writer the least reliable of all, and this statement is based on personal knowledge acquired at visits to various posts in former years, and also on the fact that the observations were — and probably still are — not made by the officers themselves, but usually by the hospital stewards, to whom this addition to their daily duties is, with few exceptions, decidedly unwelcome, and who certainly have no scientific interest in the work.[1]

The value of the records of the volunteer Smithsonian observers is, of course, very different in different cases. Some, no doubt, worked conscientiously; others did not, as is shown by the very great discrepancies between their results and those of other observers in the immediate neighborhood. The present writer can testify from personal knowledge that at some stations the instruments have been defective and the observations slovenly. In this connection it should be borne in mind that negligence or carelessness in keeping the record of the precipitation would be most likely to furnish results too low in value, so that we might expect (assuming what is in general likely to be true, namely, that the

---

[1] This is particularly unfortunate in connection with the determination of secular changes in the climate of the arid region of the United States, because almost all the earlier material which could possibly be made available for this purpose is that coming from the military posts.

idea of the necessity of accuracy has gained ground in modern times) to find that there has been, in some localities, an apparent increase in the amount of precipitation, which, however, is really due to the fact that the later observations have been taken with more care than were the earlier ones.

Another important fact must be borne in mind in considering whether our present mass of statistics is available for a discussion of possible secular change of climate. It is this: the observations of rainfall taken under various systems or for various institutions have not been made with gauges placed at a uniform height above the ground. At the United States military posts the gauges were required to be elevated eight feet above the surface; but the Smithsonian observers were directed to place theirs at a height of six inches. The later observations of the Signal Service, in fact, are taken at all elevations from a few inches up to 162 feet, and the height of the gauge is not always given in the published records. Here is an element of uncertainty introduced which entirely vitiates any conclusions which one might be inclined to draw from the comparison of records of rainfall in various localities. That the amount collected in the gauges will be less in proportion as the instrument is elevated above the ground — up, at least, to a certain height — would be admitted by all: but that this amount could be estimated and allowed for without long continued observations at each locality with gauges at various elevations, is extremely improbable.

There is another great difficulty in regard to rainfall which relates especially to our Western arid belt. It is this: that the smaller the rainfall the more irregular it is. In San Francisco the rainfall of one year is recorded as having been seven times as great as that of another; in New England in the driest recorded year it is about one half that of the wettest. In very dry regions the rainfall is extraordinarily capricious. "Cloud-bursts" are of by no means uncommon occurrence. One such event, covering perhaps only a few square miles, but happening at a locality where a rain-gauge is kept, would probably hopelessly vitiate the record for that region, for an amount of rain might fall in a few minutes more than equal to the ordinary annual average of the region.[1]

---

[1] Occurrences of this kind are more frequent in the arid region than is commonly supposed. The present writer has more than once visited localities where cloud-bursts have recently occurred. In one case, on the western border of Nevada, a family riding in a buggy was drowned from sheer inability to drive

All the meteorological material which had been collected at the Smithsonian Institution in the manner indicated above was, in 1870, placed in the hands of Charles A. Schott, for examination and elaboration, and the first results of this investigation were laid before the public in the Smithsonian Contributions to Knowledge, bearing the date of March, 1872.[1] This work, which was devoted to the subject of precipitation, was soon followed by a second volume, which related to temperature. This was issued in 1876.[2]

In 1875 a new edition of the volume on rainfall was determined on, and Mr. Schott was authorized to include in it "all the material derived from the direct labors of the Institution, together with all the accessible material from other sources up to the time of preparation for the press." As a consequence of this, this later volume devoted to the rainfall was "enriched with the addition of eight years of observations, from the beginning of 1867 to the end of 1874, for the greater portion of the stations, and in some instances includes observations to the end of 1876." [3]

---

fast enough to escape the rush of water through the cañon which they were trying to cross. In another place, not far distant from this, a stamp-mill was torn to pieces, and a steam-boiler weighing five tons carried by the raging torrent two miles down the bed of a stream which a few minutes before was almost entirely dry.

[1] The full title of this work is "Tables and Results of the Precipitation, in Rain and Snow, in the United States: and at some Stations in adjacent Parts of North America, and in Central and South America. Collected by the Smithsonian Institution, and discussed, under the Direction of Joseph Henry, Secretary. By Charles A. Schott, Assistant U. S. Coast Survey," etc.

In the Introduction to this volume it is said that "the following memoir contains in tabulated form the abstracts of all the records of observations of the rainfall which have been made from the early settlement of this country down to the close of the year 1866, so far as they could be obtained."

[2] The following statement appears in the "Advertisement," signed by the Secretary of the Smithsonian Institution, which accompanies Mr. Schott's second published volume of the results of this investigation: "The object now of the Smithsonian Institution is to render the results of these observations accessible to meteorologists by their reduction, discussion, and publication; but to give greater value to this work it has been thought advisable to incorporate in it all accessible and reliable meteorological observations that have been made in the United States since the early settlement of the country." The full title of this volume is: "Tables, Distribution, and Variations of the Atmospheric Temperature in the United States, and some adjacent Parts of America. Collected by the Smithsonian Institution, and discussed under the Direction of Joseph Henry, Secretary."

[3] This volume, which bears essentially the same title as the preceding one on the same subject, with the addition of the words "Second Edition," appeared in May, 1881.

From the manner in which the materials utilized in these volumes were collected, and from the well known ability of the person to whom their elaboration was intrusted, it is clear that we have here a source of information in regard to questions connected with the subject of the climate of this country the value and authority of which cannot be disputed. Various important memoirs have been published by the Signal Service since the meteorology of the United States became a branch of the public service, but nothing has appeared which could take the place of Mr. Schott's elaborate volumes, of which the only defect is the unavoidable one of the imperfection of the observations, as indicated in the preceding pages. That, if any rapid change were taking place in the climate of this country, as so positively asserted by the early writers on this subject, some proofs of this would have been discovered in the working over of observations extending from the time of its early settlement down to as late as the year 1875 or 1876, can hardly be doubted. At all events, the results of a systematic examination of a long series of records of temperature and rainfall must necessarily be accepted in preference to random assertions unsupported by any other testimony than that of general statements which have no basis except the recollections of the "elderly" and the "middle-aged." Mr. Schott's results may now, therefore, be taken up for brief examination.

The subject of "Secular Variations of the Atmospheric Temperature" was taken up in the volume relating to temperature,[1] and, to ascertain what these variations might have been, a number of stations were selected "possessing the requisite length of series, or from which by proper combination from several stations at no great distance apart, such a series could be produced having as few interruptions as possible." The stations thus selected for reduction and combination embrace localities extending from Maine to California, and the results are exhibited in the form of "curves of secular change in the mean annual temperature." Of these Mr. Schott remarks that their character "is that of a series of irregular waves representing a succession of warmer and colder periods, during which, however, the mean temperature deviates only about one or two degrees, in excess or defect. . . . These undulations, when compared for a number of stations exposed to similar climatological conditions, approach to parallelism over large tracts of country, and

---

[1] See pages 302-320 of that work.

exhibit considerable uniformity in their general character. . . . There is nothing in these curves to countenance the idea of any permanent change in the climate having taken place, or being about to take place; in the last ninety years of thermometric records the mean temperatures showing no indication of a sustained rise or fall."

Mr. Schott remarks that the degree of parallelism of the curves is sufficiently close to warrant an additional consolidation of results for a few characteristic stations, and for this purpose he forms two typical curves, one for the Atlantic coast, and another for the Mississippi Valley. For the former curve the undulations are longer than for the latter. The longer waves of the Atlantic stations show principal maxima in 1802, 1826, 1846, and 1865, and principal minima in 1785, 1816, 1836, and 1857, the average interval being about twenty-two years. The shorter waves of the interior States show principal maxima in 1827, 1833, 1839, 1845, 1854, and 1860, and principal minima in 1831, 1836, 1843, 1848, 1856, and 1867. These undulations are not sufficiently regular nor sufficiently distinct to serve as a basis of prediction, since they are too much mixed with subordinate fluctuations. All that Mr. Schott claims for them is that they are "a general exponent of secular change." [1]

[1] Here it becomes necessary to introduce a few remarks in regard to the meaning of the term "secular," both as used by Mr. Schott in his volumes on temperature and precipitation, and by others engaged in similar investigations. The term "secular" is properly used to designate some phenomenon continuing through an indefinite but long period of time, and which, so far as known, is not recurrent or periodical. Thus the cooling of the earth, according to the theory generally adopted by geologists, from a condition of igneous fluidity is properly designated as "secular." It has been going on for an indefinite length of time, and there is no reason for believing it to be a recurrent phenomenon. As used by astronomers, however, in the term "secular inequality," as applied to the motion of a planet, the meaning of the term "secular" is not exactly the same as that given above, since this inequality is periodic, although the period is one of excessively long duration. Mr. Schott, in his volume on temperature, a synopsis of the principal results of which has been given above, under the head of "Secular Variation of the Atmospheric Temperature," in point of fact does not attempt anything more than a discussion of the *periodic oscillations* (the "Klimaschwankungen" of Brückner), or, in other words, recurrent changes of temperature, which are periodic but of excessively short period as compared with the secular inequality of a planet. Farther on, however, he speaks of a "permanent change" of the climate, as mentioned above, and in such a way as to prove that by this phrase he means what with a strictly correct use of the word "secular" would be called a secular change, or a permanent, non-periodic increase or decrease of the mean temperature, not necessarily from year to year, but at all events from age to age, the fact that periodic oscillations of any or

In the volume devoted to the subject of precipitation there come first the records of the observations of rainfall at each station, arranged so as to show the mean amount of precipitation in rain and melted snow for each month and season, and for the year, as well as the length of each series of observations, and the time of its beginning and ending. This is followed by tables exhibiting the actual precipitation at each station for every year during which observations were made. It is from these data that the "rainfall charts" were prepared which accompany the volume, of which there are five, one of which shows the average annual precipitation in the United States, while the other four exhibit the seasonal distribution of the rainfall, or the average precipitation during the spring, summer, autumn, and winter months over the same area.

There follows next in order a discussion of the "Annual Fluctuation in the Rainfall," and by this term is understood, as we are told, "the changes from month to month," the data for this part of the investigation having been obtained "by selecting those stations where the rain record extends over the longest series of years." From these selected series of observations nine type-curves of the annual fluctuations, or the distribution of the rainfall through the year, were prepared, and the inspection of these will show at once how very differently different parts of the country are conditioned in this respect. Thus, along the Atlantic coast, from Portland to Washington, there are three nearly equal maxima, which occur about the middle of May, of August, and of December, and there is one principal minimum about the beginning of February, while the range between the monthly values is small. On the Pacific coast, however, there is a most decided minimum (amounting in fact along a large extent of the coast to an almost entire absence of rainfall) during the summer months, and a well-marked maximum late in December, the range being excessive.

The question whether this distribution of the rainfall through all the factors of climate may take place not conflicting at all with the coexistence of a permanent or really secular change of these same climatic conditions. In Mr. Schott's volume on precipitation, however, under the head of "Secular Change of the Rainfall," the following points are proposed for discussion: "Whether the annual rainfall is gradually increasing or diminishing, stationary, of a periodic character, or apparently irregular," and this inquiry is said to be "one of great interest, scientifically as well as practically." It will be more convenient and conducive to clearness to call the recurrent or periodic changes in any factor of the climate "oscillations" or "fluctuations," and any permanent non-periodic change a "secular change," as will be done in the course of the present discussion of the subject of climatic change in general.

the year — or annual fluctuation, as Mr. Schott prefers to call it — can be proved to have undergone any change during the period through which the record extends was also investigated by him, and his conclusions in regard to this point are thus stated: "The material collected which mainly refers to our own time, and hardly reaches back into the past century, is evidently insufficient for a full investigation, and obliges us to be satisfied with a less complete proof." It can, however, he adds, be shown "that the secular change, if any, in the annual distribution, must be very small." This he proceeds to do by an examination of the records at Charleston, by means of observations taken from 1738 to 1759, and from 1841 to 1861, the equations representing which "give nearly identical results," the differences being within the probable error of observation, as shown by a comparison of modern results among themselves by means of Station Fort Moultrie, in Charleston Harbor, for which locality there is a series extending from 1842 to 1859.

The discussion which follows next in Mr. Schott's volume, and is headed "Secular Change of the Rainfall," begins with the remark that comparatively few of the records extending over a number of years at any station are free from occasional interruptions, this greatly increasing the labor of reduction, and impairing the value of the investigation. The difficulties arising from carelessness and lack of skill in the observers are well illustrated by a table of rainfall observations for the same years (1853 to 1860), and at the same place (San Francisco), in which the discrepancies are very large.[1]

To facilitate an investigation of the evidence bearing on the question of an oscillation or of a secular change in the amount of precipitation, a table was prepared containing a number of selected stations in different parts of the country, as far as possible those of long record being taken, and for each of these stations the probable error in the amount of rain fallen in any one year, and also the ratio of this quantity to the average yearly amount, this furnishing an index of the amount of uncertainty which attaches to the resulting average rainfall as made out from the present record. Furthermore, another table is appended in which the

[1] The observations taken at the United States military post at San Francisco, for instance, indicate an amount of rainfall differing from that shown by the records of various scientific observers in that city by as much as from one to seven inches for various years. The figures of the observers at the military posts are always less than those given elsewhere.

ratio of each annual amount to the mean is given, in order that in different localities these may be made comparable. To free these ratios, as given in the last-named table, from the accidental irregularities, and to exhibit the nature of the fluctuations from year to year more distinctly, they were united into groups formed of stations where the annual rainfall appears to be subject to the same laws.

There are nine of these groups, of which three are said to be "tolerably trustworthy," while the others can only be accepted as being rough approximations on account of the insufficient number of stations. The groups considered as being sufficiently accurate to be made the subject of generalization are (1) that representing the Atlantic coast from Maine to Maryland ; (2) the State of New York, with some adjacent localities ; (3) the valley of the Ohio, or Ohio to Eastern Missouri. For these three regions the tabular mean results are graphically exhibited in diagrams, while for all nine of the typical groups curves are furnished which facilitate examinations made with reference either to an oscillation or a permanent secular change of the rainfall.

Of the diagrams given exhibiting the "fluctuations in the annual rainfall" in the three regions for which the data are designated as being "tolerably trustworthy," it is said, that "the irregularities in the successive annual amounts of rain are very great, yet they do not wholly obliterate the indications of a conformity to general laws." The diagrams representing the Atlantic seacoast from Maine to Maryland and the State of New York "distinctly indicate an increase of rain, on the average, since 1835, and show a certain tendency to an arrangement of groups of years of drought, followed by unusually wet years. For these regions, which are geographically so near each other, the fluctuations are shown to be so similar that these groups might have been combined and treated as one. Of the fluctuations exhibited in the third diagram (those of the Ohio Valley) it is said that they "are of quite a different character." The essential difference would seem to be, that there is no such indication of a secular increase of the rainfall since 1835 as is exhibited in the Atlantic Coast and New York diagrams, while the irregularities of the western region seem to be more marked, and less indicative of the existence of any general law by which they might be governed than is the case on the eastern edge of the country.

In regard to the peculiarities of the curves drawn to illustrate the character of the rainfall of the nine groups mentioned above, and which include the three thought worthy, on account of their superior reliability, to be specially and more elaborately treated, it is said that "the curve of Type I. (the Atlantic coast) points to a gradual increase of the precipitation from about 1818 to the present time; whether or not we have reached the maximum of this long fluctuation or secular change cannot yet be determined, but it is probable that we have passed it. Besides this greater change, which extends over several decades, and which undoubtedly is of a periodic character, there are smaller undulations covering a period of but a few years; these latter waves are superposed upon the larger one, and appear of variable parameter, those near the minimum of the greater period being greatest, and decreasing gradually to the present time."

In further illustration of the generalizations which Mr. Schott felt authorized in making with regard to secular changes of climate as indicated by these curves, the following may be quoted: "The variations in the rainfall, from year to year, in the Ohio Valley, and as far west as Missouri, are different from those just quoted, though they are not of an opposite character. Type IV. [Ohio to Missouri] indicates *no* secular increase, and the secondary waves appear larger than in Type I.; the remarkable period of drought about 1836, as well as the less conspicuous or relative one about 1855, are common to the two regions. A comparison with Type VII. of the Mississippi delta and Alabama leads to the inference that the law of succession of dry and wet years partakes largely of the character of that on the Gulf coast. On our Southern Atlantic coast the distribution is different from any of the above types; the rainfall here seems to have been on the decrease. Type IX., for the coast of California, is too limited to be analyzed."[1]

Finally, the results of Mr. Schott's investigations are summed up by himself in these words: "It must be admitted that, while they [these investigations] exhibit, in a concise form, the broader features of the laws of distribution of rain in the United States, they must still be regarded as but first approximations, considering

---

[1] These statements in Mr. Schott's memoir are followed by some remarks in regard to a possible correspondence of the sun's activity in the production of spots with the variations in the annual rainfall. His conclusions are to the effect that "either there is no such connection between the two phenomena as has been supposed, or else the accidental and local irregularities in the rainfall are not sufficiently eliminated to allow of the recognition of the law regulating the secular changes."

the irregularity of the phenomenon itself, and the comparative scantiness and frequent discontinuity of our records."

One of the most interesting results of Mr. Schott's investigation is the conclusion to which he leads us, that for the earliest settled part of the country — the part where the observations of precipitation have been longest taken and are most reliable — an increase of the rainfall during the past seventy or eighty years is "distinctly indicated." That this is the period of time during which this part of the country has been *ruthlessly* (to use the term most frequently employed by the advocates of the idea that the "devastation of the forests" is everywhere the dominant cause of climatic changes) stripped of its timber. All that had been done in this direction, in this region, previous to the beginning of the present century, is as nothing compared with what has been accomplished since that time. Along the Southern Atlantic coast, on the other hand, where during the same period much has been accomplished toward denuding the country of its forests (although by no means as much as has been done in this direction in the Northern and Middle Atlantic States), the indications point to a secular decrease of the rainfall, while in the Ohio Valley, where settlement and an active deforestation began with the present century, there is no special indication either of increase or decrease of the rainfall since that epoch. It can be safely stated, therefore, that over that part of the United States which was originally densely covered with forests, and where more has been accomplished by settlers to change the face of the country by cutting them down than either has been or could be done over any other area of similar extent within the limits of the country, there a most thorough investigation of the records of the precipitation affords no proof that any sensible change of its climate has been effected, either with regard to temperature or the amount or distribution of the rainfall, during the present century, either by natural causes or by the hand of man.

It cannot fail to have been noticed that Mr. Schott furnishes no type curves for any part of the United States where the rainfall is deficient, and enters into no generalizations with regard to the region specially connected with the subject of the present volume. The reason for this is obvious: if the data for more thickly settled and older States are by no means sufficient for the purposes of an exhaustive investigation of their climate, much more is this the case over that part of the country where the density of the population only averages two and a half to the square mile, and where, until within a very few years, there were no available records of temperature or rainfall other than those kept at the military posts.[1] As, however, thirteen years have elapsed since Mr. Schott's latest work was published, it will be desirable that there should be an examination of what has been published during that time, for the purpose of ascertaining whether this new material may possibly be utilized so as to throw any light on the problem of man's ability to influence climate.

It must also have been noticed by the reader of the preceding pages that the most sanguine expectations in regard to a possible amelioration of the climate of the arid region have been and still are maintained by many of the residents of that part of the country, and that these have been encouraged, to a very considerable extent, by some of the officials of the irrigation surveys.

The ponderous volumes of the "Report of the Special Committee of the United States Senate on the Irrigation and Reclamation of Arid Lands,"[2] are largely occupied with statements made by the citizens of the arid region, the chief object of which is to substantiate the theory that "*as settlement advances the climatic conditions will be very much improved.*"[3] The evidence brought forward in support of this theory is, in large part, so vague in its character that it defies analysis: some of the chief points only can be briefly touched upon.

Of course "reforestation" is one of the principal methods by which this climatic change is to be brought about. The term "reforestation" is used, without regard to its real meaning, to signify covering a region with trees where none grew before; for there is no evidence that the Great Plains have ever been covered with an arboreal vegetation: it is certain that they have not been since the Tertiary epoch, or at any time during the epoch designated by geologists as "Recent." Yet Mr. Fernow, "Chief of the Forestry Division," in a long preamble to a paper which he submits, and which is published as part of the evidence laid before the

---

[1] Among the forty-eight selected stations "of long record" taken by Mr. Schott to form the basis of his investigation of the secular changes in the rainfall, there are only two which are included within the arid region. These are of course both United States military posts, at one of which there was a series of observations extending over seventeen years, and at the other over twelve years.

[2] See *ante*, p. 92, for the titles and a synopsis of the contents of these volumes.

[3] See *loc. cit.*, Vol. I. p. 2.

committee,[1] thus expresses himself: "The forest, by its growth, creates its own favorable conditions of growth. The treelessness of the plains, and of much of the arid region, may possibly explain itself in this way. By the destruction of the forest which originally covered this region, the very condition of its existence and of its natural recuperation was destroyed; and thus, in a reverse manner, reforestation of parts by artificial means may make natural reforestation over the whole area possible by and by." As a conclusion from this, he maintains that "reforestation on the plains and forest preservation on the mountains is of greater national concern than the location of irrigation reservoirs."

More incorrect views than these were never expressed, even by a United States government official. Portions of the earth's surface are naturally densely covered by forests; other parts are very thinly wooded; and still others are, and have been during long ages — that is, during the whole of the present epoch — entirely bare of arboreal vegetation. Climate and soil are the regulators of this condition of things. The tundras, steppes, plains, and deserts are not the work of man's hand, any more than are the tropical forests. Where nature designed trees to grow, there, as fast as these decay and die, they are replaced by a new growth, unless this be artificially hindered. So, on the other hand, the regions naturally bare of forests can only with great difficulty be covered with them. Indeed it may be said with truth that an "artificial forest" does not anywhere exist, that is, in any other sense than as a continuation of a previously existing natural forest. Groves of trees may be planted, and, with sufficient care and with great expense, these may be kept alive, but no large area naturally destitute of arboreal vegetation has ever been converted into a forest, and it is safe to say that no such area ever will be.

The experience of the General Government in endeavoring, by means of "timber-culture laws," to cover the non-forested parts of the country with a growth of trees, is sufficient evidence of the difficulties encountered in attempting this reversal of nature's laws. As early as 1873, Congress passed an act "to encourage the growth of timber on the Western prairies," under the provisions of which any settler might obtain, without cost, a quarter-section of land "for the purpose of the cultivation of timber thereon." This act was several times amended, and finally repealed in 1891, for the reason that it accomplished nothing

---

[1] *Loc. cit.*, Vol. IV. p. 112.

toward a reforestation of the country, but only (like the swamp-land laws) opened the door to wholesale fraud.[1]

Scientific observations have also been relied on, to a considerable extent, to support the theory that the climate of the arid region is improving as a consequence of the occupation of the land by settlers. It is true that, under the direction of the Signal Service, the number of stations at which meteorological observations are taken has been considerably increased since the date of Mr. Schott's investigations; but many more than now exist are needed, and especially in the Cordilleran region. Here the topography of the country is extremely diversified. High mountain ranges alternate with much lower valleys; and the amount of rainfall being to a considerable extent dependent on the altitude of the stations, as shown beyond doubt by the observations taken on the few high points which have been occupied,[2] it follows that, before there can be any satisfactory rain-charts showing even the general features of the annual distribution of the rainfall over a large part of the arid region, a long series of observations must have been accumulated at a great number of stations, and the results laid down on accurate maps, which must necessarily be on a much larger scale than is required for the region lying to the east of the Rocky Mountains, where the topography is extremely simple.

Notwithstanding these difficulties, the Signal Service did recently prepare a work in which an attempt was made to furnish later and more reliable information with regard to the amount and distribution of the rainfall in the arid region. This volume bears the date of 1891, and was furnished in accordance with a resolution which passed the House of Representatives, May 23, 1890, and which was thus worded: "That the Secretary of War be, and is hereby, requested to transmit to the House of Representatives the reports that have been prepared under the direction of the Chief Signal Officer of the Army upon the climate of Arizona and New Mexico and other parts of the arid region, together with such tables, particularly of rainfall, temperature, evaporation, and other

---

[1] The present writer, after the timber-culture act had been several years in force, made a journey through Minnesota, the Dakotas, and Montana, partly with the object of ascertaining whether anything had been accomplished toward reforesting that part of the country by this kind of encouragement. Nowhere could it be seen that anything worthy of notice had been accomplished. Most of the trees set out, along the railroads chiefly, appeared to be but little more flourishing than so many broomsticks.

[2] See "Table of Annual Precipitation," etc., *ante*, p. 37.

matters as relate thereto, with such corrections, alterations, and additions as may be deemed advisable by the Chief Signal Officer, who will also express his views as to the value and importance of said tables of temperature, evaporation, etc., and their bearing upon the subject of irrigation and water storage."

The volumes published as authorized by the above resolution relate to California, Nevada, Colorado, Utah, New Mexico, and Arizona. For each of these States and Territories a series of maps is given, on which are shown the normal annual and seasonal precipitation, as also the normal annual temperature, and the temperature curves for January and July. In the introductory remarks prefixed to these maps, the subject of irrigation and water storage in the arid region is discussed in a very general way, without giving any information of special value to those desirous of engaging in an irrigational enterprise. Such information was indeed hardly to be expected in a work of this kind. To be of practical value the details for any specified locality where capital is to be expended must be given with the greatest fullness, and with a high degree of accuracy, as has been candidly admitted by those officials of the United States Geological Survey who are engaged in the irrigational department of that work.

The rainfall charts accompanying the Signal Service report are necessarily very imperfect. Their scale is small — not much over fifty miles to an inch — and they show only the roughest indications of topography. Indeed, accuracy, or even a moderate amount of detail of this kind, was not to be looked for, since only small portions of the arid region have ever been mapped except in the roughest possible manner. But even if accurate topographical maps did exist, and it were deemed possible to utilize them as a basis for rain or temperature charts, the lack of accurate observations at a sufficient number of stations is, as has already been explained, so great, that it would be impossible to arrive at any satisfactory result. This condition of things may be illustrated by reference to the Territory of Arizona, which has an area of about 113,000 square miles, and over much the larger part of which the topography has never been studied in any detail.[1] In the list of stations at which meteorological data have been obtained for the construction of the temperature and rain charts, there are only five

[1] Of this Territory what is called "an orographic and climatic chart" is given, but the meaning of the colors and lines displayed upon it is nowhere explained!

places mentioned at which observations have been kept up for more than twenty years, and these are all military posts, the deficiencies of the observations at which, especially in the earlier years, has already been the subject of remark. At forty-five of the stations the records are of less than two years' duration, and this in a region of which the variability of the rainfall may be estimated from the fact that at one of the stations (Fort Mojave) the precipitation was in one year (1886) 2.20 inches, and in another (1889) 21.38 inches. It is not an exaggeration to say that charts based on such a slender stock of information have neither a scientific nor a practical value.

More surprising as respects insufficiency and inaccuracy is the table given in the Signal Service volume,[1] which is headed "Annual Rainfall," and which professes to give the annual average precipitation in inches in the States and Territories of the arid region over belts lying between certain contour lines, and the number of cubic miles of annual rainfall on each of these belts.[2] Such a table, if accurate, would be of great scientific interest, but it is difficult to see how it could be made of practical value. Based on such imperfect data as at present exist, it is simply a snare and a delusion.[3]

The desire existing on the part of the authorities at Washington, at least at the time most of the various documents which have been noticed in the present volume were issued, to make things pleasant for the inhabitants of the arid region, cannot fail to have been noticed. This condition of things could receive no better illustration than that already mentioned;[4] namely, that the Chief Signal Officer considered it a sufficient reason for placing the "arid region limit" at fifteen, instead of twenty, inches of rainfall, that serious and protracted droughts occur where the average precipitation ranges between thirty and fifty inches. Again, a similar inclination to present facts under a more favorable light than is consistent

---

[1] See page 19 of that work.

[2] Thus for Colorado the areas specified are: 4,000 feet and less; 4,000 to 5,000 feet; 5,000 to 7,000 feet; 7,000 feet and over.

[3] That this statement is not one made at random may be inferred from the fact that in the Signal Service "Table of Annual Rainfall" here under discussion the amount of precipitation at 7,000 feet and over, in Nevada, is given in inches and fractions of an inch, and the number of cubic miles of rainfall over the area in fractions of a cubic mile, while there is not a single meteorological station in that State at an elevation of over 7,000 feet, and only five over 6,000 feet, the area of the State being 109,740 square miles.

[4] See *ante*, p. 219.

with truth is manifested on the part of the same officer when he says that, in his opinion, "the trans-Mississippi and the trans-Missouri rainfall is slightly increasing as a whole, though in certain localities it may be slightly decreasing," and adds: "It seems most proper for him to put forth his strong conviction, *even though it be not a certainty*, when, as in this case, it will tend to reassure the agricultural population of the lately drought-stricken districts of the West."

It will be well to inquire what is the basis of the Chief Signal Officer's happy anticipations with regard to the future of the arid region, as thus formulated by him, and as also indicated in the following additional passage quoted from the same source: "There appears no possible reason to believe that the scanty rainfall of the past year or two will not be followed by increasing precipitation in the next few years, which will maintain the annual rainfall of these sections at the average, or even increase it."[1] The evidence for the truth of this opinion appears to be the following. The later rainfall charts of the Signal Service, prepared in the manner indicated above, show the area on which the mean annual precipitation is less than ten inches as being considerably less than that so represented on the statistical maps of the tenth census, and a similar reduction of area is indicated for the part of the country where the rainfall is between ten and fifteen inches. By the use of what entirely insufficient data these later maps have been prepared has already been shown, and it is not necessary to dwell further on this matter. But the changes which have already been made on the rain charts for the benefit of the settlers on the arid lands are likely to be exceeded by those which the future has in store for them, since the Chief Signal Officer thus expresses himself in regard to the climatological probabilities of this region: "When Idaho, Nevada, Utah, New Mexico, and Arizona have been covered with rain gauges as completely as New York or New England, the final outcome of observations will indicate that the actual average of rainfall for this arid region is now understated by the census charts (Census of 1880) from twenty to forty, and by these [the latest ones of the Signal Service, namely] from ten to fifteen per cent."[2] And this is the kind of material furnished by our scien-

---

[1] See "Report on Rainfall in Washington, Oregon," p. 15.

[2] The number of rain gauges regularly observed in New England, in April, 1894, was 210, its area being somewhat more than one eighth of that of the States and Territories here designated by the Chief Signal Officer; about 1,700 stations

tific bureaus, of late years, to meet the demands for information made on them by politicians!

It is not difficult to understand how it is that Professors in Universities near the borders of the arid region of the United States should from time to time have advocated the theory that the rainfall of that part of the country was increasing, and that this presumed increase should be attributed to the settlement and cultivation of the land was quite natural.[1] The deficiency of accurate and long continued observations, which Mr. Schott found to be a sufficient reason for not attempting to generalize in regard to the climate of the country any farther west than Eastern Missouri, did not deter others from trying to discover evidence that would justify them in supporting a theory the firm establishment of which would be so desirable.

As early as February, 1880, or shortly before the publication of the second edition of Mr. Schott's volume on Precipitation in the United States, Messrs. Aughey and Wilbur, of the University of Nebraska, addressed a communication to the Governor of that State in regard to the climatic conditions of the region west of the 100th meridian, in which, after the preliminary statement that the soil of that part of the country is "chemically equal to any similar area of soil taken in any part of the American continent," water being "the only element lacking to insure complete productiveness," they proceed to assert that they hold it to be proved beyond reasonable question that "the present rate of increase in rainfall will in a comparatively short time fit this region for agriculture without the aid of irrigation." The actual increase of rainfall, they say, "is clearly demonstrated by observations taken over a period long enough to give consecutiveness to the deductions made." Farther on, it is added: "Observations, experiment and the highest scientific authority demonstrate that climates in the West are becoming moister and that rainfall is increasing steadily. This increase must extend steadily until the plains east of Denver and Laramie receive sufficient rainfall to produce farm products."[2]

---

must therefore have been established in that part of the arid region before its average rainfall will be found to have been raised from twenty to forty per cent above that indicated on the charts of the census of 1880.

[1] See *ante*, p. 239, for Mr. Newell's remarks in regard to the large rainfall of 1884 over certain districts, as having been "noticed and popularly attributed to the effects of cultivation and to other causes under the control of man."

[2] The present writer has never been able to procure a copy of the original

Without attempting to analyze the evidence on which these statements of Messrs. Aughey and Wilbur are based, it is sufficient to remark that this desired increase of rainfall has, up to the present time, not taken place; but, on the other hand, the fourteen years which have elapsed since these predictions of a more satisfactory condition of things on the Great Plains were made have been constantly occupied by endeavors to increase the water supply of that region in the various ways indicated in the preceding pages, and by irrigational surveys and investigations made at the expense of the General Government, and loudly called for by the inhabitants, who are by no means contented with the assertions made by the Professors of their Universities that the demonstrated increase of rainfall "must extend steadily," and that "any evidence of present dryness, where dryness exists, is evidence only for the present."

Since general experience justifies us in asserting that everywhere there is considerable irregularity in the rainfall of successive years, or, as Mr. Schott expresses it in discussing the conditions prevailing on the Atlantic coast, "a tendency to an arrangement of groups of years of drought, followed by unusually wet years," nothing could be more natural than that some regularity in the recurrence of these wet and dry periods should be sought for, since if any such proof of a conformity to general laws could be obtained, there would be reason to hope that a sound basis for prediction might be secured — a matter certainly of great scientific and practical importance. That up to the present time no positive result of this kind has been reached — so far at least as the working over of the Smithsonian material by Mr. Schott is concerned — has already been explained.[1] The same is the case with reference to the climatic conditions of various foreign countries where long series of meteorological observations exist and have been elaborately investigated. Nowhere has it been proved that these alternations of wetter and dryer periods were subjected to any law of periodicity.[2]

communication of Professors Aughey and Wilbur to the Governor of Nebraska, and is obliged therefore to content himself with extracts from it which have been given repeatedly in various government irrigational publications. (See Hinton's "Irrigation in the United States," p. 146.)

[1] See *ante*, pp. 303, 304.

[2] The most thorough climatic investigation ever made, unless we except that of Mr. Schott, is one relating to the climate of Geneva, in Switzerland, by Professor E. Plantamour, which forms the second part of the twenty-fourth volume of the "Mémoires de la Société de Physique et d'Histoire Naturelle de Genève," and was published in 1875-76. For this investigation fifty consecutive years of

Notwithstanding these facts, various meteorologists in the Western States have endeavored to show that the rainfall of certain regions was, as respects its distribution through a series of years, a phenomenon of regular recurrence. Thus, Mr. E. C. Murphy maintains, not only that the rainfall of Kansas is increasing in quantity, but also that periods of more and less abundant precipitation succeed each other at intervals of seven years.[1] There are only three stations for which there is a continuous record of the rainfall extending over a period of any considerable length; these are Fort Leavenworth, Manhattan, and Lawrence, which places all lie considerably to the east of the 100th meridian, and are by no means within the arid belt.[2] The Fort Leavenworth series is the longest, extending with a few breaks from 1836 on; at Manhattan observations have been made continuously since 1854, and at Lawrence since 1868. The series at Fort Leavenworth is divided by Mr. Murphy into eight periods of seven years each, alternately dry and wet, the first dry period beginning with 1836. There are five of these periods in the Manhattan series, and three in that of Lawrence, all ending with the year 1891. The differences between the means of the wet and dry periods are in all cases but one very small; this one being the years 1871–1877, the mean of which is 5.27 inches larger than that of any other period. In the case of the Fort Leavenworth series the mean rainfall of the last dry period (1878–1884) was 0.62 inch greater than that of the next succeeding wet period; in the Manhattan series the mean rainfall of the dry period 1878–1884 was 3.60 inches more than that of the next following wet period; in the Lawrence series the mean of the dry period 1878–1884 is 2.17 inches more than that of the next preceding wet period. More extraordinary than this, however, is the fact revealed in these records of the great irregularity in the relation of the annual rainfall of stations near each other, and topographically similarly situated. This condition may be illustrated by the statement that the rainfall at Manhattan during the two years 1874 and 1875 was about the same in amount (17.61 and

elaborate and accurate meteorological observations were available. A searching analysis of this accumulated material gave no support to any theory of a regular recurrence of groups of years of larger rainfall and comparative drought.

[1] See "Transactions of the Kansas Academy of Science," Vol. XIII. (1891–92), pp. 16–19.

[2] The longitudes of these three stations are, according to Mr. Schott, respectively 94° 54′, 96° 39′, and 95° 12′; the average rainfall being 33.38, 29.89, and 33.10 inches.

17.96 inches), and only a little more than half what it was at Fort Leavenworth during those years (33.81 and 31.26 inches); while during the next year (1876) it was actually greater at Manhattan than it was at Fort Leavenworth. Again, at Wallace the rainfall of the year 1880 was 34.10 inches, and that of 1881 was 8.38 inches. With such irregularities in the precipitation, records covering short periods of observation would seem to be of very little value in reference to a settlement of the question of a secular change of the climate. The general impression in Kansas, however, is that the rainfall in that State has increased considerably within the past quarter of a century, although there are some persons who do not admit this, but maintain that it has become more equally distributed through successive years, and believe that this has resulted from the increased cultivation of the soil.[1]

It will be seen from the facts which have been presented in the preceding pages how far we are as yet from having any precise knowledge of the secular changes which the climate of this or any other country may be undergoing. Instrumental records up to the present time do not authorize us to say that the average temperature or rainfall of any part of the earth has either permanently increased or diminished since accurate observations began to be taken. Nor has any regular periodicity been made out for those oscillations of the climate which are of short period, and which, though not wandering very far from the means, are yet in many regions of decided importance, where a basis for prediction would certainly be highly desirable. Still further, it may be stated with truth that the many efforts which have been made to prove that climate is something within the control of man have all proved failures. Some minor inconveniences have, in certain regions, been more or less effectually remedied by human effort: damp and marshy regions have been drained, the ravages of mountain torrents prevented, snow avalanches checked, and even the inroads of the sea restrained over limited areas, although not without immense expenditures; but no great modification of the natural physical conditions of any considerable part of the earth's surface has ever been brought about by the hand of man.

[1] Professor G. F. Becker thinks that he perceives "indications of what seems to be a 13-year periodicity" of the rainfall in California, "there being decided minima in the seasons of 1850-51, 1863-64, and 1876-77." See "Bulletin of the University of California," No. 31, for February, 1878. But at the same time he admits that "the data discussed are too few, both as to time and geographical distribution, for any very reliable generalization."

We are, however, not without abundant evidence that there have been great climatic changes during the geological ages. The zonal distribution of life, a condition so largely dependent on temperature, has been developed with the progress of time, and this, from the geological point of view, is a comparatively modern event. Furthermore, the past and present distribution of vegetable and animal life — the latter, however, in a much less satisfactory manner than the former — proves that there has been on the whole a decided diminution of temperature, the evidences of which change are naturally most marked in high northern latitudes, where once flourished the vegetation of a temperate or even semi-tropical climate. The nature and cause of this phenomenon have been the object of much investigation and discussion, but we are up to the present time far from having arrived at any satisfactory and generally admitted solution of the problem.

Still more difficult of explanation is the complicated series of climatic changes which belongs to the latest period of the earth's history, and which are grouped together as characterizing the "Glacial Epoch," during which over a considerable part of Northern and even Central Europe the glaciers had a much greater extension than they have at the present time, and when large areas in Northeastern North America, where now no permanent glaciers exist, were heavily covered by ice. While this glacial development connects itself — in certain regions at least — with the present epoch, and was perhaps everywhere synchronous with the existence of human life on the globe, yet no geologist or climatologist maintains that it was in the slightest degree the result of human agency. The causes are obscure, and the more difficult of explanation in that it was, although widespread, by no means a phenomenon of universal occurrence, and seemingly not in harmony with the more gradual and general refrigeration which the earth had been undergoing during the ages by which it was preceded.

There is a phenomenon which has been manifesting itself for an indefinite length of time, having been begun before the initiation of the Glacial Epoch, and which is still in progress, and of which the causes are as obscure as those of that epoch. Although making itself felt over a much larger part of the earth's surface than was covered by the ice at the time of its greatest glacial extension, this phase of the earth's history has thus far received but little attention, much less having been done towards its investigation than has been with reference to an understanding of the nature and causes of the Glacial Epoch. The phenomenon in question is this : over all the great continental masses, and especially in the closed basin regions, many lakes have long been and still are diminishing in area, while the volume of the water carried down by the rivers has in many cases been proved, either by direct measurement or by geological observations, to have very considerably lessened. The causes of this hitherto but little investigated, but highly important, phenomenon have not yet been explained in any way meeting with general acceptance. That it was and is a "climatic change" seems highly probable. It can hardly be otherwise than that some modification of the earth's meteorological conditions has brought about, and is still causing, this secular desiccation, the nature and extent of which have only just begun to be studied, but to which the attention of climatologists cannot fail to be more generally directed in the near future.

C.

LIST OF UNITED STATES OFFICIAL REPORTS RELATING TO IRRIGATION, AND MATTERS CONNECTED THEREWITH.

Congressional.

Report of the Special Committee of the United States Senate on the Irrigation and Reclamation of Arid Lands. 51st Congress, 1st Session. Report 928, in six parts. 1890.
- Part 1. Report of Committee, and Views of Minority, pp. 178.
- Part 2. The Northwest, pp. 459.
- Part 3. The Great Basin Region and California, pp. 573.
- Part 4. Rocky Mountain Region and Great Plains, pp. 608.
- Part 5. Statements of the Director of the United States Geological Survey. Reports of United States Consuls in Countries using Irrigation. Miscellaneous Papers on the subject of Irrigation, pp. 384.
- Part 6. A Second Edition of Miscellaneous Document No. 15, 49th Congress; essentially a reprint of Hinton's First Report on Irrigation in the United States.

Report of the Select Committee of the House of Representatives on Irrigation of Arid Lands. 52d Congress, 1st Session. Report No. 569. pp. 12.

Department of Agriculture.

ANNUAL REPORTS OF THE COMMISSIONER OF PATENTS: —
- 1854. Gardening (Watering or Irrigation, p. 332).
- 1858. Browne, D. J. Drainage, its History, Principles, Advantages to the Agriculturist, pp. 273–280.
- 1859. Clemson, Thom. G. Fertilizers, pp. 136–178 (Irrigation, pp. 146, 147.)
- 1860. Smith, E. Goodrich. Irrigation, pp. 166–224.
- 1861. Bliss, Edward. Territory of Colorado: its Soil, its Climate, its Mineral Products and Resources, pp. 154–157 (Irrigation, p. 156).

LIST OF IRRIGATION REPORTS. 319

ANNUAL REPORTS OF THE COMMISSIONER OF AGRICULTURE : —

1862. The Agriculture of Morocco. By V. D. Collins, pp. 499–508.
1867. Irrigation. By Chas. D. Poston, pp. 193–200.
1868. Irrigation (on a farm at Brattleboro, Vt.), p. 502.
1869. Irrigation and Agriculture in Utah, pp. 431, 432.
1869. Irrigation. By Horace Greeley, pp. 510, 511.
1869. Irrigation as a Renovator of Pasture Lands, p. 526.
1869. Irrigation in San Luis Park, Colo., p. 603.
1870. Irrigation in many Parts of Europe, pp. 501, 502.
1870. Irrigation Canals in California. Geo. Barstow, p. 517.
1870. Modes and Results of Irrigation, pp. 576–584.
1871. Practical Irrigation in Colorado, pp. 254–275.
1871. Irrigation Systems of Different Countries, pp. 275–287.
1872. Irrigation in England, pp. 559, 560.
1873. Irrigation, pp. 282, 283.
1873. Agriculture in Japan. By Horace Capron, pp. 364–374 (Irrigation, pp. 366–374).
1873. Irrigation and Cotton Culture in California, p. 378.
1874. Irrigation in California, pp. 352–362. Irrigation : its Evils, Remedies, and Compensations. By Geo. P. Marsh, pp. 362–381.
1876. Irrigation in Maine. D. M. Dunham, abstract, pp. 380, 381.
1881–82. Irrigation as a Remedy for Chinch Bug, pp. 88, 89.
1885. Wheat Culture in India : Irrigation, pp. 580, 581, by Rev. J. L. Hauser, pp. 569–582.
1886. Irrigation, p. 40.
1887. Irrigation, pp. 44, 45.
1888. Irrigation in Victoria, Australia, p. 469.
1889. Irrigation Problems, p. 268. Influence of Forests on Water Supplies, by B. E. Fernow, pp. 297–330. Analyses of Water, p. 497.
1890. Report of the Special Agent in Charge of the Artesian and Underflow Investigations and of the Irrigation Inquiry. By Richard Hinton, pp. 471–488.
1891. Report of the Special Agent in Charge of the Artesian and Underflow Investigations, and of the Irrigation Inquiry, pp. 439–450.

Report on the Climate and Agricultural Features and the Agricultural Practice and Needs of the Arid Regions of the Pacific Slope, etc. By E. W. Hilgard, T. C. Jones, and R. W. Furnas. Washington, 1882, 182 pp.

Artesian Wells upon the Great Plains; Report of Geological Commission appointed to examine a portion of the Great Plains east of the Rocky Mountains, and to report upon the Localities deemed most favorable for making Experimental Borings. Washington, 1882. (C. A. White and Samuel Aughey.) 38 pp.

Preliminary Report on the Forestry of the Mississippi Valley and Tree-planting on the Plains. By F. P. Baker. Washington, 1883.

Irrigation in the United States. A Report prepared by Richard J. Hinton, under the Direction of the Commissioner of Agriculture. Government Printing Office, Washington, 1887. 240 pp.

Letter from Secretary, transmitting Report of Preliminary Investigation to determine proper Location of Artesian Wells within the Area west of the 97th Meridian and east of the Foothills of the Rocky Mountains. Government Printing Office, Washington, 1890.

Progress Report on Irrigation in the United States. Part I. Prepared under the Direction of the Secretary of Agriculture by Richard J. Hinton, Special Agent Artesian Underflow and Irrigation Investigation. Washington, Government Printing Office, 1891. 337 pp. 51st Congress, 2d Session, Senate Ex. Doc. No. 53.

Progress Report of Artesian and Underflow Investigation between the 97th Degree of West Longitude and the Foothills of the Rocky Mountains, with Maps and Profiles. Part II. Prepared under the Direction of the Secretary of Agriculture by Edwin S. Nettleton. Washington, Government Office, 1891, 14 pp. 51st Congress, 2d Session, Senate Ex. Doc. No. 53.

A Report on Irrigation and the Cultivation of the Soil thereby, with Physical Data, Conditions, and Progress within the United States for 1891. By Richard J. Hinton, Special Agent in Charge. 52d Congress, 1st Session. Executive Document No. 41. 459 pp. 1892.

This forms the first volume of a series of four, the titles and contents of the other three being as follows: —

Volume 2. Final Report of the Chief Engineer, Edwin S. Nettleton, C. E., to the Secretary of Agriculture, with accompanying Maps, Profiles, Diagrams, and Additional Papers. 116 pp.

Volume 3. Final Geological Reports of the Artesian and Underflow Investigations, between the Ninety-seventh Meridian of Longitude and the Foothills of the Rocky Mountains, made by Prof. Robert Hay, F. G. S. A., Chief Geologist, 209 pp. [This volume contains sub-reports by the Assistants, Messrs. Hill, Hicks, and Culver (see p. 145 of present volume).]

Volume 4. Final Report of the Mid-Plains Division of the Artesian and Underflow Investigations between the Ninety-seventh Meridian of Longitude west of Greenwich and the Foothills of the Rocky Mountains, by Special Agent J. W. Gregory of Garden City, Kansas, and a Special Report on certain Artesian Conditions in the State of South Dakota, by Fred. F. B. Coffin, Engineer for South Dakota. 61 pp.

WEATHER BUREAU: —

Certain Climatic Features of the two Dakotas. By John P. Finley, First Lieutenant, Ninth U. S. Infantry. Washington, 1893, 204 pp.

Department of the Interior.

UNITED STATES GEOGRAPHICAL AND GEOLOGICAL SURVEY OF THE ROCKY MOUNTAIN REGION: —

Report on the Lands of the Arid Region of the United States, with a more detailed Account of the Lands of Utah, with Maps, by J. W. Powell. 2d Edition. Washington, 1879, 195 pp. (Irrigable Lands of the Salt Lake Drainage System, by G. K. Gilbert, pp. 117-126; Irrigable Lands of the Valley of the Sevier River, by Captain C. E. Dutton, pp. 133-144; Irrigable Lands of that Portion of Utah drained by the Colorado River and its Tributaries, by Professor A. H. Thompson, pp. 152-164; Land Grants in Aid of Internal Improvements, by Willis Drummond, Jr., pp. 165-182.)

UNITED STATES GEOLOGICAL SURVEY: —

First Annual Report of the United States Irrigation Survey; published as "Part II. Irrigation" of the Tenth Annual Report of the United States Geological Survey. Washington, 1890, 123 pp. (Preliminary.)

Second Annual Report of the United States Irrigation Survey; published as "Part II. Irrigation" of the Eleventh Annual Report of the United States Geological Survey. Washington,

1891, 395 pp. (Water-Supply; Surveys of Reservoirs; Bibliography of Irrigation.)

Third Annual Report of the United States Irrigation Survey; published as "Part II. Irrigation" of the Twelfth Annual Report of the United States Geological Survey. Washington, 1891, 576 pp. (Reservoir Sites; Hydrography; Irrigation in India.)

Fourth Annual Report of the United States Irrigation Survey; published in Report of the Secretary of the Interior, 52d Congress, 1st Session, Executive Document 1, Part 5; Vol. IV., Part 3. Washington, 1892, 486 pp. (Water-Supply for Irrigation; American Irrigation Engineering; Engineering Results of Irrigation Survey; Construction of Topographic Maps and the Location and Survey of Reservoir Sites in the Hydrographic Basin of the Arkansas River; Location and Survey of Reservoir Sites during the Fiscal Year ending June 30, 1892.)

ELEVENTH CENSUS OF THE UNITED STATES, 1890: —

Bulletin No. 35, Irrigation in Arizona; No. 60, in New Mexico; No. 85, in Utah; No. 107, in Wyoming; No. 153, in Montana; No. 157, in Idaho; No. 163, in Nevada; No. 178, in Oregon; No. 193, Artesian Wells for Irrigation; No. 198, Irrigation in Washington. Extra Bulletin, No. 23, Irrigation in the Western United States (containing condensed statistics of areas, values, and water-supply).

All the above were prepared by F. H. Newell. *A final report is now in preparation, and will form a part of the Census Report on Agriculture.*

Navy Department.

Narrative of the Expedition of an American Squadron to the China Seas and Japan, performed in the Years 1852–1854, under the Command of Commodore M. C. Perry, U. S. Navy, Vol. 2. Contains irrigation in Lew Chew. Washington, 1856. pp. 19, 20.)

Department of State.

Letter to the Honorable Secretary of State on the General Outline for a proposed Scheme for an International Dam and Water Storage in the Rio Grande River near El Paso, Tex., for the Control of the annual Floods, etc., and Preservation of the

National Boundary to the Gulf, and for other Purposes. Washington, December 10, 1888.

Report of the United States Commissioners to the Centennial International Exhibition, Melbourne, 1888. Published under Direction of the Secretary of State, by Authority of Congress. Washington, 1890, 452 pp. (Report on Irrigation, T. B. Merry, pp. 291–294.)

SPECIAL CONSULAR REPORTS: —

Canals and Irrigation in Foreign Countries. Washington, 1891. (Irrigation, pp. 255–494.)

Treasury Department.

BUREAU OF STATISTICS: —

Report on the Internal Commerce of the United States for the Fiscal Year 1889, Part 2. Commerce and Irrigation, by Wm. F. Switzler. Washington, 1889, 897 pp.

Report of the Internal Commerce of the United States for the Year 1890, Part 2 of Commerce and Navigation. The Commercial, Industrial, Transportation, and other Interests of Alaska, Arizona, California, Idaho, Nevada, Oregon, Utah, and Washington. Washington, 1891, 1174 pp.

UNITED STATES COAST SURVEY: —

Letter from the Secretary of the Treasury, transmitting, in Answer to a Senate Resolution of May 19, 1876, a Copy of the Report of George Davidson, on the Methods employed in irrigating Lands in India and Southern Europe. Washington, 1876, Government Printing Office, 73 pp.

War Department.

Irrigation in Egypt, by J. Barrois, Paris, 1887. Translated by Major A. M. Miller, U. S. A. Washington, 1889, 113 pp.

Irrigation in New Mexico and Arizona, by Colonel B. H. Grierson, in Report of Secretary of War for 1888–1889. Washington, 1890, Vol. I. pp. 180–188.

UNITED STATES SIGNAL SERVICE: —

Charts and Tables showing the Geographical Distribution of Rainfall in the United States, prepared under the Direction of Brig.

and Bvt. Maj. Gen. D. B. Hazen, Chief Signal Officer of the Army, by H. H. C. Dunwoody, First Lieutenant in Fourth Artillery, Acting Signal Officer. Published by Authority of the Secretary of War. Washington, 1883, 51 pp. No. 9 of Professional Papers of the Signal Service.

Tables showing Monthly Precipitation at various Points throughout the Dry Area, by Captain S. M. Mills (in Report on the Internal Commerce of the United States). Washington, 1885, pp. 212–216.

Report on the Interior Wheat Lands of Oregon and Washington Territory, by Lieutenant Frank Greene. Washington, 1888, 25 pp.

The Climate of Nebraska, particularly in Reference to Temperature and Rainfall, and their Influence upon the Agricultural Interests of the State. Washington, 1890, 60 pp. Senate Executive Document No. 115, 51st Congress, 1st Session, and is called a "Report of the Chief Signal Officer," and was transmitted by the Secretary of War, in compliance with Senate Resolution of April 22, 1890.

Irrigation and Water Storage in the Arid Regions. Letter from the Secretary of War transmitting a Report of the Chief Signal Officer of the Army, in Response to House Resolution dated May 23, 1890, relating to irrigation and water storage in the arid region. Washington, 1891, 356 pp. House of Representatives, Executive Document No. 287, 51st Congress, 2d Session.

[This document is prefaced by a brief report on the Climatology of the Arid Region of the United States with reference to Irrigation, by Gen. A. W. Greely, Chief Signal Officer U. S. Army, followed by tables of precipitation and rainfall for Arizona, California, Nevada, Colorado, and Utah, all bound in one volume, and also issued separately for the various States and Territories named, but with the same introductory matter for each.]

www.ingramcontent.com/pod-product-compliance
Lightning Source LLC
Chambersburg PA
CBHW030310240426
43673CB00040B/1119